STRATEGIC OFFENSIVE
AIR OPERATIONS

Brassey's Air Power: Aircraft,
Weapons Systems and Technology Series

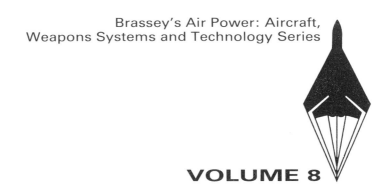

VOLUME 8

**Brassey's Air Power:
Aircraft, Weapons Systems and Technology Series**

General Editor: Air Vice Marshal R.A. Mason, CB, CBE, MA, RAF

This new series, consisting of eleven volumes, is aimed at the international officer cadet or junior officer and is appropriate to the student, young professional and interested amateur seeking sound basic knowledge of the technology of air forces. Each volume, written by an acknowledged expert, identifies the responsibilities and technical requirements of its subject and illustrates it with British, American, Russian, major European and Third World examples drawn from recent history and current events. The series is similar in approach to the highly successful Sea Power and Land Warfare series. Each Volume, excluding the first, has self-test questions and answers.

Other titles in the series include:

Volume 1. Air Power: An Overview of Roles
Air Vice Marshal R.A. Mason, CB, CBE, MA, RAF

Volume 2. Air-to-Ground Operations
Air Vice Marshal J.R. Walker, CBE, AFC, RAF

Volume 3. Unmanned Aircraft
Air Chief Marshal Sir Michael Armitage, KCB, CBE, RAF

Volume 4. Electronic Warfare
Air Commodore J. P. R. Browne, CBE, RAF

Volume 5. Air Superiority Operations
Air Vice Marshal J. R. Walker, CBE, AFC, RAF

Volume 6. Air Transport Operations
Group Captain K. Chapman, M.PHIL, BA, RAF

Volume 7. Air Defence
Group Captain M. B. Elsam, FBIM, RAF

Brassey's Titles of Related Interest

C. Chant
Air Defence Systems and Weapons: World AAA and SAM Systems in the 1990s

E. J. Everett-heath *et al.*
Military Helicopters

R. A. Mason
War in the Third Dimension: Essays in Contemporary Air Power

B. Myles
Jump Jet, 2nd Edition

P. A. G. Sabin
The Future of UK Air Power

The F-001b Stealth bomber. The US Air Force unveiled its B-2 advanced technology bomber at Palmdale, California on 22 November 1988. The stealth aircraft combines all the best attributes of a penetrating bomber—long-range, efficient cruise, heavy payload, all-altitude penetration capability, accurate delivery, and reliability and maintainability. (*US Air Force*)

The Northrop B-2 'Stealth' bomber on its maiden flight from Palmdale, California on 17 July 1989. After the successful completion of functional checks on the basic sub-systems of the aircraft, it was brought in to land at the USAF's Edwards Air Force Base. (*US Department of Defense*)

STRATEGIC OFFENSIVE AIR OPERATIONS

Air Chief Marshal Sir Michael Knight, KCB, AFC, FRAeS

BRASSEY'S (UK)
(a member of the Maxwell Pergamon Publishing Corporation plc)

LONDON · OXFORD · WASHINGTON · NEW YORK · BEIJING
FRANKFURT · SÃO PAULO · SYDNEY · TOKYO · TORONTO

U.K. (Editorial)	Brassey's (UK) Ltd., 24 Gray's Inn Road, London WC1X 8HR, England
(Orders, all except North America)	Brassey's (UK) Ltd., Headington Hill Hall, Oxford OX3 0BW, England
U.S.A. (Editorial)	Brassey's (US) Inc., 8000 Westpark Drive, Fourth Floor, McLean, Virginia 22102, USA
(Orders, North America)	Brassey's (US) Inc., Front and Brown Streets, Riverside, New Jersey 08075, USA Tel (toll free): 800 257 5755
PEOPLE'S REPUBLIC OF CHINA	Pergamon Press, Room 4037, Qianmen Hotel, Beijing, People's Republic of China
FEDERAL REPUBLIC OF GERMANY	Pergamon Press GmbH, Hammerweg 6, D-6242 Kronberg, Federal Republic of Germany
BRAZIL	Pergamon Editora Ltda, Rua Eça de Queiros, 346, CEP 04011, Paraiso, São Paulo, Brazil
AUSTRALIA	Brassey's Australia Pty Ltd. P.O. Box 544, Potts Point, N.S.W. 2011, Australia
JAPAN	Pergamon Press, 5th Floor, Matsuoka Central Building, 1-7-1 Nishishinjuku, Shinjuku-ku, Tokyo 160, Japan
CANADA	Pergamon Press Canada Ltd., Suite No. 271, 253 College Street, Toronto, Ontario, Canada M5T 1R5

First edition 1989

Library of Congress Cataloging in Publication Data
Knight, Michael, Sir.
Strategic air operations/Sir Michael Knight.—1st ed.
p.   c.m. — (Brassey's air power ; v. 8)
Bibliography: p.
Includes index.
1. Bombing, Aerial—History.   2. Strategic forces—History.
I. Title. II. Series.
UG700.K65   1989   358.4′2′09—dc20   89-9835

British Library Cataloguing in Publication Data
Knight, Michael, Sir.
Strategic air operations—(Aircraft, weapons systems and technology series).
1. Air operations, history.
I. Title.   II. Series.
358.4′14′09
ISBN 0-08-035806-3 Hardcover
ISBN 0-08-035805-5 Flexicover

The front cover shows the F-00lb Stealth bomber. The US Air Force unveiled its B-2 advanced technology bomber at Palmdale, California on 22 November 1988. The stealth aircraft combines all the best attributes of a penetrating bomber—long-range, efficient cruise, heavy payload, all-altitude penetration capability, accurate delivery, and reliability and maintainability. (*US Air Force*)

Printed in Great Britain by BPCC Wheatons Ltd., Exeter

Preface

There are obvious pitfalls in penning a book which is some way down the numerical order in a series covering any generic and cohesive subject. Such a subject is undoubtedly air power and one of the difficulties faced by the author of Volume 8 in the series will be obvious to those who have eagerly devoured Volumes 1 to 7. Quite simply, the authors of previous volumes have already covered many of the basics—the physical, aerodynamic, meteorological and other 'givens' which are naturally common to aviation (and specifically, military aviation), whatever the combat role being discussed.

In an attempt to ensure that the Air Power and Technology series accommodates within its span of volumes a broad cross-section of releasable information, the author has elected to expand this volume in three ways: firstly, by devoting two chapters to the history of strategic offensive air power—a history that is of absorbing and still, in many ways, very relevant interest to any student of air power.

Secondly, the book includes some study of strategic missiles. Although these do not qualify as elements of air power in the view of some analysts, they do form a natural progression from the longer-range stand-off missiles released from manned aircraft. Indeed, there are few members of today's air forces who could take their stand as proponents of exclusively manned flight for military purposes.

Thirdly, some areas which are of more general interest than merely that of strategic operations have been included: crew environment and escape, some advanced navigational systems and the still relatively unknown science of 'stealth technology'—the bases of which are already in the public domain, though the details of their application are still heavily classified. It is hoped that, in these ways, readers of the series will appreciate just how manifold are the interests involved in a study of air power and technology.

Acknowledgements

I am indebted to a number of people who have offered me help and advice in putting together this modest volume. A number of them are mentioned in the book itself, where their contributions—either on a personal or commercial basis—are duly acknowledged. Among others, I would specifically thank a number of friends in the aerospace industry, including Sir Roy Austen-Smith of Boeing Operations International; and Messrs Peter Hearne of GEC Marconi Ltd, R J Lowin of Plessey Microwave Ltd, J R Morgan of the Naval and Electronics Division of British Aerospace plc and John Wragg of Rolls-Royce plc. The late Geoffrey Dollimore of Hunting Engineering Ltd offered his customarily generous encouragement; whilst Air Vice-Marshal Peter Howard of the Royal Air Force Institute of Aviation Medicine and Dr Geoffrey Pope of the Royal Aerospace Establishment have also offered sound advice, as has Air Commodore Henry Probert of the Air Historical Branch.

Various dedicated and enthusiastic librarians have been of immense help, with the loan of books and articles. Among their number I include Mr John Andrews and his colleagues of the Ministry of Defence Library Services, Mr Chris Hobson of the RAF Staff College Library and members of the staff of the Air Warfare College at Cranwell. Photographs and illustrations have come from a variety of sources; but Reg Mack of the Royal Air Force Museum, Jane Carmichael of the Imperial War Museum and Barry Wheeler of the Ministry of Defence have been particularly helpful. Crown Copyright photographs are reproduced by kind permission of the Controller, Her Majesty's Stationery Office. Air Vice-Marshal John Walker offered sound advice on Chapter 7, where the majority of the illustrations are based on his originals. In the matter of illustrations, I acknowledge also, the help of Victor Bertolaso.

I also owe a particular debt of gratitude to the tireless spare time efforts of Colin Smith, whose meticulous work of collation and presentation could not have been bettered.

My thanks to them all—and to whom I have inadvertently omitted from this list.

Finally, the representation of facts and opinions in the following chapters is solely the author's own responsibility and implies endorsement neither by the British Ministry of Defence nor by any other agency.

M W P K

About the Author

Air Chief Marshal Sir Michael Knight has enjoyed a particularly varied career in the Royal Air Force since joining as a National Service Officer in 1954. His flying career has covered a broad spectrum of roles—including day-fighter ground attack, interdiction and strike/attack, tactical reconnaissance and survey, target-marking, light- and medium-bomber, tactical and strategic transport and air-to-air refuelling. In nearly 5,000 hours of flying on well over a hundred types of aircraft he has served in the United Kingdom, Germany and the Near and Far East.

As Air Officer Commanding No 1 Group of the RAF's Strike Command, he saw the introduction of the Tornado GR1 into service and guided the preparation for active service in the South Atlantic of the RAF's bomber, tanker and reconnaissance forces.

His staff appointments have included those of a Director of Operations in London, the Senior Air Staff Officer at HQ Strike Command and the Air Force Board member with responsibility for all the RAF's logistics, support and security functions. Most recently he has served as the United Kingdom's Representative to NATO's Military Committee.

A Fellow of the Royal Aeronautical Society, a member of the International Institute for Strategic Studies and a former Council member of the Royal United Services Institute for Defence Studies, Air Marshal Knight is a frequent speaker and writer on defence and related subjects.

Contents

List of Figures

List of Plates

List of Acronyms

AAA	Anti-aircraft artillery
AAR	Air-to-air refuelling
ABM	Anti-ballistic missile
ADP	Automatic data-processing
AI	Airborne intercept
ALCM	Air-launched cruise missile
AMSA	Advanced manned strategic aircraft
AOA	Airborne Optical Adjunct
AOA	Angle of attack
APU	Auxiliary power unit
ASAT	Anti-satellite missile
ASMP	*Air-sol moyenne portée*
ATB	Advanced tactical bomber
AWACS	Airborne warning and control system
C^{3}I	Command & control communications and intelligence
CEP	Circular error probable
CEPS	Central integrated test expert parameter system
CG	Centre of gravity
CITS	Central integrated test system
CRT	Cathode-ray tube
DAS	Defensive avionics suite
DEW	Directed energy weapon
DR	Dead reckoning
DSO	Defensive systems operator
ECM	Electronic countermeasures
EMP	Electro-magnetic pulse
EMUX	Electrical multiplex
ETA	Estimated time of arrival
EVS	Electro-optical viewing system
FLIR	Forward-looking infra-red
GCI	Ground-controlled interception
GEANS	Gimballed electrostatic airborne inertial navigation system
GHz	Giga-hertz
GLCM	Ground-launched cruise missile
GPS	Global positioning system
HE	High Explosive

HF	High frequency
HUD	Head-up display
ICBM	Inter-continental ballistic missile
IN	Inertial navigation
INS	Inertial navigation system
INU	Inertial navigation unit
IP	Initial point
IR	Infra-red
IRBM	Intermediate-range ballistic missile
JATO	Jet-assisted take-off
J-STARS	Joint surveillance target attack radar system
JTIDS	Joint tactical information distribution system
km	Kilometre
kts	Knots (nautical miles per hour)
LP	Low pressure
LRCA	Long-range combat aircraft
M	Million
m	Metre
m²	Square metre
MEWSG	Multi-service electronic warfare support group
MHz	Mega-hertz
MIRV	Multiple independently-targetable re-entry vehicle
NEACP	National Emergency Airborne Command Post
NOX	Oxides of nitrogen
nm	Nautical mile(s)
OAS	Offensive air support
OAS	Offensive avionics system
OSO	Offensive systems operator
POD	Probability of detonation
psi	Pounds per square inch
RAF	Royal Air Force
RAM	Radar-absorbent material
RCS	Radar cross-section
REM	Rapid eye movement
RLG	Ring-laser gyro
RPE	Relative price effect
RPV	Remotely-piloted vehicle
RV	Re-entry vehicle
SAC	Strategic Air Command
SAF	Soviet Air Force
SALT	Strategic Arms Control Treaty
SAM	Surface-to-air-missile
SAR	Synthetic aperture radar
SCAD	Subsonic cruise armed decoy
SDI	Strategic Defence Initiative
SFC	Specific fuel consumption
SG	Specific gravity

SHF	Super-high frequency
SLAB	Subsonic low-altitude bomber
SLBM	Submarine-launched ballistic missile
SRAM	Short-range attack missile
TEL	Transporter-erector-launcher
TERCOM	Terraincomparison, terrain contour-matching
TERPROM	Terrain profile-matching
TI	Target indicator
UHB	Ultra high by-pass ratio
USAAF	United States Army Air Force
USAF	United States Air Force
USMC	United States Marine Corps
USN	United States Navy
VLF	Very low frequency

1

The Development of Strategic Bombing—the Role

It might be helpful, first, to indicate the author's view as to precisely what the term 'strategic' means, when applied to offensive air power. It is, indeed, an often misused adjective in this context.

One way of looking at the differences between the strategic and tactical in offensive air operations is to consider the metaphorical distinction contained in one of the source documents on the subject—the scholarly *United States Strategic Bombing Survey* which was carried out immediately after World War II.[1] Marginally light-hearted for such a serious study, the analogy of the cow and the pail is nevertheless apposite. As the Survey suggests:

> Strategic bombing bears the same relationship to tactical bombing as does the cow to the pail of milk. To deny immediate aid and comfort to the enemy, tactical considerations dictate upsetting the bucket. To ensure eventual starvation, the strategic move is to kill the cow.

As the German Luftwaffe probably knew in the summer of 1940 (but fortunately was not allowed to carry through with the necessary determination and single-mindedness) the way to beat the Royal Air Force and, thus, open the way to a German invasion of the United Kingdom, was to destroy the capacity of British industry to produce fighters. Instead, the combination of a marvellously spirited defence, some adverse weather at critical periods, less than coherent German direction at the political level and mounting frustration combined to ensure that a great deal of the Nazi offensive effort was spent in attacking fighters and their bases, radar and other installations and eventually—less effectively than all—the British people in their towns and cities. Thus was the Battle of Britain lost by the Luftwaffe—and the opportunity for invasion denied its political masters. But that is the story of air superiority—already well told in an earlier volume of this series.

For a rather 'heavier' treatment of the strategic definition, it is necessary to pass from cows to Clausewitz. Over 70 years before the first flight by a heavier-than-air machine, the great Prussian writer and philosopher of conflict, Carl von Clausewitz, had defined strategy as 'the employment of the battle as the means towards the attainment of the object of the war'. More than a century later, in his introduction

1

to *Makers of Modern Strategy*,[2] the American Edward Mead Earle extended that definition beyond the bounds of war—as indeed Clausewitz and, before him, Machiavelli had also done in their day. Earle wrote of strategy in the mid-twentieth century as:

> ... the art of controlling and utilizing the resources of a nation—or a coalition of nations—including its armed forces, to the end that its vital interests shall be effectively promoted and secured against enemies, actual, potential or merely presumed.

However, when applied to air power, the term 'strategic' has acquired a more specific and inevitably more chilling connotation. The modern dictionary definition of strategic bombing as 'designed to disorganise the enemy's internal economy and to destroy morale' clearly reflects that crucial directive issued by the Combined Chiefs of Staff at the famous Casablanca Conference in January 1943, when the war with Nazi Germany was at its height. In the clearest possible terms, it directed the commanders of the British and United States air forces that:

> Your primary object will be the progressive destruction and dislocation of the German military, industrial and economic system and the undermining of the morale of the German people to a point where their capacity for armed resistance is fatally weakened.[3]

EARLY HISTORY

The detailed history of strategic bombing is not the province of this book, but it is perhaps worth pausing to examine exactly why such a directive came to be couched in such a way. As Professor Lee Kennett has so well chronicled in his *History of Strategic Bombing* (1982), the idea of aerial bombardment was, for many years, the stuff of science fiction. Although the potential for massive aerial attack had been foreseen by leading military thinkers for a century or so before Messrs Jules Verne, Albert Robida and H G Wells, it was works such as their *Clipper of the Clouds* (1873), *War in the Twentieth Century* (1883) and *War in the Air* (1908) which brought into the public domain visions of an apocalyptic 'bolt from the blue', a massive airborne attack which would bring untold destruction on its defenceless victims; destroying at once their homes, their lives and—for those who actually survived the onslaught—their very will to resist. It is clear from even the most cursory study of contemporary writings, from professional military works to the science fiction of the day, that the bomber was considered, in the early years of the present century, to pose every bit as terrible a threat to civilisation as does the nuclear missile today. But in those early days, the bomber was in fact almost totally unproven as a weapon or war. In the absence of proof, speculation reigned supreme—and the so-called 'fantasy factor' began to endow the bomber with a semblance of complete invincibility.

It is true that such early proponents of air power as Hayne, the Montgolfier brothers, Uchatius and von Zeppelin did at times allow their respective enthusiasms to get the better of their proven judgements: but that is not unknown when men of action become impatient with the pace of technological change. And later, when the world's first infant air forces were taking their first figurative steps, it was both right and natural that their leaders and chief exponents should foresee capabilities far beyond what the technology of the day might offer. Thus did Trenchard of the Royal Air Force, Douhet in Italy, Mitchell in the USA and others take all that was placed before them and extrapolate well into the future, foreseeing in the process rather greater degrees of power, precision and invulnerability in their burgeoning air fleets than were, in the event, then remotely possible. That is not in any way to decry the visions of men without whom such capabilities would have been later in the coming. It is merely to suggest, with all the infallible wisdom of hindsight, that the claims made for air power in the very early days of its development were too often exaggerated.

But such was (and, indeed, probably still is) the power of aviation to dazzle and attract, that very many people of influence in the 1920s and 1930s—politicians and writers among them—came to believe implicitly in the power of what were still rather crude weapons. The cry that 'the bomber will always get through' may have been voiced in England; but it was echoed around the world.

And, of course, the pace of change was in all conscience swift. A mere eight years after the Wright Brothers' first-ever flight in a heavier-than-air craft, the war between Italy and Turkey produced a number of 'firsts' in aviation—as Professor Kennett has duly recorded. 1911 saw the first ground-to-air radio transmission—appropriately carried out (from the ground) by Guglielmo Marconi himself. Before the end of that same year, Gunner Lieutenant Giulio Gavotti had flown the first bombing mission, dropping four rather small projectiles in the general vicinity of Turkish positions in Libya and eliciting a slightly hysterical headline in the *Gazzetta Del Popolo*: 'Aviator Lieutenant Gavotti throws bomb on enemy camels. Terrorised Turks scatter upon unexpected celestial assault'. Six months later came the first night bombing raid by the adventurous Italians; and it is recorded that, in the absence of lights on the instrument panel, the pilot in question wore an electric lamp attached to his helmet. In these early air raids 2kg Cipelli bombs, of about the size of large oranges, were carried suspended on each side of the aircraft by a cord around the pilot's neck. Having pulled the pin with his teeth, the intrepid aviator would simply toss each bomb over the side (Plate 1.1).

WORLD WAR I

In the same short war, a greater weight of attack would, at least in theory, be mounted from airships (or dirigibles) which could carry rather larger loads aloft and which presaged the Zeppelins (Plate 1.2) which were to be used in World War I—a mere 2½ years later. The first Zeppelin raid (on Liege on Day 3 of that war) was followed 24 days later by the first air attack on a city, when a single German Taube monoplane (Plate 1.3) dropped five small bombs over the Gare de l'Est in Paris (apparently, the target) killing one civilian, but causing little damage. Early Allied raids were mounted on the great Zeppelin sheds of the Ruhr but, on 4 December 1914, bombers of the French Air Service attacked the railway station at Freiburg, 50 miles or so behind the German lines. The bombing was inaccurate and several civilians were killed—making the French, in the words of one German commentator, 'the first power to introduce the horrors of the air war to a peaceable community'.

PLATE 1.1   Precision bombing, *circa* 1914. In this case, flight safety is enhanced by the delegation of bomb-dropping duties to the observer. (*Imperial War Museum*)

It is clear that civilians were not the target of the French bombers. However, in the raid on Freiburg we see the beginnings of a problem which was to affect the whole course of strategic bombing. The unpalatable fact was that the equipments used to ensure accurate navigation and bombing were then—and continued for very many years to be—just too crude and ineffective for precision attacks on specific military targets. And as many of those targets, in both world wars and in many other campaigns, were situated in or near centres of population—inevitably, civilians living in their vicinity would suffer as a direct consequence of air attack. It may be a little simplistic to suggest, as some historians have done, that the shortcomings of tech-

PLATE 1.2   A typical Zeppelin, L.30 pictured in flight. (*Imperial War Museum*)

PLATE 1.3   The bird-like Taube was responsible for some distinctly unfriendly
'droppings' on Paris in the early days of World War I. (*Bundesarchiv Koblenz*)

nology led directly to the concept of 'area bombing'; but in practical terms, that was
certainly the effect.

It was Imperial Germany that was the first to embark on a sustained programme
of bombing beyond the battle area—in other words, to engage in a bombing campaign that was the precursor of that agreed upon in far-off Casablanca nearly 30
years later. In this, the German High Command elected to carry out raids which
could properly be classed as strategic—in scope and aim. In the great Zeppelin
airship it had the best, if not the only weapon then capable of such action. At the
outbreak of war, in August 1914, Germany had no more than ten Zeppelins available, though more were under construction. However, although few in number,
they had the range and potential payload to carry over two tons of bombs per sortie
to the British Isles. From January 1915 through to the end of the war, a total of 51
Zeppelin raids was mounted against England, though increasingly effective defences
ensured that attacks were very infrequent after 1916. Nor were they ever particularly
accurate—Zeppelin commanders finding, as did their colleagues in the heavier-than-
air machines, that the combination of searchlights, anti-aircraft guns and, later,
fighter aircraft forced them ever higher; and that the ill-forecast effects of wind,
both on the bombs and on the machines from which they were released, were such
as to spread the weapons rather liberally around and seldom accurately upon their
targets. By the end of 1915, the Allies had calculated that their bombers had less

than a one-in-four chance of hitting as large and distinctive a target as a Zeppelin shed: the percentage success of strikes against something like a railway junction was a miserable 2%.

Despite that—indeed, in a sense, because of it—the effect of such raids on the people of those cities under attack was always regarded as critical. Even when it had been conclusively proven that civilian morale was very much more resilient than the planners of the day had assumed, there was still what R. P. Hearne, a contemporary writer on such matters, called 'the principle of psychological influence'. Writing in 1916 in his book *Zeppelins and Super-Zeppelins* (for reference to which I am again indebted to Professor Kennett) Hearne commented that:

> It is particularly humiliating to allow an enemy to come over your capital
> city and hurl hombs upon it. His aim may be very bad, the casualties may
> be few, but the moral effect is heavily undesirable. When the Zeppelins
> came to London, they could have scored a galling tactical triumph over us
> if they had showered us with confetti.

It was not confetti which Germany was to use in the next phase of its aerial assault on the United Kingdom; and 1917 marked the year in which a new form of terror came to its islands. The first of the Gotha raids saw a force of 21 of these G-type aircraft killing 95 innocent shoppers and injuring twice that number in Folkestone. In fact, these were G-IV model Gothas, the most potent variants of what had hitherto been a rather undistinguished line of long-range bombers. John Terraine has commented in his excellent book on technological development in World War I[5] that the Gotha was not a pretty aircraft (Plate 1.4); yet it was to become the most successful German bomber of the war. For the period, it was large—over 40 ft long

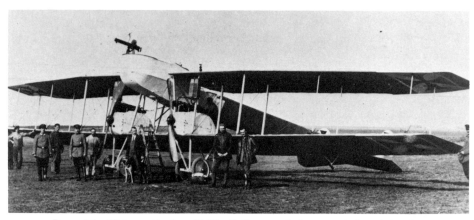

PLATE 1.4 'Not a pretty aircraft'. The Gotha nevertheless came to be rated as the most successful German bomber of World War I. (*Royal Air Force Museum*)

and with an upper wingspan of nearly 78ft. Its two 260hp Mercedes engines gave it a top speed of only about 87 mph. However, its success as a bomber derived from its defensive armament of three machine-guns (one rearwards-firing) a bomb-load in excess of 1,000lb and the famous Goertz bomb-sight. By June 1917 the first Gotha raid had taken place on London, when 14 aircraft succeeded in killing 162 people and injuring more than 400, of whom 16 killed and 30 injured were infants attending class at an East End primary school. In fact, although it caused great and understandable consternation, this first raid was to be the most effective for the Gothas in terms of aircraft lost and civilian casualties inflicted. British air defences, at first virtually non-existent, became steadily more effective in deterring—if not too often destroying the enemy bombers.

As always, an offensive weapon had led to the development of defensive counters; as always, those defences were now threatened by a more capable adversary. The

PLATE 1.5   Yet another German bomber. Staaken-Aviatik's 'Riesenflugzeug' R.16 lifts off. (*Imperial War Museum*)

new *Riesenflugzeug* or R-plane was a giant by any standards (Plate 1.5). Owing not a little in concept to Sikorsky's massive *Ilya Mourametz* of the Russian Air Arm, its wingspan of 138ft 5½in was only 3 ft less than that of the B-29 Superfortress which was to be used so devastatingly on incendiary (and, eventually, atomic) bombing raids on Japan nearly 30 years later. Its four engines were mounted in pairs—one pushing and one pulling from each of two nacelles. Capable of carrying no fewer than six guns (though normally, three), usually—and interestingly—of the British Lewis variety, its range was close on 300 miles, its ceiling 12,500 ft and its speed a relatively sedate 80 mph. However, its bomb-load of 4,500lb was impressive for its time—and, indeed, for several years later. To quote again from John Terraine:

> Interesting elements of its equipments were the gyro-compass for navigation, which was also assisted by directional wireless; the bomber could send out a signal which was plotted by two ground stations, which then transmitted its exact position back to the aircraft. The wireless operator was a regular member of the (7- or 9-man) crew, and sat in the control cabin. In one of the machines... a pneumatic tube carried messages from one part of the aircraft to the other—a light warning the receiver that a message was in the tube. Six 'Giants' operated against England; two crash-landed on return in March 1918—this was always a hazard—and a massive

undercarriage consisting of no fewer than sixteen large wheels was devised to combat it. No 'Giant' was brought down by Air Defence.[6]

In the face of mounting anger among its people, the British Government was forced to resort to reprisal. In the words of Prime Minister David Loyd George: 'We will give it all back to them, and we will give it to them soon. We will bomb Germany with compound interest.[7]

The problem was that Britain's two military air arms (the Royal Flying Corps and the Royal Naval Air Service) consisted almost entirely of short-range fighter reconnaissance or 'spotter' aircraft, which were totally unsuitable for bombing raids against Imperial Germany. In 1916 one exception (and even then, in no way compar-

PLATE 1.6   De Havilland's DH-4—the first British aircraft designed for the day bombing role—pictured in 1916. (*Royal Air Force Museum*)

able to the German G- and R-planes) was the de Havilland DH-4 (Plate 1.6), the first British aircraft actually designed for the day bombing role. Operating out of eastern France, its range of more than 400 miles and top speed of some 136 mph were advantages to offset a strictly limited bomb-load of only 460 lb. Even so, it was greatly superior in all-round performance as a bomber to the already obsolescent FE-2b (used, with very limited success, in the night-bombing role); or to the ill-fated DH-9 which had been rushed all too precipitately into service.

The only genuine exceptions to the rule in Britain's steadily more capable air arm in the second half of World War I were, in fact, a series of Handley Page designs, starting with the twin-engined 0/100 in 1916 and followed by the 0/400, with a useful performance for its day of nearly 100 mph and a bomb-load of 2,000 lb carried over a 650-mile range. In May 1918 came the V-1500, powered by four 375 hp Rolls Royce engines and capable of carrying two 3,000-lb bombs a distance of 1,200 miles—as Terraine rightly suggests, 'a true strategic weapon' (Plate 1.7). But, as he goes on to say:

'It was designed to attack Berlin, but it arrived just too late: three V-1500s were actually standing by, bombed-up, when the Armistice was signed.'[8]

By contrast, the French Army Air Service had had some experience of strategic bombardment—from the time of that first none-too-successful raid on Freiburg in December 1914. Its *Groupe de Bombardement* No 1 was, indeed, the first unit of any of the belligerents to be formed specifically for the bombing role. Despite the obvious danger of German retaliation against actions which caused civilian casualties, French bombers did have some limited success in raids against specific military targets in Germany. Among the more notable were daylight attacks on the chlorine gas plants at Ludwigshafen and Oppau and the great Mauser works at Oberndorf; and, over a 2-year period, no less than 1,800 tons of bombs were dropped, by day and night, against the vast rail network of the Briey Basin, near Metz.

But despite numerous proposals by some obviously very daring young men, no bomber was to strike the German capital—Berlin. By the war's end, the only aircraft capable of mounting such a raid (the Handley Page V-1500) was barely in service.

PLATE 1.7   A Handley Page V-1500, pictured over Cricklewood, England, in 1918. This was, for Great Britain, the first genuine strategic bomber. (*Royal Air Force Museum*)

Yet, as a footnote to this short survey of strategic offensive air operations in World War I (a survey which has, incidentally, necessarily omitted much detail and completely ignored the activities of the Italian and Russian air arms) one exploit cannot be overlooked. As early as June 1916 a single Allied aircraft—a specially modified Nieuport, flown by Lieutenant Antoine Marchal of the French Army Air Service— did make the long journey to Berlin. His plan, which had French High Command approval, was to fly right across Europe, from the Western Front to the Russian lines, passing over Berlin *en route* during a flight of some 14 hours. The gallant Lieutenant actually reached the German capital where he threw out leaflets proclaiming that the French also had a bombing capability, but would not make war on women and children. Continuing eastwards, Marchal was eventually forced to land because of a misfiring engine. He was in the process of changing his spark-plugs when he was captured by a German patrol, only some 60 miles from the Russian lines. Truly the embodiment of the spirit of an age; but, at the same time, an age which had seen the rise of an ever more powerful form of war—the strategic air offensive—to set beside the horrors of the trenches and the high seas but, unlike those two environments, also to bring civil populations well within the sound and reach of battle.

THE INTER-WAR YEARS

In the years between 1918 and 1939 there were sporadic outbursts of bombing activity in various parts of the globe, as man maintained his unfortunate predilection for showing inhumanity to his fellow-man. In Morocco, in China, in Abyssinia, on the North-West frontier of India and elsewhere, aerial bombardment was added to the growing list of disasters with which people—and by no means all of them military people—had to contend. In Spain, the Civil War brought the bombing of civilian populations once again to world attention—none more so than the attack by the so-called Condor Legion on the unprotected Basque town of Guernica. On 26 April 1937, German bombers inflicted heavy casualties on the population of that small and relatively compact place. The facts were that the attack was unexpected and unopposed, that the participating bombers had only short distances to travel without any real fear of anti-aircraft opposition, and that the bombing took place when the streets were full of market-day shoppers. Much of this was overlooked, however, as the Civil Defence planners of Europe calculated the likely damage to a major city on extrapolations of Guernica.

There were miscalculations, also, from a less than adequate study of the bombing of London in 1917 and 1918. Taking the number of casualties suffered in 16 night raids over that period, the planners arrived at a likely figure of 50 casualties per ton of bombs dropped and a prediction of 25,000 casualties a month. In fact, over 40% of the total casualties included in this count had resulted from two raids—one of which involved an extraordinary sequence of events when 38 people had been killed and 85 injured at the Odhams Printing Works in Long Acre. The works had, in fact, been designated a public air raid shelter (and thus held many more people than normal during the raid). It was struck by a single 660-lb bomb, which penetrated the printing-room floor and caused the heavy presses to fall on the heads of those taking refuge below—hardly a 'statistically normal' occurrence to be used as a basis for accurate civil defence planning.

For reasons such as this, magnified by a quite unjustified assessment of the likely success of German bombers in reaching and striking their targets, it is small wonder that something approaching resignation—if not frustrated panic—set in among the inhabitants of some of the larger cities of Europe. But of course not every bomber would reach its target. Of those that did, many would not bomb accurately—if at all. Every bomb dropped would not hit densely populated areas—let alone a printing works doubling as an air-raid shelter. In consequence, expert opinion held that the Germans would drop 100,000 tons of bombs on London in 14 days—a figure greater than that actually received by the city during the whole course of the impending war.

It is easy to be critical. But the fact of the matter was that people and their political leaders were driven into making individual and collective decisions on evidence that was assumed to be the best available. In consequence, when Prime Minister Chamberlain made his dramatic dash to Munich the fear of air attack had, in the words of Winston Churchill, 'become obsessive in men's minds.'[9] When it was widely held that war would involve the destruction of the nation and the very ruin of civilisation, it was at least understandable that its prevention, in 1938, was widely acclaimed—whatever the cost to Czechoslovakia. One year later it had become clear that, despite all dangers, appeasement was no response to the growing demands of the Reich.

WORLD WAR II

The Second World War was to see the almost unrestrained growth of strategic air bombardment. Much has been written of all this; and it is beyond the scope of this book to do more than summarise the principal technological developments which laid the foundations for the strategic offensive air power of today—and, indeed, of tomorrow. In truth, such is the short historical timespan of air power as a component of man's war-fighting capability and so close has been its relationship to developing technology, that the past 50 years can be seen as no more than rapidly evolving scene-setting for the future. It is certainly impossible to ignore a period so important to an understanding of the subject as is World War II in the context of strategic bombardment. The least that can be done is to highlight some of the ways in which the technology of the day assisted in the development of a genuinely strategic role for the air forces of the principal combatants.

During the inter-war years the role of the bomber had become a topic of serious and, occasionally, bitter debate among the many protagonists of air power. Today, there are many who would see the effectiveness of long-range air attack as calling for large formations of aircraft, scheduled in 'packages' to provide real-time information on the enemy; to seduce, divert or destroy his defensive radars; to combat his electronic warfare capability; to offer defensive fighter cover to and from the target area; and to carry out the attack itself. At the same time, there are those who would put their faith in smaller numbers of attacking aircraft, themselves capable of electronic self-protection, anti-radar strikes and, in the last analysis, limited self-defence with air-to-air missiles—able to penetrate at very low levels and at night or in poor weather, with a combination of aids to terrain-following, night vision and target acquisition. There is a parallel here with the 1930s. And, given that technology was then immeasurably less complex or costly, room could be found, even in some of the comparatively modest defence budgets of the day, for experimentation and the development of differing concepts of air power projection.

The idea of the bomber as a specialist load-carrier, with a range and payload sufficient to give it true strategic reach, was espoused by some. The R-plane and the Handley Page V/1500 of 1918 had, less than 20 years later, spawned the Italian Caproni 90PB and huge American XB-15 (Plate 1.8)—the latter swiftly superseded by Boeing's classic B-17 Flying Fortress. That aircraft, in turn, owed something to another school of thought—that which proclaimed that the bomber should rely for its self-protection on heavy all-round defensive armament as, to a degree, had the Gotha of World War I. A series of French bombers of the 1930s was built on this same principle—aircraft such as the Amiot 143 (Figure 1.1) entering the war of 1939–45 heavily armoured and relatively heavily laden; but lacking the range, height and particularly the speed to operate effectively against the type of opposition

PLATE 1.8   Boeing's massive XB-15 development was to be overtaken by the very much more successful B-17 series of 'Flying Fortresses'. (*The Boeing Company Archives*)

already available in the inventories of the enemy. An interesting (though in the event almost unique) concept was that of the Russian engineer Vladimir Vakimistrov. His *Zveno* or 'linked flight' project was an attempt to compensate for the limited range of the bomber's escort fighters by strapping them to the parent bomber, from which they could be launched as required. The massive four-engined Tupolev-designed TB-3 could carry no fewer than five fighters in this way (Plates 1.9 and 1.10). Where, once launched, they would eventually land was not entirely clear; and—to the presumed relief of the fighter pilots—interest died with the increased range of the newer Soviet fighters[10].

Others, again, argued the case for the multi-role aircraft; yet others, that of speed as an essential requirement for the bomber. Led by the Germans with their concept of a *schnell* bomber, designers of aircraft like the Heinkel He 111 looked to aerodynamically clean shapes, the internal carriage of bombs, relatively light defensive armament, all-metal construction and powerful engines. Initially designed in 1935 as a thinly disguised 10-passenger transport aircraft, the He 111 was in action less

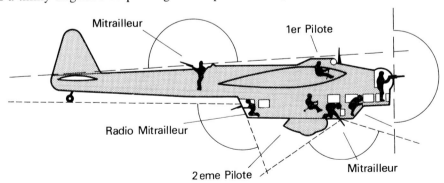

FIG. 1.1   The Amiot 143—work-horse of France's bomber squadrons on the eve of World War II. Its lack of speed was in part, compensated by its self-defensive armament—the arcs of fire which are illustrated here. (*Service Historique de l'Armée de l'Air Française*)

PLATES 1.9 and 1.10   Vakimistrov's 'Zveno' project. A massive Tupolev-designed
TB3-bomber, capable of carrying no less than five assorted escort fighters, pictured
in flight and on the ground in 1935. (*The Eyermann Collection, GDR*)

than two years later as a highly effective medium bomber, with a range of about
1,000 miles, a top speed of more than 250 mph and a very respectable bomb-load
of nearly 4,500 lb. But, as in so much else, the design of bomber aircraft in the 1930s
and beyond represented a series of compromises; and it is interesting to note that
the greatest success stories of those stirring times were with aircraft which combined
attributes of more than one of the various schools of bomber thinking. The Boeing
B-17 Flying fortress, for example, can be seen as a compromise between the capabilities of a large, long-range bomber and those required for all-round self-defence.

Even more successful than the He 111 was the de Havilland Mosquito, an aircraft
which not only went much faster and further than its German predecessor (over 400
mph at 26,000 ft and nearly 1,500 miles with a 5,000-lb bomb-load) but which was

capable of very many more operational roles than had been envisaged by even the headiest exponents of the multi-purpose bomber in the 1930s. Originally designed as a fast day-bomber which would rely on speed for its protection, the Mosquito was to see action also as a night-bomber, an exceptional 'pathfinder' of the RAF's Light Night Striking Force, an anti-shipping aircraft, a night-fighter and—perhaps as well-tailored a role as any—a photographic reconnaissance platform of unequalled effec-

PLATE 1.11   A sight to put the pulses of any red-blooded airman into over-drive! The beautiful (and extremely versatile) Mosquito. Pictured here is a Mk B16 of No. 571 Squadron, Royal Air Force, operating in the 'Pathfinder' role. The photograph dates from September 1944, when the Mosquito was in its heyday as a front-line aircraft.
(*Royal Air Force Museum*)

tiveness (Plate 1.11). And it is worth recalling that the Mosquito was built largely of wood—not only to conserve weight (and, incidentally, scarce resources of metal) but to allow the skills of those earlier aircraft-builders to be carried through into another generation of combat machines.

In terms of design development, a most striking example of triumph born of failure was the brilliantly successful Lancaster, with its four Merlin engines, derived from the disastrous Manchester with its two double-engined Vultures. And to prove that disaster knew no national boundaries in the matter of aircraft design, it is perhaps salutary to consider the following extract from an official report on a bomber variant taken into service by the Royal Air Force in the early war years. It may serve to offer some insight into the complexities of long-range air warfare even the best part of half a century ago; and of the desperate efforts of technology to catch up with the ever more demanding requirements of operational aircrew in war. Quoted by John Terraine in his book *The Right of the Line* (an excellent history of the RAF's crucial role in World War II) the report[11] read:

> ... the bomb-sight was not fully automatic above 20,000 feet, and therefore bombing accuracy still depended on the human element; armament consisted of heavy, manually-operated machine guns, and to operate the beam guns large blisters had to be opened, reducing the internal temperature of

the aircraft to the order of –50°C; armour was inadequate, but if augmented would lower the (aircraft's) ceiling; its turbo-blown engines, though giving a higher ceiling than any other bomber, took it up to 35,000 feet, not to the stratosphere; it made great demands on the physiology and mentality of its crew at such heights;... weather conditions limited its operational scope; it formed contrails, and would do so until it could exceed 40,000 feet; its radius of action[12] at 30,000 feet was still only 500 miles; its engines developed defects in the rarefied atmosphere near its ceiling; and its atmospheric oxygen supply needed to be replaced by a pressure cabin system.

Another disaster? In fact, this was the Boeing Fortress I—the RAF designation of the modified B-17C in which crews of Bomber Command's No. 90 Squadron flew a total of 51 daylight bombing missions over a four-month period in 1941. Of these, less than half were even claimed as effective and the aircraft was withdrawn for less demanding maritime reconnaissance tasks.

Such is the imperative for progress in war that, within a year, later derivatives of the B-17 (the E, F and ultimately G models) were giving impressive service, though often at great cost, in the strategic air campaigns over Europe. In the process, the earlier C models had been transformed (Figure 1.3) by many hundreds of modifications. These included major structural alterations to the nose section, rear fuselage, fin and rudder and the fitting of rear-gun and under-fuselage 'ball' turrets. Also introduced were self-sealing fuel tanks, additional sources of internal electric power, improved navigation and communications equipments, improved cockpit layout, a much improved crew oxygen system and more powerful engines (the R-1820-97 engines of the B-17F having an emergency rating of a massive 1,320 hp). As a result of all this, the aircraft's gross take-off weight rose to some 65,000 lb which, in turn, called for the strengthening of the undercarriage and the fitting of a dual braking system. Compared with any other bomber, before or since, the Flying Fortress (Plate 1.12) was aptly named. Each carrying 12 0.5-in guns capable of firing up to 14 rounds a second over an effective range of some 600 yards, the standard 36-aircraft formation (adopted from early 1944 onwards) could bring to bear no fewer than 432 defensive guns and a total of almost four million rounds of ammuntion. The strength of the Fortress's firepower was not matched by its protective armour—though this was steadily improved over the years and the aircraft was, it is true, capable of sustaining great damage. But, of the 15,000 heavy bombers (the great majority of them B-17s) sent by the United States Army Air Force (USAAF) to the European theatre of war, no less than 8,000 (53%) were lost to enemy action and a further 1,000 or more to 'other causes'—mostly, accidents in training. In each of the last two years of the war, almost one-third of the American bomber force in Europe had to be replaced.

Of course, none of these statistics is quoted in any way to denigrate the part played by the USAAF B-17s in the prosecution over three grim and difficult years of the strategic bombardment of Hitler's Third Reich. Nor is the B-17 deserving of any singling-out as an especially vulnerable aircraft for its role. Over the 5¾-year period of the war in Europe, the RAF's Bomber Command sustained over 47,368 casualties in operations alone—more than 67% of the total of RAF officers, NCOs and airmen aircrew killed or missing in action—together with a further 8,305 lives lost in the

XB–17

YB–17

B–17B

B–17C

B–17D

B–17E

B–17F

B–17G

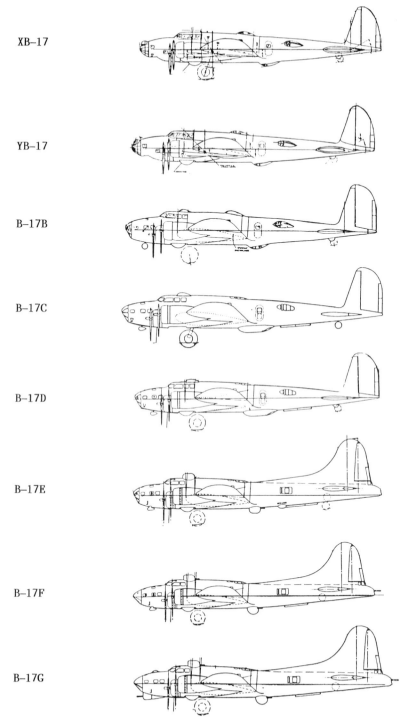

FIG. 1.3   Showing the evolution of the Boeing B-17 'Flying Fortress', from early prototype to fully-fledged war machine. (*Historical services, the Boeing Company*)

PLATE 1.12   The 'Flying Fortress'. Boeing B-17Fs of the USAAF's 8th Air Force pictured in dramatic fashion en route to their German target. (*Boeing Aerospace Company*)

Command's non-operational flying, as a result of accidents in training. These stark figures serve only to underline the very hazardous nature of war in the air—particularly when that war is taken, by night and day and in virtually all weathers, to an enemy whose homeland and whose invading armies are well defended and whose leadership is both determined and increasingly desperate. Were any future war to break out in Europe, the losses in the air would not be so great nor the war so protracted; but the destruction might, as a consequence of modern weapons, well be incalculably greater. Hence, the primary purpose of strategic air power from the 1950s onwards—as a deterrent to war and, in a very real sense, a safeguard of the peace.

2

The Development of Strategic Bombing—the Equipment

TECHNOLOGICAL DEVELOPMENTS OF THE 1930s AND ONWARDS

The costs of the bombing offensive in Europe were enormous—whether assessed in terms of aircraft lost or, far more tellingly, of gallant young airmen killed, wounded or missing in action. There has been endless debate as to the relative value of that offensive to the ultimate winning of the bloodiest war in history. Military historians and others have argued their respective cases over the years—indeed, were doing so while the war still raged. The proponents of daylight precision bombing, large formations, bomber self-defence, the need for long-range escort fighters, night-attacks, area and 'carpet' bombing, pathfinder techniques—all have had their say; and the student who wishes to learn more of these important issues of the day will find plenty on which to bite in the many books and studies since published. In this one, he will hopefully learn a little of the technology which is used to ensure the viability of modern and future strategic weapons systems. But there is merit in studying some of the ways in which the technology of the day helped the aircrews of the 1940s and 1950s to carry out the daunting, often highly dangerous and always challenging tasks which were demanded of them.

Early Bombs

Firstly, let us look briefly at the development of the weapon itself—the bomb, in all its many forms. We have already seen how, in the earliest days of air power, these were little more than grenades, which the pilots and observers of the first generation of true bombers would carry aloft by hand or loosely attached to their flimsy aircraft; and would drop—again by hand—with the only aid to sighting being that of the all-purpose 'Mark 1 eyeball'. The lower the height of the attacking aircraft, the steadier it could be flown and the less the effects of wind or—worse—anti-aircraft barrage, the more accurate would be the bomb-strike. With bombs weighing only a few pounds in all, accuracy was the essential pre-requisite of success. Of course, the ideal conditions for bombing accuracy were seldom realised; and those early pioneers of bombing were compelled to take the most awful risks with enemy defensive fire if they were to stand any chance of success. Even in those early days, alternatives to high explosives had been used—though with only limited success. Canisters of small darts (or *flechettes*) were the precursors of generations of anti-personnel weapons. Dropped in quantities of several hundred at a time, they were meant to strike troops and pack-animals with the force of latter-day rifle bullets. However, as such momentum demanded that they be dropped from heights of at least 5,000 ft, accuracy was very poor; and the *flechettes* themselves were so small (only a few inches in length) that success called for nothing less than a direct hit.

Crude incendiary devices were also available to both the Royal Flying Corps and their French and German counterparts of the 1914–15 era. These generally consisted of nothing more than petrol cans, into each of which had been inserted a cartridge of modest charge. On impact, the firing of the cartridge would ignite the petrol. At least, that was the theory. In practice, there was quite a high rate of cartridge failure and, in any case, the ballistic properties of the petrol cans were not such as to ensure the effective accuracy of the weapon.

However, the challenge of war to scientists, designers and manufacturers—every bit as much as to the politicians and their generals—ensured that the development of new weapons was as swift as that of their carriers and of the tactics used in their employment. As early as 1915, Zeppelins were carrying over two-thirds of their weapon loads as incendiary bombs for use against cities; and by the end of 1917 a newly designed 10-lb incendiary weapon was ready to be delivered by the hundred from the Gotha bombers launched principally against London. Fortunately for that city, the new weapons suffered from problems of ignition; and their effect on the mass of the civilian population was negligible. Meanwhile, inventive German scientists had developed a variant of the earlier phosphorous bomb (used mostly for the generation of smoke and local heat on the battlefield) and had produced the *Elektron* weapon—a bomb consisting almost entirely of pure magnesium which would burn at temperatures approaching 3,000°F and which was calculated to raise massive, uncontainable fires on target cities. By mid-1918, thousands of these weapons had been manufactured; but London was spared by the realisation of the German High Command that the war was then as good as lost and that their use would only have attracted further and unnecessary opprobrium (and possible Allied retaliation) on the German nation.

Just as incendiary weapons had been increasing in size and power during the war years, so had high-explosive bombs. The 2-lb grenades of late 1914 had become, first, 20-lb bombs; then 112- and 230-pounders on the old Handley Page 0/100s and Short bombers of 1916/17; and so to 550-pounders, designed to penetrate the concrete protection which the Germans were then affording their shore-based gun batteries and submarine pens. By the end of the war, the Handley Page V/1500 could carry no fewer than thirty 250-lb or two specially developed 3,300-lb bombs slung under its massive fuselage. As has already been noted, this genuine strategic bomber was destined never to take to the air in anger—either with one of those huge loads or with the 1,000 lb total it was designed to carry to Berlin. Nor had the Kaiser's Germany been inactive in bomb development during those same years of war. The Gotha G-IV could lift six 110-lb bombs across the North Sea to London and a total of 1,100 lb carried internally and externally for shorter-range bombardment. The massive R-plane had room for eighteen 220-lb weapons carried within the fuselage, with larger-sized weapons (up to a 2,200-pounder) carried externally. A maximum load of 4,500 lb could only be lifted over the shorter ranges, but the lighter loads could be carried for 800 miles by the fitting of external fuel tanks. It is easy to imagine the drag effect of these otherwise useful encumbrances on a machine which was both ungainly and, by all accounts, rather difficult to fly.

Bombing Equipment

As with bombs—so with the means of their carriage, aiming and release: World War I saw a steady improvement in both capacity and capability. From the earliest rudimentary 'nail sights' at the beginning of the war, experts in physics and ballistics combined with combat aircrew to resolve the mysteries of how to hit a target with a bomb dropped from a height, at a speed and with a wind effect which could never be measured with the precision demanded by the exercise. (A simplified diagram,

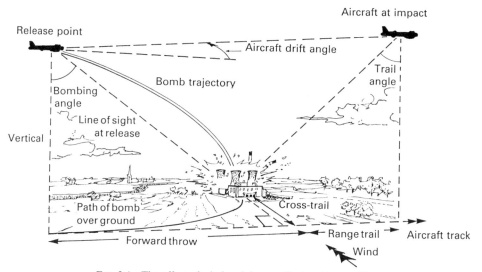

FIG. 2.1   The effect of wind and drag on the bombing problem.

Figure 2.1. indicates some of the problems) Perhaps the most promising design was that of Lieutenant Commander Wimperis of the Royal Naval Air Service, whose Course-Setting Bomb-Sight, came at the very end of the war but remained standard RAF equipment for the next 20 years. The fact that this was due more to the continuing pressure on defence funds than to the excellence of Wimperis' design is not to criticise what was, for its day, a very brave attempt to produce a bomb-sight which could take into reasonable consideration the effects of an aircraft's height above target, air- and ground-speed, drift and direction of attack relative to the prevailing wind.

Between the wars, the USAAF not only sponsored the development of a series of long-range bomber types (the most successful of which were to be the lineal descendants of Boeing's Y1B-17 Fortress and B-24 Liberator) but also took delivery of a sophisticated bomb-sight (the Norden) which, in its various forms, was to see service throughout World War II and beyond. The

Norden (Plates 2.1 and 2.2) was a tachometric sight, designed to measure the changing values of directly observable quantities, such as the relative positions of aircraft and target, and the angles thus required to compute aiming allowances for

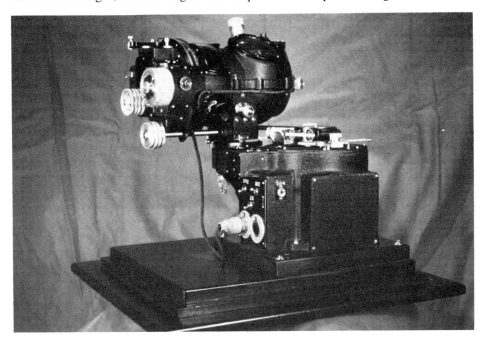

PLATES 2.1 and 2.2   Norden's tachometric bomb-sight, which saw extensive service in World War II. Here, the actual sight and some of its accompanying equipments are shown on display and, more dramatically, in use. (*United Technologies—Norden Systems*)

wind velocity, drift etc. The basic principle of a tachometric (or, as it is sometimes known, a synchronous) sight is illustrated in Figure 2.2. With bomb ballistics already set, a line of sight, established between aircraft and target, is turned in azimuth to allow for the drift of the aircraft over the ground. The sighting angle (*ie* the angle between the sighting line and the vertical) is altered at a rate which is dependent on the setting of controls to measure aircraft height and ground-speed. These controls are so adjusted until the sight graticule coincides (and thereafter remains coincident) with the target. The consequent 'tracking' of the target with the line of sight produces the data required to determine the bombing angle. When this coincides with the sighting angle, the aircraft will have reached the point of bomb release. The Norden sight was said to be able to determine the bombing angle so accurately that its manufacturers claimed its user could 'drop a bomb in a pickle barrel from 25,000 ft'. To assist him in attempting to match this brochure claim, the bombardier could physically control the lateral movements of his aircraft through an Automatic Flight Control Equipment. To avoid undue anticipation or 'freeze' on his part (he could, for example, well be under enemy fire as his aircraft approached its target), the bombs were released automatically.

In theory—and indeed in practice in the generally clear skies of the USA—the Norden was a fine precision instrument, used to achieve excellent bombing results. But such conditions were not the norm in the European theatre of war in which it was first to see action. There, cloud was all too frequently encountered between the target and the high-flying US bomber; and if it was not cloud, then industrial haze was often to be found. On average these two conditions were met on some 65% of days in a North-West European year. And when nature was kind to the bombers, man frequently put a metaphorical spoke in their wheel by generating smoke or false fires which served to blanket their targets.

Very early in the war, the RAF had been forced to accept that close formation flying and concentrated defensive fire were inadequate for its bomber forces in daylight operations. By the end of 1940 the increasingly effective anti-aircraft defences mounted by the Third Reich had ensured that, for every sortie planned by

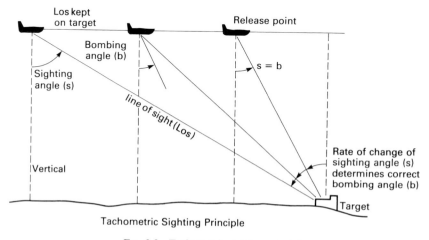

Tachometric Sighting Principle

FIG. 2.2   Tachometric sighting principle.

day, Bomber Command was mounting twenty in the hours of darkness. But, given the then technological state of the art in aircraft navigation and weapon-aiming systems, that option brought its own problems—primarily those of target acquisition, compounded again by nature. Comparatively short summer nights put practical constraints on the bomber's radius of action, if it was to have the refuge of darkness between crossing the enemy coast inbound to and outbound from its target. Again, even on those nights free of cloud or industrial haze (the latter, very frequent in and around the enemy's great industrial centres of the Ruhr) only about one in four afforded the assistance of a 'bomber's moon' for the identification and acquisition of targets.

The challenge was met on three different fronts: by improvements in sighting systems and navigational aids; with the arrival of more capable aircraft—of greater range, speed, service ceiling and load of ordnance; and in the development of advanced bombing tactics.

March 1942 had seen the entry into service of the first of Bomber Command's Lancaster heavy bombers. The bomb-sight developed for it was the Mark XIV—a stabilised vector sight mounted over a large panel of reinforced glass in the nose of the aircraft. The principle of the vector (or impact) bomb-sight differs from that of the tachometric sight in that it depends on the setting up of the sight with calculated values of those variables which cannot be directly observed in flight—for example, the true airspeed of the aircraft or the wind velocity (which itself varies between bombing height and impact). In considering an attack on a fixed target, the effect of a change in windspeed would be seen as a change in the velocity of the aircraft relative to target, whether that change was a result of a changed head- or tail-wind or of a drift-inducing cross-wind. In a tachometric bomb-sight such as the American Norden, the effective rate of change in the relative positions of aircraft and target would be noted by the bombardier, who would effect the necessary adjustments by continuous tracking of the target with the line of sight. In a vector bomb-sight, the new (observed or calculated) values would be fed into the sight during the run-up to the target.

As seen in Figure 2.3, the principle of the vector sight lies in the prediction (using

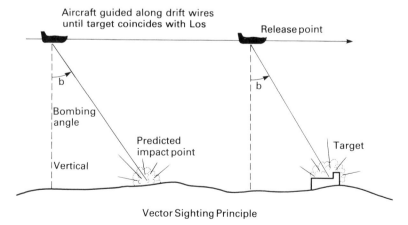

Vector Sighting Principle

FIG. 2.3   Vector sighting principle.

pre-set data) of the impact point of a bomb at the moment of release. This is set as a bombing angle, *ie* the angle between the vertical (aircraft to ground) and the line of sight (aircraft to impact point), taking into account bomb ballistics, the true heights of aircraft and target and the ground-speed of approach of aircraft to target. The azimuth of this line of sight (in relation to aircraft heading) required knowledge of the drift component, *ie* the effect of cross-wind on aircraft and bomb. Bomb release-point was attained by guiding the aircraft in such a way that the target appeared to move along the drift-wires of the bomb-sight until it was on the line of sight itself. For practical purposes, at least 10 seconds of straight and level flight were necessary before bomb release; but the gyro-stabilisation of the Lancaster's Mark XIV sight did allow evasive action to be taken on the final approach to the target—a very necessary requirement on many of the highly defended targets selected for attack by Bomber Command. An important component of the Mark XIV

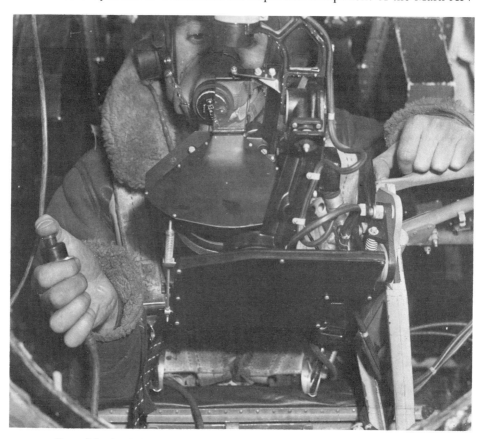

PLATE 2.3   A Mark XIV bomb-sight as fitted in an Avro Lancaster of Bomber Command during World War II. (*Imperial War Museum*)

sight (Plate 2.3) was its computer—a crude device by today's standards, but capable of correlating and feeding into the sight itself the more important parameters of each attack. A collimeter, within the sighting head, projected a graticule on to the reflector glass; and it was the job of a bomb-aimer so to direct his pilot that the target moved steadily down the longer (fore and aft) axis of the graticule until it was bisected by the shorter (cross) axis. At this point the weapons would be released.

In practice, accurate bombing called for a heady mixture of skill, experience and luck—even in training on undefended bombing ranges in good weather conditions. The effects of cold, poor visibility, fear and adrenalin-flow could all play their part in deciding whether or not the bombs actually hit their intended targets. And that is to say nothing of the combined efforts of searchlights, anti-aircraft guns and enemy fighters to affect the aim; the last-minute obscuration of target by cloud, smoke or the effects of other aircrafts' bombs; or the often violent movements of the bombing platform itself, as pilots sought to dive, climb, weave and corkscrew their way clear

PLATE 2.4   . . . when it really counted. Lancasters over Germany, some time in 1943. (*Imperial War Museum*)

of the many threats which beset them (Plate 2.4). Whether by night or day, the life of the bomb-aimer in the skies over Europe in the early 1940s was one of almost continuous stress. Given the extreme youth of most of their number, the results they achieved were little short of remarkable. What they did have, for comfort and mental balance, was the knowledge that they were members of a crew, dependent on each other not only for results but for their very lives; each sharing the full measure of danger with the other; every man clear as to just what was expected of him. In consequence, they were able to enjoy the easy familiarity and close comradeship which is reserved for those trained together to face situations of great danger.

Aids to Navigation

The placing of bombs on target was, of course, the objective of the bomber crew. But to achieve that objective, it was necessary to find the target—and more than desirable to return safely from it. As has been noted, the aids to precise navigation in the late 1930s—certainly, those that were considered acceptable for military aviation—were crude by the standards of today. Again, however, they developed with great rapidity under the pressure of all-out war.

A comparison of the experience of two combat air forces, the British and the German, is instructive in the matter of precision navigation in the early 1940s. For the RAF at the outbreak of World War II, the primary navigational aid was still 'dead reckoning' (DR). This was the process by which a navigator took into the air a precisely calculated flight plan, accurately drawn on his maps and taking into account not only known factors (distance, positions of base, check-points and target) and those variables which could be fairly accurately predicted (aircraft speed, planned height, fuel consumption etc), but also a number of rather important features which, given the existing state of the art, were often no more than educated guesswork. These features were primarily meteorological—windspeed and direction at all heights flown by the attacking aircraft, air temperature and pressure throughout the flight regime, cloud cover, precipitation and icing. All were critical to the precise calculation of the aircraft's flight path, and any inaccuracies in the forecasting of them would lead to errors in navigation. But the greatest problem was that of calculating the wind vector—a calculation that had to be repeated throughout the flight, given a wind constantly changing with aircraft height and location. The perennial problems for the often unjustly maligned met forecaster were compounded in war by his inability to obtain all the information needed on weather patterns over a wide area. Understandably, there was precious little of that information available about the conditions over large tracts of enemy territory. In the circumstances, the 'met men' of the 1940s did, as always, every bit as well as could be expected of them; but (again as always) expectations were unreasonably high and the inevitable errors often bitterly resented. The aircrew of the day certainly needed as much help as they could get. To give the reader a more vivid feel for the problems of DR navigation in war, I can do no better than quote from a footnote in a definitive work on the subject, *The Strategic Air Offensive against Germany, 1939-45* by Sir Charles Webster and Noble Frankland:[1]

> Pilots could not hold heavy aircraft constantly on precise headings; and their attempts to do so were often vitiated by the need to take evasive action, during which magnetic compasses tended to swing aimlessly and gyro-compasses often 'toppled'. Moreover, instruments did not give true readings. Air-Speed Indicators had to be corrected for position error, temperature and altitude; altimeters for barometric pressure; magnetic compasses for variation caused by the magnetic field of the earth and for deviation caused by that of the aircraft; and gyro-compasses for 'wander' caused by the spin of the earth. Navigators had to work fast, in somewhat cramped and poorly lighted conditions. They also had to draw straight lines on vibrating surfaces.

Bomber aircrew were not, of course, launching off into some 'black hole', reliant entirely on the weather forecast and their skills in DR navigation. There were, even then, a few useful aids to navigation—albeit not reliable in all circumstances. Radio aids to navigation were at an early stage of development—certainly for military use—and, in any case, unlikely to be of use out of range of the home base. Nevertheless, they did exist. Then there was the aforementioned 'Mark I eyeball'—in fact, several pairs of those rather flexible instruments in each aircraft. Given reasonable visibility and the absence of cloud cover, fix-points could be seen and overflown—allowing the navigator both to update his aircraft's true position and, by back-plotting, to calculate the actual wind conditions which had affected its flight path thus far. This was all very well by day—except that, as Bomber Command dicovered all too soon, daylight also favoured the increasingly effective enemy defences, both ground-based and airborne. When the bombing was carried out by night, the problem with visual fixing was that most of the recognition points normally available had, in fact, been blacked out for the duration of the war. Towns, villages, lighthouses, airfield beacons and road traffic—all were, more or less, denied to the navigator as a source of in-flight information; and lakes and rivers required a 'bomber's moon' before they could be relied upon as useful features for night navigation. The sober fact was that, operating by day and above cloud, DR could not be guaranteed to take an aircraft nearer than 50 miles to its target: by night, errors could be even greater.

By 1939, some bombers had been fitted with astrodomes—plexiglass bubbles on the top surface of the fuselage—in which a navigator could stand and through which he could use a sextant to 'shoot' the stars. In ideal conditions, this was in fact an extremely accurate form of navigation: for a bomber navigator in war, it was less than ideal. Not only did astro-navigation demand the initial absence of cloud between aircraft and stars: it also called for extremely careful in-flight calculation which was severely disadvantaged by the effects on the navigator of cold and fatigue. Added to that, the technique involved several minutes of very precise straight-and-level flying while each observation was being made—and for some time thereafter—before the navigator could complete his calculations and establish a fix—by that time, inevitably, several minutes out of date. Furthermore, the accuracy of the sextant was entirely dependent on the absence of aircraft acceleration, deceleration or turning forces for a little time before and throughout the process of star-shooting. In normal circumstances, this called for both accurate and very smooth piloting, and the enemy was all the while trying to ensure that circumstances were far from normal. In short, in those aircraft equipped for it, astro-navigation could offer a useful adjunct to DR navigation before crossing the enemy coast inbound to the target: thereafter, its utility was strictly limited.

First into the field (or, more correctly, the air) with improved aids to navigational accuracy for the bomber was the German Luftwaffe. Throughout most of the decade preceding World War II, British and German scientists had been attempting to harness radio waves to the cause of aviation. The British, working in the growing shadow of the dreaded 'knock-out blow' by an increasingly powerful German offensive air arm, had concentrated on the development of equipment which, as a first priority, would detect the direction and range of approaching enemy aircraft. Such equipment, using short-wave radio emissions which could be bounced back from the aircraft they struck, was of course Radio Detection and Ranging (or radar).

The Germans were more interested in the offensive aspects of the problem and experimented with radio as a bombing aid.

The German Lorenz company had designed a system by which airborne receivers, picking up two slightly overlapping radio beams transmitted from ground stations on an airfield, could put a pilot on course between them to establish a direct line of approach to land, whatever the weather. In fact, one of the beams transmitted the dots and the other the dashes used in signalling by Morse code. The narrow overlap of the beams came over to the approaching aircraft as a steady tone which, if maintained whatever the aircraft heading, enabled it to track towards the airfield of landing—thus compensating for the effects of cross-wind or drift (Figure 2.4).

This system was developed as a bombing aid by the German signals giant, Telefunken GmbH. Again two beams were used, the first to keep the pilot on course to his target by following the same steady note, transmitted via his headphones, with Morse dots and dashes to indicate when he had strayed left or right of the required track; the second, transmitted from a site well away from that emitting the director beam, would intersect it to indicate the point of bomb release (Figure 2.5). The transmitters were large radio arrays, moveable on three axes to allow extremely accurate alignment of beam to target. The system could be used by any number of aircraft fitted with the Lorenz airfield approach aid, as was standard in all German bombers by 1940.

Later developments of this basic *Knickebein* (or dogleg) system sought to improve on its accuracy—an accuracy dependent in large part on the distance of target from ground radio emitter, because the radio beam naturally widened with range to about two miles in width at 360 miles from the point of transmission. In consequence, at such a (typical) range, the bomber could be anything up to a mile either side of its target—in fact a marked improvement on the results obtainable by navigational DR, but scarcely precision bombing. More complex systems involving up to four beams (one along and three across track) and relatively sophisticated tuning devices installed in the bombing aircraft, made it possible accurately to time the bomber's speed over the ground and automatically to release its bombs at the calculated release point. The Germans achieved some notable successes with the system (known as *X-Verfahren*). However it was not only dependent on high levels of crew training and co-operation; it was also prey to counter-measures which (as is described with authority and immediacy in Professor R. V. Jones's *Most Secret War*) were devised by British scientists in the very nick of time.

It was the scientists, too, who developed British systems to help carry the strategic air offensive deep into Nazi Germany—and with increasing accuracy. In order of entry into squadron service, the best-known of these equipments were Gee, Oboe H2S and G-H. Although often classed together as radar devices, the first of these was not, strictly speaking, so derived. In fact, Gee depended on the direct transmission and reception of radar pulses. But there were similarities in the techniques used and it was the radar technique which offered Bomber Command the first regular and reliable method of navigational fixing. In the development of Oboe and G-H, it was also important in solving the problems of bomb-aiming; and, given the often encountered conditions of cloud cover or poor visibility in the target area, 'blind' bombing by radar was, by a very large margin, more accurate than bomb-release at the bomber's estimated time of arrival (ETA) over its target.

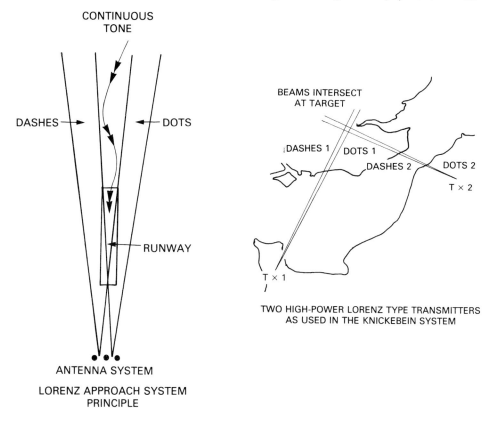

FIGS. 2.4 and 2.5   The Lorenz approach and its application to 'Knickebein'.

A brief description of these four important technological developments is required. Gee involved the reception by suitable equipment within the bombing aircraft of pulsed transmissions from three ground stations sited on a base line of some 200 miles in length. Each transmission from the two 'slave' stations (B or C) was locked to a transmission from the master (or A) station. The difference in time taken to reach the aircraft by A and B and by A and C signals was measured and displayed on a cathode-ray tube at the navigator's station. The effect was to locate the aircraft on two discrete position lines (the Gee coordinates) and the point of intersection of the lines corresponded to the ground position of the aircraft (Figure 2.6). Each crew carried a set of special charts on which the Gee coordinates were printed as a grid (hence the code-name—G for 'grid'); and aircraft-fixing was thus a matter of a minute or less for any trained navigator. The best of them could, in favourable circumstances, fix the aircraft's position to within half a mile; but accuracy deteriorated with range from the transmitting stations and with a decrease in the angle of cut between the two position lines. It could, like the German system, be used at ranges up to about 400 miles, though this meant that it ceased to be of value much beyond the industrial Ruhr. However, it could be used as a homing device on return to base—the nearer the aircraft approached the transmitting

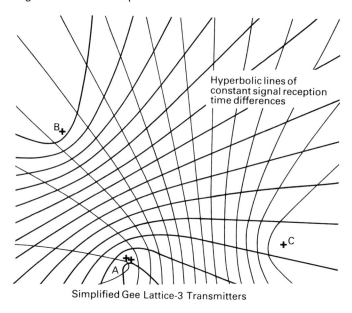

Simplified Gee Lattice-3 Transmitters

FIG. 2.6   A simplified 3-transmitter GEE lattice.

stations, the more accurate its Gee readings. Of course, just like the German *Knick-ebein* and *X-Verfahren*, Gee was susceptible to enemy jamming: it could also be used (indeed, with greater accuracy) by German bombers homing in on the United Kingdom, with the result that its pulses had eventually to be coded and the time taken to obtain a fix inevitably increased.

Oboe was devised as a blind-bombing system, again featuring signals from ground stations. Two stations (known as 'Cat' and 'Mouse') transmitted pulses which were received, boosted and retransmitted by aircraft equipment—thus enabling the ground stations to measure the range of the aircraft concerned. 'Cat' described the arc of an imaginary circle, on the circumference of which would be the target. By the customary dot/dash method, it indicated when the pilot was on a final track to his target. 'Mouse' measured the across-track component for the calculation of bomb release-point. So as not to hold for too long a precalculated track to the target (*ie* by flying the arc against which 'Cat' was measuring the aircraft's range), navigation to the general target area was usually achieved by other means—the Oboe equipment only being switched on for about the last 10 or 12 miles before bomb-release. The equipment's range was limited by the fact that the pulses it produced travelled tangentially to the Earth's surface and thus offered greater ranges only at the greater aircraft altitudes—typically, some 270 miles at 28,000 ft. And that was the sort of altitude which the heavily-laden bombers just could not reach *en route* to their targets. It was extremely accurate for its time—at best, to within a few hundred yards—but it suffered a further limitation in that each pair of Oboe stations could control only one aircraft at a time. For these reasons (and others) Oboe was success-fully used by the lighter, far more manoeuvrable Mosquito, acting in the role of pathfinder or target-marker for the main stream of heavy bombers. Again, it could be jammed. But its value was maintained by the development (in late 1943 and 1944) of centimetric radar to replace the original specification of a more easily jammable 1½-metre wavelength.

H2S offered a form of radar map reading which would be used for the purposes of both navigation and blind bombing. It made use of the principle that radar transmissions return distinctive echoes from different surfaces—whether land or water, buildings or open fields. A downward-looking radar antenna, mounted in the bomber itself, could thus provide a form of map on the navigator's cathode ray tube—a map that was difficult to interpret in those early days and subject to much ground clutter, but which was more than useful in conditions of overcast or haze. Indeed, it offered early experience of the sort of equipment which, in highly developed form, remains in use to this day. By measuring bearing and distance from the more readily identifiable features (lakes, coastlines and river bends were particularly useful for this purpose) the navigator could fix his position with some accuracy. If the target was radar discrete (*ie* could be positively identified on the tube), then H2S could even be used as a blind-bombing aid. More usually, some readily identifiable

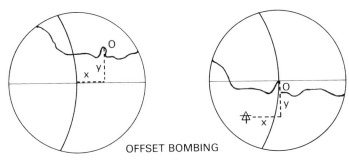

OFFSET BOMBING

(a) TARGET NOT IDENTIFIABLE ON SCREEN, BUT SELECTED OFFSET AIM POINT 'O' CLEARLY VISIBLE. OFFSETS NOT SELECTED

(b) WITH OFFSET COORDINATES x, y, SET IN BOMBING COMPUTER OFFSET POINT 'O' IS USED AS AIMING POINT TO STEER AIRCRAFT TO TARGET.

Fig. 2.7   The principle of offset bombing.

feature was taken—either for offset bombing (Figure 2.7 or as a point from which a time run could be made against the target, its bearing and distance from the identification point having been accurately measured before flight. Nearly 40 years later, this same technique was to be used by the Vulcan crews sent to attack targets in and around the airfield at Port Stanley in the Falklands—though the range of target from base was, in that particular case, increased by a factor approaching ten on that of the typical World War II raid on the Ruhr and beyond.

Although H2S had the advantage over equipments like Gee and Oboe in being independent of ground stations, it did have a number of inherent disadvantages. As already noted, the quality of picture was not good, particularly over land features or large conurbations. Further, because the H2S transmitter was carried by the bomber itself, it could be jammed or (worse) used by enemy night fighters to home in on the bomber stream. Later in the war, equipment specifically designed to detect H2S was fitted in German fighters and was successful enough to enforce a virtual H2S silence on the aircraft of Bomber Command: certainly it could no longer be used as a continuous aid to navigation. But, by then, it had not only proved its value but had pointed the way to future developments in airborne radar.

Last among the four equipments to be studied here is G-H—a sort of amalgam of Gee and Oboe. Indeed, in practice, it differed from the latter only in that it could be used by many aircraft at the same time. Its advantage over Gee was that its accuracy did not suffer with increased range. That said, its effective range was no greater than that of either of the two earlier equipments, although the principle it used was rather different—H being a kind of reverse Oboe, with an airborne radar transmitter/receiver measuring aircraft distance from two ground stations. In fact, this brought to light another limitation of the equipment (as Webster and Frankland have well described),[2] for it was clearly easier to make the necessary calculations and adjustments from the safety and relative comfort of an Oboe station in the UK than in a cold, draughty, noisy and often bumpy bomber—even one that was, temporarily, unengaged in evasive manoeuvres.

Assorted Countermeasures

Before leaving this brief survey of some of the more important equipments used to assist the bomber crews of World War II, it might be useful to mention some of those developed to counter radio and radar aids—because it is in this development that we see the birth of the highly-specialised art of counter- and counter-counter-measures which play (and will continue to play) such a major role in the tactics of war in the air.

It is clear that offensive air power in World War II came of age only with the development of a series of aids to navigation and bomb-aiming. On the other side of the coin, the Battle of Britain could not have been won without the early warning provided by Britain's newly developed radar installations: nor would Bomber Command and the USAAF have sustained anything like their huge losses over Germany and German-occupied territories had the German anti-aircraft and night-fighter forces not benefited from the continuing application of technology to their own defensive battles.

As has been noted, however, both radio and radar aids are capable of being jammed, or turned to the advantage of the enemy. The battle for supremacy between offence and defence is a continuing struggle in peacetime: in war, it is heightened by the fear of defeat. In consequence it becomes a battle that is sharply fought and which works alternately—and often rather smartly—to the advantage first of the attacker, then the defender. Each struggles to develop equipments and to evolve techniques that will, first, counter those employed by his adversary, then pose him yet more difficult problems which he in turn must solve.

Even in the early 1940s the technical problems presented first by one, then the other protagonist were complex in the extreme: and we shall see later how much more complex they have become. The difficulty lies not only in determining the detailed nature of the threat, without which it would be impossible to respond:

rather is it that the response (and its eventual recognition by the enemy) could allow him an advantage to be used against one's own forces. Thus, measures developed to assist the air offensive could prove damaging to the defensive forces of the same side.

The methods employed by the Allies during the strategic offensive of 1940–45 came under four main headings: interference, deception, warning and counter-attack. For the first, interference or jamming could be directed either against the communications links which served to coordinate the various components of the enemy's defensive system, or against his early warning and tracking radars. Of the latter, perhaps the best known (and certainly one of the most effective) was 'window'—lightweight strips of metal foil, cut to exactly half the known wavelength of the enemy's radars and dropped in huge quantities to clutter his radar picture with false returns. For the disruption of the enemy's communications links—both within ground and air elements and as between them—techniques of interference and deception were used. Space does not permit a detailed examination of the long-running cut-and-thrust of the radio countermeasures war, but it makes fascinating reading for the student of modern electronic combat.[3] Suffice to say that, by the end of 1943, a specialist Group of Bomber Command had been formed to develop, evolve and practise radio countermeasures techniques. Under the third and fourth heads of 'methods', equipments were duly developed to offer the bombers warning of enemy radar activity, and to enable fighters to home in on the enemy's airborne intercept (AI) transmissions. And it goes without saying that such developments were undertaken, with varying degrees of success, by both sides. Indeed, it is likely that no three-year span in history will ever see such varied, almost frenetic development of technological counters to increasingly sophisticated military threats as did the period between mid-1942 and May 1945 in the air war over Europe.

Back to Bombs

To complete this short survey of the history of strategic bombing—a history which is, incidentally, unusually full of pointers to the future—let us return briefly to the principal weapon of offensive air power—the bomb. We left it some pages ago, at the end of World War I. As might well be imagined, the powerful incentive of war was again to produce improvements; and, before it was over, World War II had literally revolutionised not only man's understanding of the power of the strategic air offensive, but his very perception of the place it would play in future world conflict—as a deterrent, rather than as a purely destructive force. But before that was to happen, the world of the 1940s was to suffer a succession of horrifying assaults. Already, ten years before the outbreak of war, scientists and designers were collaborating on airborne weapons that were larger, or had higher charge-to-weight ratios, were more effective and (perhaps above all) more specialised than before.

Basically, World War II saw the use of three main types of high-explosive (HE) bomb, a series of increasingly powerful incendiary weapons, a family of target indicators and of course, at war's end, two variants of the world's first atomic weapon. Briefly, HE bombs could be broadly divided into General Purpose (GP), Medium Capacity (MC) and High Capacity (HC) weapons, the main differences between the three classes being their varying charge-weight ratios—*ie* simply the weight of explosive expressed as a percentage of the total weight of the bomb. In general, the higher the capacity of the weapon the lighter (probably, thinner) its casing, thus offering greater blast effect but less penetration—the weapon disintegrating on impact. Compromise between blast and penetration was provided in the GP bomb, a weapon designed for attack against a wide variety of targets and, in consequence, not being optimised against any one of them. In size, they ranged from 20-lb to 4,000-lb during World War II; and Bomber Command alone dropped over 830,000 of them during the course of the war—over half a million being of the mid-range 500-lb variety. However, these impressive figures conceal less than impressive results. As Noble and Frankland have chronicled,[4] most British GP bombs of World War II suffered the worst effects of compromise. Not only were they low in charge-weight ratio (about 27% as compared to the German average of 50%) but they were relatively inefficient and, all too often, defective. Large numbers of them simply failed to detonate.

By the end of 1940, work had begun on the development of a MC weapon for use by Bomber Command. With charge-weight ratios nearer 40% and, when available, a more efficient explosive content, they should have given the RAF the weapons that would justify those hazardous flights to and from its targets. In practice, although later MC variants were extremely effective, too many of the earlier weapons tended to break up on impact and (again) as many as 30–40% failed to detonate at all. Their initial reputation with bomber crews and analysts alike was thus suspect, and it took the later development of larger weapons—primarily the 1,000-lb MC—to restore faith in this class of bomb. At the furthest extreme of bomb size, two MC weapons were developed by that most famous exponent of the trade, Dr Barnes Wallis, for specific use by the Lancasters of Bomber Command (Plate 2.5). The 12,000-lb Tallboy was made up of three 4,000-lb charges placed inside a case of sufficient strength for reasonable penetration and with a stabilising tail. The total weight of the weapon was, in fact, 14,000-lb. As described by W. J. Lawrence in his history of Bomber Command's No. 5 Group:[5]

> It was an extraordinary weapon, an apparent contradiction in terms, since it had at one and the same time the explosive force of a large high-capacity blast bomb and the penetrating power of an armour-piercing bomb. . . . On the ground it was capable of displacing a million cubic feet of earth and made a crater which it would have taken 5,000 tons of earth to fill. It was ballistically perfect and in consequence had a very high terminal velocity, variously estimated at 3,600 and 3,700 feet a second—which was, of course, a good deal faster than sound so that, as with the [German] V-2 rocket, the noise of its fall would be heard after that of the explosion.

The 22,000-lb Grand Slam was also excellently streamlined and had great penetrative power. Designed for attacks on 'hardened' targets such as U-boat submarine pens, it was also used (like Tallboy) to great effect against important railway viaducts such as that at Bielefeld. This first use of Grand Slam on that particular target (on 14 March 1945) was highly successful, the weapon detonating deep underground and causing such extensive shock-waves that much of the surrounding structure was completely undermined.

PLATE 2.5   22,000-lb 'Grand Slam' and 12,000-lb 'Tallboy' bomb casings pictured outside Dr Barnes Wallis's office at the Vickers factory site on Brooklands Airfield, near Weybridge, England. (*Royal Air Force Museum*)

For maximum blast effect, the HC bomb was brought into the inventory of Bomber Command with charge-weight ratios of more than 80%. To achieve this exceptional destructive value, bomb casings were extremely thin; and, because terminal velocities were designed to be comparatively low, bomb ballistics were often indifferent. Shades of developments yet to come, the first HC bombs were actually fitted with parachutes; but aiming accuracy was so poor that the parachute was replaced by a conventional metal tail. The first light-case HC bomb was a 4,000-lb weapon nicknamed in macabre (but descriptive) fashion as the 'cookie'. In effect it consisted of a mild steel drum, filled with powerful RDX explosive and with front-mounted windmill fuses. Later variants were the 8,000-lb and 12,000-lb 'blockbuster' weapons. Among the various special types of HE bomb, the best known is undoubtedly the cylindrical rotating weapon designed by Barnes Wallis specifically for the attacks by No. 617 Squadron on the Mohne and Eder dams in May 1943 (Plate 2.6).

PLATE 2.6   Another Barnes Wallis creation—the famous 'bouncing bomb' used by No. 617 (Dambusters') Squadron of the Royal Air Force against the Ruhr dams in May 1943. Here, a trials drop is being carried out from a Lancaster. (*Imperial War Museum*)

Incendiary Weapons

The extreme accuracy of these weapons (an accuracy which was as much a function of tactics as of bomb design) contrasts sharply with the relative inaccuracy of the incendiary weapons which were used in such vast numbers, primarily against German and Japanese cities. The 4-lb magnesium incendiary, which was the primary weapon of its type used by the RAF in World War II, was too light to be accurately aimed from normal bombing heights. The solution lay in the clustering of these weapons in 350-lb, 500-lb and 1,000-lb containers of reasonable ballistic design; but that development came rather late in the conflict in Europe. Of course, incendiary bombing was a policy which attracted very many critics—and for obvious reasons. True, it did cause significant damage to enemy industrial production, but seldom without great loss of civilian life and, certainly, the destruction of whole swathes of often historic cities—Coventry, Hamburg and Dresden being those most vividly remembered in Europe. However, it was in Japan that the greatest damage and loss of life was sustained by fire—a fact that owed a great deal to the comparatively lightweight, earthquake-resistant design of Japanese buildings and their close proximity to each other in the teeming major cities of the Japanese island chain.

The aircraft used to most devastating effect in the war against the Japanese homeland was the Boeing B-29 Superfortress (Plate 2.7). Designed initially for use in the European theatre it was, in fact, confined to the war in the Far East—not only because of its exceptional range but because, by the time it had begun to join the USAAF in significant numbers, the strategic offensive in Europe was being

PLATE 2.7   The Boeing B-29 Superfortress, as used extensively in HE, incendiary
and, ultimately, nuclear raids on Japan during World War II. (*United States Air
Force*)

adequately prosecuted with the earlier generation of heavy bombers. It was not only
the B-29's range which made it an exceptional aircraft for its day. Its wing-span
measured in excess of 141 ft (about half the length of an American football field);
At 67½ tons, its maximum take-off weight was twice that of the heaviest mark of B-
17; and its four 2,200-hp engines drove propellers that were an enormous 16½ ft in
diameter. However, despite its size, the Superfortress was a very clean aircraft, both
aerodynamically and actually. Its skin was flush-rivetted and, by late 1944, its shining
silver aluminium alloy finish was devoid of friction-inducing (and, incidentally,
heavy) camouflage paint. To enable it to operate routinely at heights in excess of
30,000 ft, its nose section, centre fuselage and tail area were all pressurised to 6.5
psi, giving an equivalent cabin pressure of 8,000 ft and enabling the crews of the
giant bombers to fly without oxygen masks—at least, by day: as night vision is
critically affected by a reduction in oxygen intake, the luxury of unmasked flying by
night was denied the crews even of the sophisticated B-29. Its defensive armament
benefited from an early type of computer control though, in the effort to increase
range and payload, most of the guns were progressively stripped out. This, together
with the reversion of the aircraft to night attack, when it could be flown at lower
altitudes, helped overcome a persistently worrying unreliability of its Wright R-3350
engines.

By January 1945, the B-29 was poised to launch its ordeal by fire against the
Japanese islands. Four months later, over 75% of the bomb-loads carried by the
Superfortress were incendiary weapons, dropped in clusters of up to 5,000 lb in
weight or, more effectively, in the 500-lb M76 variants filled with a lethal cocktail
of jellied oil, petrol, sodium nitrate and magnesium powder. Once ignited, these
incendiary weapons were virtually impossible to extinguish in the predominantly

wooden cities of Japan; and their effectiveness against such targets has been calculated as some five times that of the comparable weight of HE bombs. In perhaps the
most terrible raid of all (on the night of 9/10 March 1945) 334 B-29s carried some
2,000 tons of bombs (for the most part, incendiaries) to Tokyo. The target was
marked at midnight and the last bombers left the target a full three hours later. By
that time, 16 square miles of the city had been destroyed and 84,000 people killed.
At a distance of 150 miles, the tail-gunners of the returning B-29s could still see the
glow of the fires they had helped create in this, the most destructive air-raid ever
carried out—not excluding those two rather better remembered B-29 raids when
atomic weapons were released—for the first and, so far, only occasions in anger—
on the cities of Hiroshima and Nagasaki.

Target-Marking

So much for the incendiary weapons used for destructive purposes: they had
another role. The inability of World War II bomber crews to navigate their way
with sufficient accuracy to strike targets with precision, particularly at night, has
already been noted. It was, in truth, due far less to the inadequacies of the aircrew
than of the equipments then available for their use; and we have seen how developments in navigational and bomb-aiming equipments began to give the hard-pressed
airmen greater practical assistance as the war progressed.

Tactics also played their part; and although it is not the aim of this book to detail
the many tactical shifts and experiments which have affected the course of past
bomber wars, the development of pathfinder techniques was of such central importance to the conduct of the strategic offensive in World War II that it cannot be
ignored. These techniques relied on a combination of the right aircraft (in the case
of the RAF, primarily the Mosquito and Lancaster), the right equipment
(essentially Oboe and Gee H) and the right method of marking a target accurately
and long enough for the main bomber stream to release its weapons. At the
beginning of the war, no target-indicating weapons were available to the RAF,
although the need had been foreseen in some quarters several years earlier. The
official view was that crews were deemed to be able to find their targets individually,
with only some rather ineffective illuminating flares to help that process by night.
As it became clear that expectation had far exceeded capability in the matter of
target acquisition, incendiary bombs were sometimes used for target indication—
initially as a by-product of their primary purpose: later, in the form of specially
developed target-marking incendiary devices. Early in the RAF inventory was a
250-lb benzol, rubber and phosphorous-filled bomb; to be followed by a 4,000-
lb version which ignited with an unmistakable pink flash, giving it the typically
euphemistic slang name of Pink Pansy.

However, what was clearly needed was a weapon with excellent ballistics, which
could be accurately aimed at the centre of a given target and which would burn with
a long-lasting flame that would be readily recognisable to the bomber crews which
followed up the attack. In attempting not only to perfect the design, but also to
defeat the efforts of the German defences in simulating target indicators some distance away from likely target areas, no less than 40 variants of the basic target
indicator (TI) were produced in the 2½ years from early 1943. TIs consisted, in

essence, of ballistically shaped cases from which could be ejected, at pre-determined heights, powerful pyrotechnic 'candles' of various colours. The release of the pyrotechnics was usually governed by a straightforward barometric fuse, which could be adjusted before flight to the required height above target. They were thus used at heights ranging from ground-burst to 8,000–9,000 ft above target—at which latter heights they were, of course, more useful for general target direction than for target indication. Even so, they offered a welcome sight to any bomber crew anxiously seeking confirmation of its position; and, in combination with true target-marking weapons, they added greatly to the effectiveness of the bomber crews—particularly those operating by night. To give just one example of many: on 5 March 1943, a Mosquito of the Light Night-Striking Force dropped a stick of TIs from a height of 30,000 ft over the giant Krupps factory in Essen. Forty minutes later, 400 main force bombers had laid waste more than 600 acres of the plant. Equally significant, the ability of the bombers to carry out genuine first-run attacks, comparatively free of the need for last-second jinking on to target, had increased the effective striking rate of the force from the customary 5% or 6% to around ten times that figure. Although used operationally by the RAF for the last time during the Suez campaign of 1956, TIs were considered useful enough to remain in the inventory for another 10 years beyond that.

The First Missiles

Before drawing to a close this brief historical view of strategic offensive operations and of the technology brought to bear in their application, it is necessary to consider two other developments which, together, have come to symbolise the ultimate in strategic power in the 1980s—the inter-continental ballistic missile (ICBM), which is so powerful and potentially so destructive that its effect is achieved without its ever being used. The deterrent power of the ICBM is of course dependent in part on advanced avionics, navigational systems and protective measures; but, basically, it consists of a ballistic missile and a nuclear warhead—both, not only available but actually used 'for real' more than 40 years ago.

First the missile—or, rather, two missiles: one an early version of the contemporary 'cruise'; the other, a true ballistic weapon. In the battle for the control of Italy in August 1943, the Germans had made the first determined use of a tactical glider-bomb—the air-launched HS 293, which looked like a miniature aircraft and was capable of delivering a 1,100-lb warhead at 550 mph over a range of some 3½ miles. With a similar terminal velocity, the larger, radio-controlled FX 1400, released at heights of up to 18,000 ft and at ranges of over 8 miles, had an armour-piercing capability and was virtually immune to the defensive fire of the day. The next step for the Germans lay in the development of unmanned weapons systems capable of attacking strategic targets—notably the United Kingdom. The so-called *Vergeltung-swaffen* (or reprisal weapons) had been under development from the early years of the war at the Peenemunde experimental station on the German Baltic Coast. The V-1 (Plate 2.8) was literally a flying bomb (the Fieseler Fi 103), with a 1,870-lb Trialen warhead, powered by a primitive Argus pulse-jet and capable of a 400 mph top speed—which made it a difficult target for all but the fastest Allied fighters of

PLATE 2.8   A German V-1 'doodlebug', seen leaving its launcher in 1944. (*Royal Air Force Museum*)

the day. Indeed, just as effective against the V-1 were anti-aircraft guns fitted with proximity fuses. The 'doodlebugs' (as the V-1s came to be known) were inherently inaccurate, because their targets were whatever happened to lie beneath them when their engines stopped; range was purely a factor of the (albeit carefully measured) amount of fuel carried. But, however inaccurate as a terror weapon, the V-1 certainly had its effect on the perception of civilian populations in the south-east of England. They were also capable of being air-launched from the Heinkel He 111H, but by the time that technique had been perfected (and 800 V-1s so launched) Hitler had available a newer and infinitely more frightening weapon—the V-2.

A development of the A-4 liquid-fuelled rocket, the V-2 (Plate 2.9) had a 2,145-lb Amatol warhead and attained a maximum speed of nearly 3,500 mph, making it invulnerable to British defences. Although fairly inaccurate (it was radio-controlled over only a part of its flight regime), the only warning of its arrival was its explosion on impact—followed a few moments later (for those still able to hear it) by the noise of its own shock-wave. Its very lack of warning, coupled with the size of its warhead, led to many civilian casualties in south-east England; over two-thirds of those killed and nearly three-quarters of those seriously injured by the two weapon systems fell victim to the V-2, though eight 'doodlebugs' had been launched to every one rocket.

As a footnote to the story of Hitler's reprisal weapons—if only to prove yet again that desperate threats warrant desperate measures to combat them—there is the story of the Allies' own flying bomb. As one method of attacking the very difficult hardened targets which were the V-weapon sites in the Pas de Calais region of northern France, time-expired B-17 and B-24 bombers were loaded with explosives (up to 27,000 lb per aircraft), fitted with a number of fairly crude impact fuses, taken into the air by pilots who baled out as their steeds crossed the English coast, and left to the radio-guidance of a control aircraft which homed them in on their targets.

PLATE 2.9   The last of the operational *Vergeltungswaffen*: A V-2 rocket being prepared for launch. (*Royal Air Force Museum*)

The Atomic Weapon

No such indignity befell their cousins, the mighty B-29s, which were selected to
take the world into the nuclear age in just two attacks on Japan. The second key
element of what was to be developed as the ultimate deterrent to war was brought
vividly to the attention of a world which knew little or nothing of the awesome power
which could be released by the fission of tiny particles of matter. Only a tightly
guarded body of exceptional scientists, working in New Mexico on the top-secret
Manhattan project, had any real idea of what could be achieved by a controlled
nuclear explosion. After more than five years' work, two types of atomic bomb were

ready to be dropped from specially modified B-29 aircraft. The first, codenamed Little Boy (Plate 2.10), weighed more than 9,000 lb—much of that weight being attributable to the device used to explode one part of the fissionable Uranium 235 into the other, to produce the supercritical mass necessary to sustain the required chain reaction. Fat Man (Plate 2.11) was the other weapon developed by the team at Los Alamos. Twice the diameter of Little Boy it would only just fit into the huge

PLATES 2.10 and 2.11   America's first two atomic weapons—Little Boy (*top*) and Fat Man (*bottom*). (*Imperial War Museum*)

bomb-bay of the Superfortress and its fissionable material was Plutonium. The yields of the two weapons were broadly in the same range—around 20 kilotons (or the equivalent of 20,000 tons of TNT).

Yet, although dreadful at the time (and certainly causing more casualties by the longer-term effects of nuclear radiation), the devastation caused by the only two atomic weapons ever to be released on cities was not markedly greater—and, in at least one case, less—than that inflicted in some of World War II's more destructive raids by conventionally armed aircraft. The obvious differences lay in the fact that such mayhem had been wrought by just one aircraft, and in the clear indication of how such destructive power might be developed in the years to come. Against the latter consideration, it is perhaps pointless to argue whether or not the 110,000 lives lost at Hiroshima and Nagasaki could be set against the estimated 5 million (4 million of them, Japanese) deaths which might have occurred during a full-blown and tenaciously resisted invasion of the Japanese islands. The point was that war on a global scale could never be the same again. When single weapons could achieve, in developed forms, orders of magnitude more than had hitherto been achieved by great armadas of aircraft, then the awful prospect of man-made cataclysm entered the realm of the possible. And with it came the prospect of a world held back from all-out war by fear of what might be. The age of strategic offensive air power was not over; but its power would henceforth be harnessed to the deterrence of world war.

3

The Survival of the Strategic Bomber

A few explanations of terms are helpful in any consideration of the present and future of the manned strategic bomber in the air forces of the world. Whilst 'manned' is a fairly explicit term, the words 'strategic' and 'bomber' are not quite as simple as they may seem. In fact, 'strategic' and 'tactical' are words used to define not types of combat aircraft, but the missions on which they fly. It is a negation of that very flexibility which is the essence of air power to pigeon-hole its assets according to a set of preconceived ideas. Examples abound of military aircraft designed for one specific role but performing admirably in several. And if that has been so in times past, it is becoming ever more necessary, given the cost escalation of modern military equipments.

In the past, interceptor fighters have been adapted for ground attack roles, bombers for long-range reconnaissance, or transport aircraft for air-to-air refuelling because they were available—either in the current inventory for conversion or merely available 'on the day'. That short, sharp conflict in the South Atlantic in 1982 saw the RAF's close air support Harriers being 'navalised' for operations from ships; Victor tankers being fitted out for maritime reconnaissance; Vulcan bombers becoming long-range missile-carriers and, later, air-to-air refuellers; Hercules tactical transports used also for this last role and, again, for maritime surveillance; and Nimrod maritime patrol aircraft, not only being equipped for in-flight refuelling but—perhaps most unlikely of all—actually acquiring a modest air-to-air missile capability.

For the future, combat aircraft will increasingly be designed for multi-role operations—as today's Tornado, F-16 Falcon, F/A-18 Hornet and MiG-29 Fulcrum have already been. The tendency will also be for good airframe designs to be run on ever longer in service—with uprated engines, advanced avionics and new offensive/defensive packages enhancing and extending the range of their capabilities. Not too many aircraft designed in the early 1990s will be in service in their original designed role nearly 50 years later, as are today's Tu-4 Bulls of the Air Force of the People's Republic of China. As one swallow doesn't make a summer, so a squadron of Bulls probably doesn't make a point—but those aircraft first saw life as Boeing B-29 Superfortresses.

It is far more likely that future military aircraft will be either designed or adapted (or both) for a variety of roles; but even when they are not, tactical aircraft can easily be employed on missions which are, in a very real sense, strategic. Again, examples abound. From the relatively recent past, we can note the Israeli Air Force's pre-emptive strike against Arab airfields in 1967; the same nation's F-16 raid on Iraq's developing nuclear power plant at Tuwaitha in 1981; and the later attack on the Palestinian terrorist headquarters in Tunis—all examples of tactical aircraft being used in a strategic role. The controversial American air raids on Libya in April 1986 certainly involved the use of aircraft (such as the F-111) which were designated as tactical, but which were operating over in-flight refuelled distances of strategic proportions, in the other sense of that word. And in-flight refuelling has certainly played its full part in breaking down the divisions between roles and enhancing the flexibility of air power. When, both before and immediately after its entry into front-line service, the tri-national Tornado was being unfairly criticised for its lack of 'legs', the RAF was able to make a point by mounting (in November 1982) a Tornado sortie from the United Kingdom to Cyprus and back—the 12½-hour flight involving a round trip of some 4,300 nautical miles, 600 of them at low level into and away from a simulated operational attack on the Akrotiri air base.

THE ROLE OF AIR-TO-AIR REFUELLING

Air-to-air refuelling (AAR), as a key component of air power, is properly dealt with elsewhere in this series. Here we will merely touch on its value in enabling shorter-range tactical aircraft to stretch their legs in pursuit of targets at what are commonly considered to be strategic distances. In the next chapter, we will note that the AAR technique has proved of immense value in extending the already impressive in-built combat radii of the strategic bomber with the missions flown to and from North Vietnam by mid-Pacific-based B-52s. One other example deserves closer attention, if only because it offers the most recent example of a genuinely strategic offensive capability by the air force which had, for so long, held that capability at the very core of its being.

When Argentinian troops invaded the nearby Falkland Islands on 2 April 1982, the prospects of their being challenged by forces from the United Kingdom, nearly 8,000 miles away, seemed remote indeed. However, as history reveals, such forces were despatched in short order to undertake one of the most remarkable counter-attacks ever undertaken. Already well chronicled are the parts played in the South Atlantic conflict by naval and merchant ships and their crews, by carrier-borne fixed and rotary-wing aircraft, and by brave and highly trained soldiers, sailors, marines and civilians. So too in the context of the South Atlantic have we read of land-based air power in the roles of maritime and electronic surveillance, transport, reconnaissance, close air support and air defence. Critical to the successful prosecution of virtually all those roles was the technique of AAR which had, significantly, been pioneered in the United Kingdom. For it was AAR which allowed the ageing Vulcan bombers of No 1 Group of RAF Strike Command to begin their 27th year of front-line service with an unforeseen 'first'. After 26 years of unqualified success in helping to deter war, the mighty Vulcans were about to release their first bombs against a real enemy—not, of course, the nuclear weapons which had been their primary source of deterrent strength; but the still impressive warload of 21,000lb of conventional bombs which had long comprised their secondary offensive capability.

Operating out of Wideawake airfield on the mid-Atlantic island of Ascension, Vulcan sorties (codenamed Black Buck) were flown against targets in and around the only Falkland Islands airfield then worth the name—outside the tiny capital of Port Stanley. Over a 6-week period, Vulcans were tasked on only seven occasions—of which one was cancelled before take-off, when forecast headwinds *en route* to the Falklands made an already complex refuelling plan impossible to guarantee. Three of the last raids (one of which had to be aborted) were mounted against Argentinian radars, using hastily constructed pylons to mount American Shrike missiles under the Vulcan's wings. The remaining sorties were tasked against the runway and installations of Port Stanley airfield itself. However, the capability of the aircraft's bombing and navigational equipment (designed, many years before, for a nuclear release which did not require such pin-point accuracy) was not such as to guarantee a direct hit by other than an angled cut of the runway. And the minimum stick-spacing between bombs was such that if one were to strike the runway it was extremely unikely that any other could do so. Indeed, it would be theoretically possible for that runway to be straddled by two bombs and to remain unscathed. In the event, Black Buck 1 achieved its objective and the Port Stanley runway was duly cratered.

There was, inevitably, much ill-informed criticism of this feat; and in truth the effort required to place a single bomb on a runway appeared at first sight excessive. To enable one Vulcan to mount an attack on the Falkland Islands, no fewer than 15 Victor sorties (from a total force level of 23 aircraft in service) had to be tasked, with a further two standing 'ground reserve' for both outbound and inbound legs. The complexity of the refuelling plan is hinted at in the excessively simplified diagram at Figure 3.1. Briefly, the outbound phase comprised two waves. Wave 1 consisted of the Vulcan and a long-range support Victor, together with two-short-range tankers and both Vulcan and Victor airborne reserves. Wave 2 (six Victors and a reserve) climbed to a higher altitude than the first wave, achieving a rendezvous at approximately 1,800 nm out of Ascension Island. After successfully refuelling, the primary Vulcan and three fully replenished AAR Victors continued towards the Falkland Islands—the final outbound refuelling bracket being completed at around 3,000 nm south of Ascension. On completion of its attack, the Vulcan undertook a 1,750 nm transit to its recovery rendezvous. During this phase of the mission, four AAR Victors took off from Ascension, positively to guarantee two operationally serviceable tankers at that last rendezvous. All the shorter-range Victors were able to recover without replenishment and, despite some rather low fuel states on landing, the later refuelling plans proved to be nearly perfect.

It is perhaps worthy of note that, to accomplish each mission (for the Vulcan, a more than 7,000 nm round trip), a total of nearly 300 tons of fuel was transferred between aircraft in no less than sixteen separate refuelling brackets. Five of these brackets involved the Vulcan, which took on board over 75 tons (predominantly at night and, from time to time, in conditions of severe turbulence and adverse cloud) which, like the upper winds between Ascension and the Falklands, could not be precisely forecast from 'one end only' of the route.

And what did all this effort achieve? Certainly not just one crater on the Port Stanley airfield and the collateral damage of destruction of airfield installations and defensive radar positions. It is clear that the psychological effect of the Vulcan

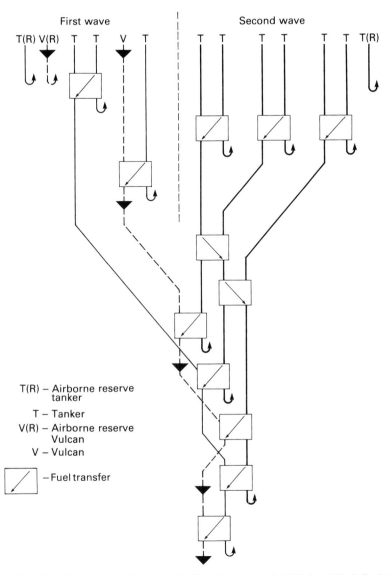

First wave   Second wave

T(R) V(R) T   T   V   T   T   T   T   T   T   T   T(R)

FIG. 3.1   The complex air-to-air refuelling plan for the RAF Vulcan 'Black Buck'
raids on the Falkland Islands, May-June 1982. (*Crown Copyright*)

raids—particularly of that first, entirely unexpected attack—was profound. Not only
was that effect experienced, in dramatic fashion, by those on the ground at the
airfield; it was also felt by those on the mainland, who came to the disheartening
realisation that they might also be targeted. As a direct result, the squadron of
Argentinian Mirage III interceptors, which had been operating near the Falklands,
was re-deployed for the defence of the mainland; and one very significant threat to
British operations was thereby significantly reduced. For the Vulcan, there was
another twist to the story. Not only was the old bomber, in its last few weeks of
planned front-line service, forced to demonstrate 'for real' a capability which it had

for so long sustained purely to deter: ironically it was then held, for a 2-year extended in-service life, duly modifed for a role for which it had never been designed—that of AAR tanker. Perhaps it is fitting that, in so doing, it followed precisely the example set by its two erstwhile stable-mates in the RAF's inventory of V-bombers— the Valiant and, companion to the end, the ageing Victor.

But, AAR or no AAR, aircraft that are dedicated to the role of strategic bombing are, nowadays, almost as rare as hen's teeth. Indeed, large and truly strategic bombers remain in the inventories only of the world's two superpowers and, less definitively so, in the air forces of China and France. In examining why this is so, the opportunity will be taken to assess the likely development of the manned strategic bomber and the ways in which technology may assist such development in the years ahead.

SOME SOVIET BOMBERS

The Soviets have one aircraft narrowly qualifying as strategic (the Tupolev Tu-26 Backfire), and one reputed now to be entering service (the variable-geometry Blackjack—again from the Tupolev design bureau). Doubts have been raised as to the genuine strategic reach of the Tu-26: indeed, that very issue became a long-running *cause célèbre* in the bi-lateral US/Soviet Strategic Arms Limitation Talks of the mid-1970s. Early Soviet assertions of a less than 1,200 nm range and a purely in-theatre capability were treated with great scepticism, even when the aircraft's refuelling probes were removed in an attempt to reassure the sceptics. It is now generally accepted that Backfire has a maximum unrefuelled combat radius of some 2,160 nm, which would make it only a marginal candidate for a strategic role in the strict sense of the word. In other words, as it stands (or, rather, flies) it is less than a realistic threat to the continental USA; rather is it a very potent and flexible weapons system for multi-directional theatre attack. However, as we have seen, the terms strategic and tactical (or 'theatre') relate more to missions than to specific aircraft. In the case of Backfire, in-flight refuelling is still an option to extend radius of action—as is the carriage of stand-off missiles such as the AS-4 Kitchen (Plate 3.1) which can strike targets up to 160 nm beyond the radius of action of its carrier aircraft. *En route* staging and recovery could also extend Backfire's reach, with the result that it might justifiably be considered for long-range tactical missions rather than what the Soviets would judge to be strategic use.

No such caveats will surround Blackjack when it enters front-line service. This massive aircraft has clearly been designed from the outset as a strategic bomber for the 1990s and beyond. It will be treated in more detail in a later chapter; but there is no denying the impressive nature of a bomber which is known to be longer than either the B-52 or Tu-95 Bear; and which has been variously assessed as some 13% larger, 60% heavier and 50% faster than the USAF's latest B-1B bomber.

Three other Soviet aircraft, all by Tupolev and all still in service, have been (and in certain variants still are) classed as strategic bombers. They include the ageing Tu-95/TU-142 Bear (Plate 3.2), the H model of which carries the 1,600 nm range AS-15 Kent air-launched cruise missile to add reach to its already impressive 4,475 nm unrefuelled combat radius. The fact that it can be (and is) in-flight refuelled (Plate 3.3) adds point to the argument. However, Bear H is, by any current stan-

PLATE 3.1   Tupolev Tu-26 Backfire-B, of the Soviet Long-Range Air Force, carrying a single AS-4 Kitchen air-to-surface missile. Note the multiple bombracks fitted beneath the engine intake ducts; and the twin 23-mm radar-directed defensive guns in the tail.

PLATE 3.2   The mighty Bear a Soviet Tu-142 development of a well-proven design seen here in its ('H') variant. On operational missions, long range cruise missiles (including the AS-15 Kent) would be carried under the inboard wings.
(*US Department of Defense*)

dards, both slow and comparatively vulnerable—which is scarcely surprising for a turbo-prop aircraft which first flew in 1954. And, although it remains a truly strategic offensive weapons system, other models in the Bear series are now used for maritime surveillance, reconnaissance, strategic communications and anti-submarine warfare.

The Tu-16 Badger (Plate 3.4) was first flown in 1952 and some 2,000 were built for the Soviet Air Forces and Naval Aviation, as well as for export. Indeed, the aircraft is reported still to be in production in China (as the Xian H-6). The many variants of this twin-engined subsonic medium bomber have seen service in roles as varied as strike/attack, anti-shipping, reconnaissance, maritime surveillance, stand-

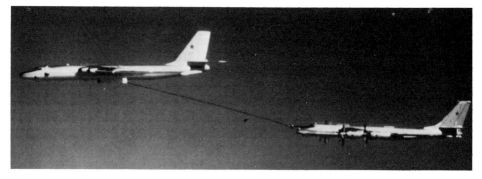

PLATE 3.3   Another Bear H—this time being refuelled by a Soviet Myasishchev M-
4 Bison tanker. (*US Department of Defense*)

off or escort electronic countermeasures (ECM), electronic intelligence-gathering and stand-off missile-carrier (Plate 3.5). For this last role Badger has carried, over the years, AS-1 Kennel, AS-2 Kipper, AS-5 Kelt and AS-6 Kingfish—the last of these conferring an added 200 nm or so to Badger's own 1,200 nm radius of action. However, its days as a front-line bomber in the Soviet inventory have long passed; and its claim to be considered a true strategic offensive aircraft were, anyway, always suspect.   Historically, the supersonic Tu-22 Blinder (Plate 3.6) has not been the most successful product of the Tupolev design bureau and has been given other roles besides that of strategic offence—including reconnaissance, ECM and possibly electronic intelligence-gathering. With an estimated maximum refuelled combat radius of less than 1,600 nm, it is again barely in the class of the true strategic bombers. But it deserves to be mentioned here because of the sensation it created when it first appeared at an Aviation Day flypast in Moscow as long ago as 1961; and because it became the first front-line Soviet aircraft to carry the liquid-propelled Mach 3 air-to-surface missile Kitchen (AS-4)—of which, in various forms, more than 1,000 were probably built.

—AND SOME AMERICAN

The history of the manned strategic bomber in the air force of that other superpower, the United States, has been in some ways rather less coherent than that of the USSR. Indeed, it is fair to say that the modernisation of the USAF's strategic bomber force has been a recurring and controversial issue since the early 1950s. This debate has certainly had its effect on the provision of hardware for the USAF, and sets the scene for a more in-depth examination of the influence and potential of technology in maintaining the manned strategic bomber as a component of the United States' future front-line strength. That said, it is instructive to note that the high hopes of the American manned bomber lobby at the end of World War II were to be much reduced by the development of the ICBM. In fact, for those very few nations that can afford it, both are essential elements of deterrence. And, as with that other fiercely-fought contest (between the proponents of the manned fighter and the advocates of the surface-to-air-missile), both are right and both capabilities needed— because they are inter-dependent and mutually compatible. In both cases, the mix

PLATES 3.4 and 3.5   A pair of Badgers. The Tu-16 in two variants—(above), a 'G' model of the Soviet Naval air force, which can carry both AS-5 Kelt and AS-6 Kingfish air-to-surface missiles: in the Kelt fit, two missiles could be carried, as well as a selection of free-fall bombs, chaff etc. Below, is a modified 'G', equipped to carry two AS-6 Kingfish air-to-surface missiles, but pictured here with a single AS-5 Kelt under the port wing.

of manned and unmanned systems confers a degree of flexibility which is welcome to politicians and commanders alike—though, it has to be said, for rather different reasons.

For the United States, concerns about supposed or actual 'missile gaps' between the superpowers have been a recurring pattern of events since the late 1950s. Probably the most dramatic expressions of such concern followed the successful launching of the Sovets' Sputnik 1 satellite (on 4 October 1957) and the shooting down of the American U-2 in May 1960. The first of these events gave an undoubted spur to American ICBM development; the second, as already noted, gave ammunition to

PLATE 3.6   The supersonic Tu-22 Blinder photographed by an interceptor-pilot of
the Royal Norwegian Air Force. The aircraft which was first revealed publicly in 1961,
was the Soviet Union's first supersonic bomber; and has also seen service with the air
forces of Iraq and Libya.

those who claimed that the missile had proved its superiority over the manned
aircraft and that the latter, certainly as a weapon of war, would shortly be relegated
to history. Fortunately for successive generations of airmen, such predictions were
at least 30 years ahead of themselves—and the run seems set to extend by many
decades yet.

The fact is that each component of offensive air operations has its place in the
armouries of a nation—though only in one or two can those places be assured. In
favour of the missile is its still relative invulnerability, its short reaction time, its *en
route* survivability (which eases the task of the planners) and its accuracy. It is also,
in terms of life-cycle costs or cumulative cost of ownership, certainly cheaper than
the manned bomber—the latter having to bear the recurring expenses of crew training and replacement, structural fatigue and its prevention, mid-life updating, and
all the costly infrastructure to back those inherently expensive requirements. In
favour of the manned aircraft, the best argument is undoubtedly its flexibility. Not
only can it be used with an almost infinite variety of basing, routeing, evasion, re-
targeting and recovery options; but it can also be recalled, once committed—a
factor which must weigh heavily with any politician given the awesome responsibility
of prosecuting war in the late twentieth or early twenty-first century.

The manned aircraft can also be used in ways positively denied the ICBM. It can
be put at ever higher alert states (including airborne alert) as a clear indication to
any potential aggressor that he is being watched and warned. It can be deployed
forward to operating areas against which that aggressor might be less able to defend.
It can be withdrawn and stood down from alert, to show that conflict is not inevitable
and that reason will be matched by reason. It can also be used in sub-strategic and
conventional conflict, in ways in which the nuclear-tipped ICBM cannot—it being a
weapon only of all-out war. As a final thought: even for the hard-hearted financiers,
on whom defence ministers and commanders alike depend for their equipment,
there must surely be attraction in the concept of a re-usable, rather than a one-shot
weapons system. At least it is an argument to set beside the earlier one of the
comparative costs of long-term ownership. Of course, the sharpest of financiers

could turn it against the advocates of the manned bomber by proclaiming that if the deterrent really worked as well as advertised, neither system would be used in war and the missile would therefore be cheaper. But that is possibly a counsel of perfection—even in the eyes of a financier.

Such arguments were undoubtedly tossed back and forth in the United States during the 1960s and 1970s—a period which, incidentally, saw comparatively little activity in the modernisation of the USAF's bomber force. The B-70 programme was cancelled and the B-52 production line closed down. B-47 Stratojets and B-58 Hustlers were phased out of the inventory; and in 1977 the Carter Administration cancelled the B-1 bomber programme, with the argument that air-launched cruise missile (ALCM)-carrying B-52s would offer a more cost-effective option. In retrospect, that might be seen as the right decision taken for the wrong reasons. Hindsight has shown that some of the more exciting features of the original B-1A have been carried through into the B-1B, which has also benefitted in ways not available to the earlier design—notably by the incorporation of very much more advanced avionics and a variety of features to reduce observability.

The USAF now has three very different varieties of strategic bomber, with a fourth currently under design. All four will be examined in greater detail. For now, let us merely record the existence of the FB-111A. Let us dwell a little on the venerable, but still very potent Boeing B-52 nuclear and conventional bomber (affectionately, if rather impolitely, known to its crews as the 'Buff'), which also carries the AGM-86B ALCM and will be capable of carrying its successor system. With genuine inter-continental radius of action (the –G model claiming over 3,250 nm unrefuelled and the later –H model a daunting 4,350 nm plus) the B-52 is also used by the USAF as a long-range maritime reconnaissance aircraft and for conventional mining operations, where its impressive weapon-carrying capability can also be used to excellent effect.

The Rockwell B-1B entered USAF front-line service in July 1985 after a remarkably rapid and intensive 2½-year development based on the use of the two prototypes of the earlier B-1 programme, cancelled six years previously. Taking into consideration merely the publicly available details of this remarkable aircraft, there is no doubt that a great deal of development has in fact taken place. We are now seeing an almost new concept of a strategic bomber, which will point to even more dramatic progress in the design of its eventual successor, the Advanced Tactical Bomber (ATB). Capable of carrying a large number and wide variety of weapons—conventional free-fall and 'smart', nuclear gravity bombs, short-range attack missiles and ALCMs—the B-1B is credited with inter-continental range, assessed in a number of specialist publications as implying an unrefuelled combat radius of at least 3,000 nm; and with a supersonic dash capability approaching Mach 2 at altitude. Both B-52 and B-1B will be covered more fully in later chapters.

The General Dynamics FB-111A (Plate 3.7) will not be treated in such detail— though, in truth, it lays claim to strategic bomber status. Developed in the late 1960s as a slightly larger, heavier and longer-range variant of its older cousin, the F-111 tactical fighter-bomber, the FB-111 is a two-seat, medium-range swing-wing strike/attack aircraft capable of operations up to some 60,000 ft and of speeds in excess of Mach 2. The terrain-following radar which it shares with the F-111 permits low-level penetration to and escape from the target in all conditions of weather and

PLATE 3.7   A 'tanker man's' view of the General Dynamics' FB-111A—the Strategic Air Command member of the very flexible F-111 family. (*United States Air Force*)

light. Its payload can consist of six AGM-69A short-range attack missiles or six B61 free-fall/retarded nuclear bombs or a combination of the two. In the conventional role, it can carry an impressive 31,000 lb of weapons. As compared with contemporary variants of the F-111 series (*ie* excepting the slightly later –F model), the FB-111A featured improved avionics—including attack radar, inertial navigation system, digital computers and advanced cockpit displays. It also carried more fuel and was, after a series of false starts, eventually fitted with the planned Pratt and Whitney P-7 variant of its TF30 engine. To cater for its increased all-up weight, a more robust landing gear was fitted.

The FB-111A remains in USAF service as a still very capable component of its strategic offensive arm. However, its days may be numbered; and proposals to develop a significantly more effective and longer-range variant (the FB-111H) were killed by the decision to fund the B-1B/ATB programmes. The F-111 family will survive for some time yet in the tactical –D and –F models and in the Grumman-developed ECM variant, the EF-111A. But these aircraft lie outside the scope of the present volume.

LE BOMBARDIER FRANÇAIS

To complete the short list of those truly credible strategic bombers which exist today in the inventories of just three nations, mention must be made of the one which presses its candidature by allocated role rather than performance—the French Air Force's Dassault Mirage IV. Entering front-line service in late 1964 as the airborne element of France's *force de frappe* (later, *force de dissuasion*), the original Mirage IVA was purpose-designed to carry French nuclear bombs and is only now being modified (as the Mirage IVP (P for *penetration*) with the *Air-Sol Moyenne Portée* (ASMP) missile, offering stand-off ranges, on weapons release, of up to about 135 nm.

No second glance is needed to confirm that the Mirage IV is indeed a large variant from the famous Dassault stable (Plate 3.8) which has been producing excellent

PLATE 3.8   A Mirage IVP of the French *Armée de l'Air*, launching an ASMP missile—its new contribution to the French *force de dissausion*. (*Service d'Information
et de Relations Publiques des Armées*)

combat aircraft since the early post-war years. Development work on the IV was begun as long ago as April 1957—the requirement being to scale up the existing

Mirage III fighter by some 50% overall, including a virtual doubling of both wing area and maximum all-up weight, and the addition of a second SNECMA Atar engine. In fact, the original concept was for an interim bomber that would remain in service only until such time as an even larger (some claim as much as three times larger) genuine strategic bomber could be developed. And let it not be forgotten that the remarkable Dassault, in his pre-war existence as Marcel Bloch, had designed not a few big bombers. Thirty years on (and in an experience shared with others) the costs and complexity of the 'super Mirage' eventually foreclosed on its development by any medium power working in isolation; and the Mirage IV was left to soldier on—like many another interim design which eventually became its own successor. In this, the French were certainly not alone. Indeed, the recurring theme of the best of the big bombers since the mid-1950s has been their staying power—even when requirements, tactics, employment, weapons, avionics and defensive systems all round were changing. Think only of the British Vulcan, a late 1940s design which saw service as a high-altitude, high-speed component of the nation's independent nuclear deterrence; a low-altitude deliverer of nuclear or conventional bombs; a stand-off missile-carrier (in which development it was never fully exploited); a maritime surveillance aircraft of some distinction; and, finally, as an air-to-air refueller developed in a mere 35 days (and in squadron service 15 days later) to meet the pressing and unforeseen requirements that followed the Falklands conflict of 1982. Think of the United States' venerable B-52, the eighth production variant of which is still in front-line service 37 years after the flight of the first prototype and planned to be there for several years yet to come. Think of the Soviets' Tu-95/142 and Tu-22—to say nothing of those Chinese Bulls. In that company, the Mirage IV is still a comparative youngster.

It, too, has undergone the change from high-altitude penetration to low-level under the radar approach and escape, from deliverer of free-fall bombs to launcher of stand-off missiles. In consequence it has, over the years, been subject to many of the same modifications and developments as have others of its breed. Straight engineering has played its part, in the strengthening of structure and the extension of fatigue life well beyond anything even conceived of as being necessary. In this, the Mirage IV found itself with similar advantage and disadvantages to the Avro Vulcan, whose delta-wing shape it shared in principle, if not detail. Given the all-up weight of the Mirage IV, the size of its 60°-swept delta allowed its designers to construct a moderately loaded wing—the low thickness-to-chord ratio of which made high supersonic dash a practicality.[1]

By constructing those same wing surfaces of continuous skin, carefully milled and tapered, it was also possible to incorporate leak-free integral fuel tanks in both wings and fin. However it was pragmatism and finance which combined to bring Boeing C-135Fs into the French orbit, specifically to extend the radius of action and/or survivability of the Mirage IV.

Given that designers and engineers had combined to produce a basically very good aircraft, it was up to the manufacturers of power-plants and avionics to endow it with an acceptable capability for its role. France's largest aero-engine specialists, the *Société Nationale d'Etude et de Construction de Moteurs d'Aviation* (SNECMA), produced the Atar 09K variant, with a dry thrust of some 10,360 lb and a reheated value of 14,770 lb. To reduce take-off run at the higher all-up weights, provision was also made for 12 jet-assisted take-off (JATO) rockets, mounted in rows of six under each wing (Plate 3.9).

PLATE 3.9   Jet-assisted take-off helps an ASMP-loaded Mirage IV into the air.
(*Service d'Information et de Relations Publiques des Armées*)

The avionics of the Mirage IV have naturally undergone the most extensive modernisation over the quarter-century of the aircraft's service life, specifically since the decision was taken to run on the Mirage IV as one of the French Services' there ASMP-carriers (the others being the tactical strike/attack Mirage 2000 in its N (or *nucléaire*) version; and the carrier-borne Super Etendard). For the Mirage IVP this had identified the need to feed very accurate positional data into the ASMP up to the moment of missile release, after which it is guided to the target by its on-board inertial platform. Naturally enough, the navigational systems of the early Mirage IVA would find it difficult to achieve compatibility with the late 1970s technology of ASMP. In consequence, the IVP now boasts a Thomson-CSF ARCANA[2] pulse-doppler radar, providing very high-resolution all-weather mapping as an adjunct to the Mirage's twin inertial navigational (IN) system. However, as we shall see, radar emissions are not compatible with unobserved approach to the target—a problem on which French industry is doubtless now engaged. For self-protection the Mirage IV is, as one would expect, equipped with a comprehensive ECM suite—the details of which are classified, but which are thought to include a Thomson-CSF TMV 015 self-protection jammer and a Philips BOZ 100 chaff and flare dispenser. Antennae fitted in pods on the outboard wing and in an extension of the cooling air intake for the after-burner section of the two Atar engines are likely to afford the crew of the Mirage IV warning of enemy radar illumination.

The original operational concept for the Mirage IV has, similarly, been re-thought a time or two during its years of service. The 860 nm radius of action of the early aircraft was distinctly limiting for the delivery of free-fall weapons from bases confined strictly to metropolitan France. The concept was therefore of a high-low profile through the enemy's defensive systems, with acceleration to high subsonic speed at target approach, followed by rapid climb and supersonic dash (minimum Mach 1.7) over target, weapon release and aircraft recovery to the nearest friendly base. All very exciting! The acquisition of C-135F tankers somewhat eased the problem—as did the later development for low-level delivery of a lay-down version of the Mirage's AN 22 nuclear weapon and, more recently, with the acquisition of the ASMP. To complete this thumb-nail sketch of France's last strategic bomber, a word on that weapon is appropriate.

As its name suggests, ASMP (Plate 3.10) is not a long-range extended stand-off weapon, but it does endow its releasing aircraft with a degree of protection hitherto

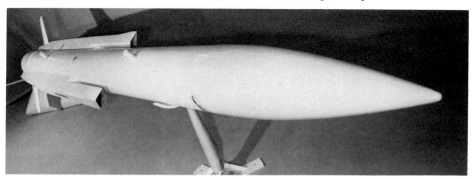

PLATE 3.10   The Air-Sol Moyenne Portée (or ASMP), carried by both the Mirage IVP and Mirage 2000N of the French Air Force. (*Service de'Information et de Relations Publiques des Armées*)

denied it. ASMP is a winged missile, powered by a two-stage rocket/ramjet. The rocket element consists of a powder propellant which accelerates the missile to Mach 2 in about 5 seconds after it has attained free flight. Very shortly thereafter, an ONERA ramjet opens up to sustain that flight. The missile is programmed before take-off and target data is inserted by cassette. Up to the point of weapon release, the ASMP's on-board inertial system is continuously updated, as already noted, by the more powerful twin IN system of the Mirage itself. Missile range obviously depends on height of release, but it can be as much as 135 nm from altitude. Lacking a terrain-following capability ASMP can make up, in some measure, by intelligent pre-flight programming—which of course pre-supposes the absolute accuracy of both mapping and missile launch-point.

Suggestions are now being freely made that ASMP might offer a basis for the development of a later-generation air-to-surface missile for the sort of stand-off ranges which are sought by some of France's allies. After all, air-to-surface missiles have, in the past, been joint ventures—witness the Anglo-French Martel, to name but one. In theory, there seems no reason to doubt that ASMP's current ranges may not be doubled and more; and that developments of the missile might not make it very much smarter than it currently is—and, in consequence, better able to survive the inherently bumpy ride from release to target. We shall see.

In the meantime, there is a little footnote which indicates that, as in many developments in military aviation, *plus ça change, plus c'est le même chose*. When the RAF (and the British aviation industry) suffered the cancellation of its extremely

PLATE 3.11   What might have been! A purposeful TSR-2 of the British Aircraft Corporation, piloted by Wing Commander Roland Beamont on one of its all too few sorties from the United Kingdom's Aeroplane and Armament Experimental Establishment before the project was cancelled in April 1965. (*British Aerospace plc, Military Aircraft Division*)

promising TSR-2 (Plate 3.11) project on 6 April 1965, the race was on to find an alternative successor to the then ageing Canberra and, in time, to the remaining V-bombers. Among the many options investigated was an anglicised version of the Mirage IV. Tentatively christened Mirage IV*, this aircraft was to be fitted with two Rolls-Royce Spey 25R reheated turbofans, each of 21,000 lb static thrust; and a suite of nav/attack, avionics and reconnaissance systems which were already under development for TSR-2. In the event, the project failed to attract the necessary political support; but it is nice to think it was even tried.

4

Something Old, Something New': the 'Buff' Flies On

Having established the relative paucity of examples available to us in considering the application and potential of technology to the role of modern strategic offensive air power, let us now examine some current (and one planned) aircraft which can properly be included in that category. In so doing we will be able to trace the way in which modern technology has helped, is helping and will, in the future, help those aircraft to sustain the role for which they are designed.

A summary of the principal attributes of the American Boeing B-52 'Stratofortress' was contained in the first volume of this series—Air Marshal Mason's *Overview of Roles*. If my own introduction to that aircraft draws on some of that earlier material, it will be not only a compliment to my colleague's succinct presentation of fact; but a help to the reader in avoiding the need for detailed cross-reference. There are, anyway, only a few ways in which facts can be presented; and some repetition is therefore unavoidable.

THE NATURE OF THE BEAST

From preliminary design in late 1947, the earliest mark of B-52 entered USAF squadron service in June 1955. Eight marks and the best part of 35 years later, it is still one of the mainstays of Strategic Air Command (SAC). In the process it has seen off such rivals as the even larger Convair B-36 (Plate 4.1) (the maximum bombload of which was greater than the all-up weight of a fully loaded Lancaster); the B-47 Stratojet (Plate 4.2) and the Mach 2 stainless steel B-58 Hustler (Plate 4.3). By the time it is eventually retired from service, the B-52 (Plate 4.4) will have been a front-line bomber for half the span of fixed-wing military aviation history. It will be as if the Lancaster had only recently been retired from squadron service with the RAF; or, perhaps more dramatically, as if the Bleriot monoplane had been used during the Korean war. Why this great longevity in an aircraft which might well be thought too cumbersome, rather too slow and too easy a target for the defences of the late 1980s?

Part of the answer lies in the very size of the aircraft (Figure 4.1) which has allowed successive generations of designers to install ever more potent electronic defensive

PLATE 4.1   Four burning and six turning': a huge Convair B-36 in flight near Eglin AFB, Florida in May 1956. (*United States Air Force*)

PLATE 4.2   A B-47 Stratojet, using rocket-assisted take-off from Eglin Air Force Base, Florida in 1954. (*United States Air Force*)

systems and even smarter weapons. The airframe, too, has been subjected to much modification over the years, to make the B-52 stronger, more survivable and more capable of operations in a very different environment from that for which it was first designed. With its 161-ft length, the 185-ft span of its high aspect ratio wing and a wing area of 4,000 sq ft, the B-52 is certainly the sort of aircraft to get itself noticed— –which is, of course, not always an advantage in modern air warfare. Its eight Pratt and Whitney TF-33P-3 turbofan engines, generating an impressive total of some 136,000 lb of static thrust, can drive the B-52 along at speeds up to Mach 0.9 at

PLATE 4.3   A supersonic Convair B-58 Hustler of the USAF's Strategic Air Command. (*United States Air Force*)

altitude. For low-level penetration, it is restricted to about 360 knots. It must therefore rely on advanced penetration and defensive aids if it is to survive in war: more of this, later. The aircraft does enjoy a genuine strategic reach—in the -H model, an impressive 10,000 mile unrefuelled range, capable of being greatly extended by AAR. As long ago as August 1959, a B-52G completed a 28-hour non-stop of 12,942 miles.

B-52 ROLES

Of course, the B-52 had been originally designed as a high-altitude carrier of free-fall weapons—a role which, in essence, differed little from that of the big bombers of World War II. The heights and speeds were very much greater and the bombs were likely to be of the nuclear variety, but the basic idea was much the same. Within five years of its entry into squadron service, things began to change. As already noted, the increasing effectiveness of Soviet defensive systems, particularly of surface-to-air missiles, was brought into sharp relief by the shooting-down in May 1960 of an American U-2 reconnaissance aircraft at a height estimated to be nearly 90,000 ft. From then on, the penetration of enemy defences became progressively viable only at low level—'under the radar' as it became known in the jargon of the day. For aircraft like the B-52, this called for extensive (and expensive) modification. Over the next few years it was the recipient of a hundred or more structural alterations designed specifically to cater for the additional stresses of low-level flight. At a glance, a B-52H does not appear much different from its earlier -A or -B variants, but under the skin they are very different animals; indeed, the skin itself has been changed with new metals, of different gauges from the original, being extensively used.

General Arrangement Diagram

Compartment Diagram

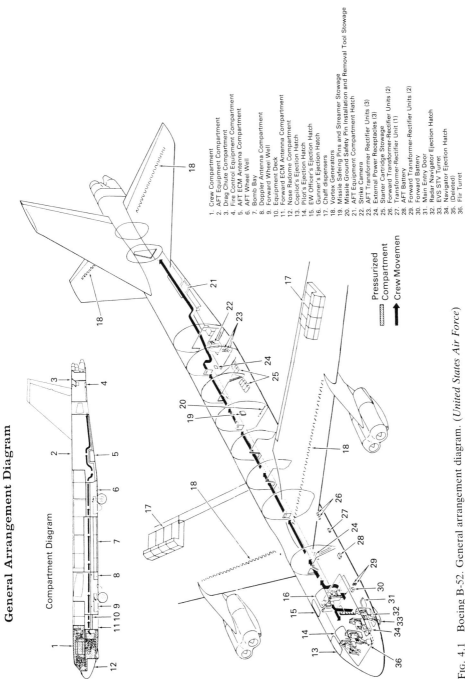

1. Crew Compartment
2. AFT Equipment Compartment
3. Drag Chute Compartment
4. Fire Control Equipment Compartment
5. AFT ECM Antenna Compartment
6. AFT Wheel Well
7. Bomb Bay
8. Doppler Antenna Compartment
9. Forward Wheel Well
10. Equipment Deck
11. Forward ECM Antenna Compartment
12. Nose Radome Compartment
13. Copilot's Ejection Hatch
14. Pilot's Ejection Hatch
15. EW Officer's Ejection Hatch
16. Gunner's Ejection Hatch
17. Chaff dispensers
18. Vortex Generators
19. Missile Safeing Pins and Streamer Stowage
20. Missile Ground Safety Pin Installation and Removal Tool Stowage
21. AFT Equipment Compartment Hatch
22. Strike Camera
23. AFT Transformer Rectifier Units (3)
24. External Power Receptacles (3)
25. Starter Cartridge Stowage
26. Forward Transformer-Rectifier Units (2)
27. Transformer-Rectifier Unit (1)
28. AFT Battery
29. Forward Transformer-Rectifier Units (2)
30. Forward Battery
31. Main Entry Door
32. Radar Navigator Ejection Hatch
33. EVS STV Turret
34. Navigator Ejection Hatch
35. (Deleted)
36. Flir Turret

Pressurized Compartment

Crew Movemen

FIG. 4.1   Boeing B-52. General arrangement diagram. (*United States Air Force*)

PLATE 4.4   Big and ugly—but certainly effective. A B-52G coming in to land.
(*United States Air Force*)

As a result, the original 5,000-hour fatigue life of the aircraft has been trebled; but conservation of those hours remains a very necessary element of fleet ownership—as, indeed, it does with all modern combat aircraft. The ever more widespread use of sophisticated flight simulators and the flying of crews in other, less expensive and less valuable aircraft to build up and maintain the necessary levels of flying experience are but two of the ways by which modern air forces seek to husband their precious resources. In the end, however, it is time in the air, in front-line aircraft undergoing realistic operational training, that really counts; and that, of course, consumes fatigue life. Hence the need for expensive strengthening and life-extension modifications. There is little doubt that the cumulative cost of the progressive modification of the B-52 is many times that of the original aircraft cost: and that is true of any modern military aircraft—particularly if, as so often happens, its time in service is extended way beyond original plans.

However, that is only part of the story and, in the context of survivability in war, probably only a small part. More telling in the ceaseless battle for the predominance of offence over defence are the complex and powerful penetration aids which have been incorporated in and on the B-52's great bulk. Over the years there have been many—a number, inevitably, still shrouded in the mists of national confidentiality. Among the more obvious examples is the B-52's defensive armament. In the older - G model, this consists of four 0.5-in (12.7-mm) M3 machine guns firing armour-piercing incendiary, which are replaced on the B-52H by a single-barrel 20-mm T 171 Vulcan cannon, operating on the Gatling principle of rotating barrels and, at maximum rate of fire, pouring an impressive 6,000 rounds a minute on target. That said, guns would certainly represent the last ditch of the B-52's defences in war: they would come into operation when all other techniques of deception, tactical routeing, ECM defence suppression, warning of attack and missile seduction had been invoked.

Evidence of the existence of some of those systems can be adduced from the various blips, bumps and blisters which serve to make the old B-52 even less attract-ive a beast than ever it was. On the underside of the fuselage and in the area beneath the nose radar (Plate 4.5) are the sensors for the Electro-Optical Viewing System (EVS) which offers the crew unrivalled assistance in the difficult art of night low-level penetration in a big bomber.The standard AN/ASQ-151 EVS in the latest

PLATE 4.5   'Full frontal' view of a B-52H, showing the external components of the powerful electro-optical viewing system (EVS). Under each wing are fitted AGM-86 air-launched cruise missiles. (*Boeing Aerospace Company*)

marks of B-52 has been a feature of the aircraft for over half its in-service life. It incorporates a Hughes AAQ-6 forward-looking infra-red (FLIR) on the starboard side and a Westinghouse AVQ-22 low-light television camera to port. Each is con-trolled through a steerable housing, to give the B-52's crews high confidence in their clear and impressive cockpit displays. The demanding task of aircraft handling at low level is further eased by the read-out on the B-52's EVS displays of alphanumeric symbols depicting aircraft altitude, height above terrain, airspeed and time to weapons release—all of which, in earlier times, would have required either the extrapolation of data from a scan of a number of flight instruments or some rapid and continuous calculation by another crew member—navigator or bomb-aimer.

ROLE EQUIPMENT

Although performance details of some of the B-52's advanced avionics equip-ments are naturally classified, enough has appeared in specialist publications to indicate the variety of those equipments and the tasks they would perform in war. The so-called Phase VI avionics package has now been incorporated in most of

SAC's operational B-52 force. In essence, it extends signal coverage, enhances threat-warning and provides new and updated countermeasures, including more and better flares. The Phase VI installation is said to incorporate an ALQ-122 Smart Noise Operation Equipment, an ALR-46 digital radar warning receiver and an ALQ-153 pulse-doppler tail-warning radar—in addition to advanced and improved ECM and satellite communications equipments. As part of an Offensive Avionics System (OAS) for the later marks of B-52, Boeing has improved the aircraft's capa-

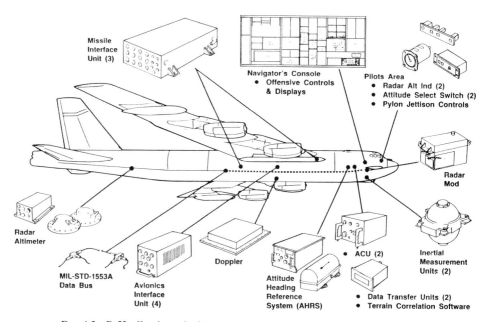

Fig. 4.2   B-52 offensive avionics system. The major elements of this complex system are here identified with their location on board the big bomber. The total system is claimed to improve the accuracy of both navigation and weapons delivery, to reduce operational and support costs and to enhance reliability. (*Boeing Aerospace Company*)

bility for long-range navigation and weapon delivery (Figure 4.2). Open sources indicate that new digital, solid-state equipments include terrain contour-matching (TERCOM) guidance; the Honeywell AN/ASN 131 gimballed electrostatic air-borned inertial navigation system (GEANS); a new Teledyne Ryan doppler radar; new and improved equipments for altitude heading and reference; radar altimeter height reference; and the IBM/Raytheon OAS digitally-processed bombing and navigation system. In installing these and possible future equipments such as the Navstar Global Positioning System, account will continue to be taken of the need for protection against the effects of heat, blast and electro-magnetic pulse (EMP) were the big bomber ever to be committed to operation in a nuclear conflict.

ELECTRO-MAGNETIC PULSE

As an aside: heat and blast, whether from the detonation of conventional or nuclear weapons, are readily understandable phenomena. EMP may need some explanation. In essence, it is a very intense electronic signal of extremely short duration—similar in kind to a radio transmission, but immensely stronger. It can occur as a product of nuclear detonation. When a suitable antenna picks up such a transmission it is, in fact, sensing the changes in the electro-magnetic field which are caused by the radiated signal. Because of its power, intensity and extreme concentration in time and space, EMP radiation can cause severe damage to ground installations and to aircraft. A simple diagram (cf Figure 4.3) indicates that an EMP signal can be very much faster than a bolt of lightning; will usually be of greater intensity;

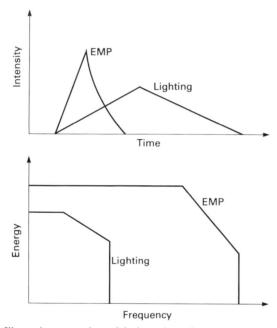

FIG. 4.3   Illustrative comparison of the intensity and energy of lighting and electro-magnetic pulse (EMP). (*Author*)

and may well produce greater energy over a longer timeframe. An aircraft, in effect, acts as a sort of antenna over a part of the frequency spectrum within which EMP signals will travel; and, because of the power involved over periods of some hundreds of nano-seconds, damage to the aircraft's electronic systems is a very real possibility. Current flows may be conducted via cables, down mechanical linkages or through holes, cracks and conduits to burn out connectors and wiring, damage or destroy the circuiting of navigation or weapons systems and even to fire explosive detonators. Modern integrated circuitry is particularly susceptible to such damage; and the program memories of sophisticated on-board computers are also likely targets. Obviously at risk are equipments which depend on microprocessors—such as stores management and weapons release systems and, every bit as alarmingly, digital fly-by-wire aircraft controls. Arcing within near-empty fuel tanks could also ignite fuel/-air mixtures, leading to fire or explosion. Clearly the EMP protection of a modern combat aircraft must be very much in the mind of its designers.

B-52 DEVELOPMENT

Back to the B-52 which, if committed to future combat operations, would have to survive a number of additional hazards. It seems certain that, before it is finally retired from service, the old bomber will be subject to still further extensive modification in both offensive and defensive avionics; enhancements of reliability and maintainability; and, possibly, a re-engining programme, if it is to maintain its viability and capability as a weapons system. There is, of course, a great deal of scope for such modification on an aircraft the size of the 'Buff'.

There have, over its many years of service, also been some fairly dramatic develop-

PLATE 4.6   A B-52G of Strategic Air Command, with a representative array of its possible weapons, with the accent on maritime roles. Included here are 500- and 750-lb conventional 'iron bombs', sea-mines, special weapons and Harpoon anti-shipping missiles. For other roles, equally impressive 'mixes' of weapons could be displayed. (*United States Air Force*).

ments in the weapons carried by the venerable B-52 (Plate 4.6). As we have already noted when it first entered service the aircraft's primary role was the delivery, from high altitude, of free-fall (or gravity) nuclear weapons. In those days, such weapons were invariably large—the Mark 17 bomb reputedly weighing as much as 42,000 lb and requiring some extensive re-working of the aircraft's bomb-bay doors to permit carriage. Over time, these weapons became progressively smaller—science, technology and manufacturing techniques (including the micro-miniaturisation of electronic components) combining to produce equivalent (often improved) results from within a much smaller compass. Depending on weapon size, the giant B-52 could carry a score or more of today's nuclear weapons; and free-fall bombs remain very much a part of the USAF's inventory.

However, over the years, the aircraft has also had to be prepared to contend with

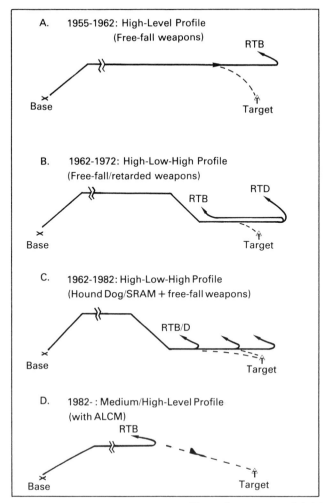

A. 1955-1962: High-Level Profile
(Free-fall weapons)
RTB
Base
Target

B. 1962-1972: High-Low-High Profile
(Free-fall/retarded weapons)
RTD
RTB
Base
Target

C. 1962-1982: High-Low-High Profile
(Hound Dog/SRAM + free-fall weapons)
RTB/D
Base
Target

D. 1982- : Medium/High-Level Profile
(with ALCM)
RTB
Base
Target

FIG. 4.4   Typical B-52 profiles 1955 to present (illustrative purposes only). (*Author*)

increasingly capable and sophisticated enemy defences—both ground-based and air-launched. In consequence, the tactics have moved away from penetration and target over-flight towards stand-off bombing (Figure 4.4). Indeed, such tactics have been part of the USAF's philosophy for many years. As long ago as March 1956 the requirement was laid for a medium-range air-to-surface weapon for carriage under the wings of the B-52. Such a weapon (or, in the case of the B-52, such weapons) would today be launched against enemy targets or defensive systems from the relative security of stand-off range; and might, if circumstances so decreed, be followed by the bomber's penetration of degraded defences to deliver either internally carried free-fall or stand-off missiles. The concept of decoy weapons was also introduced—small free-flying missiles with deliberately enhanced radar cross-section (RCS) to simulate the radar return of a B-52 itself, and thus both confuse the enemy's defences and cause him to expend surface-to-air missiles on a relatively low-cost, unarmed (and absolutely harmless) 'threat'.[1]

STAND-OFF MISSILES

The first of the stand-off missiles to be introduced into service with the B-52 was the North American GAM-77 Hound Dog (later re-designated AGM-28) (Plate 4.7). Operational between 1961 and 1976, it was a comparatively large weapon—

PLATE 4.7   A B-52 carrying two North American GAM-77 'Hound Dog' stand-off missiles during early carriage and release trials in the late 1950s. The weapon was eventually carried in front-line service by E, F, G and H-model B-52s. (*United States Air Force*)

over 40 ft long and with a wingspan of some 12ft, as a result of which only two could be carried by each B-52, on underwing mountings between each pair of inboard engines and the fuselage itself. Armed with a nuclear warhead, Hound Dog was capable of penetration up to about 650 nautical miles from point of release at high altitude—obviously rather less from a low-altitude launch (Plate 4.8). Flying at speeds over Mach 2, the missile was powered by a Pratt and Whitney J52-P-3 turbojet and guided to its target by a self-contained inertial navigation system (INS). Because of their weight, the carriage of two Hound Dogs restricted the fuel uplift of the B-52 on take-off; but there were a number of advantages in this. Firstly, the missiles' J52 engines could be used to boost the bomber's take-off power or, indeed, to augment its thrust in flight. AAR was (and remains) a standard feature of B-52

PLATE 4.8   'Hound Dog' in flight over White Sands Missile Range, New Mexico.
(*United States Air Force*)

operations; and the lower all-up take-off weights, which could thus be accepted, served to reduce airframe fatigue and the stresses to which wheels, undercarriage landing gear and wings were inevitably subjected. Fuel could be readily transferred from the bomber's fuel tanks into those of the Hound Dog, with the result that the underwing load of the missile could itself be reduced for aircraft take-off and cruise and the missile topped up for maximum penetration range at some convenient point before release. All in all, a very flexible arrangement indeed. The Hound Dog was eventually phased out of the SAC inventory in favour of the smaller and more accurate short-range attack missile (SRAM)—of which, more later.

The first operational decoy missile to form part of the B-52's armoury was the McDonnell Douglas GAM-72 (later designated ADM-20) Quail. A mere 13 ft long with a wing-span of 5 ft 6 in, it is remarkable that this diminutive missile (Plate 4.9) could in fact replicate the radar return of its B-52 mother aircraft. However, some clever design work ensured that it could appear virtually identical to a B-52 on the radar screens of a waiting enemy. Furthermore, as four Quails could be carried by each B-52, it is easy to visualise the confusion of enemy defences by the sudden acquisition of a mass of targets released simultaneously by the approaching bomber force. Powered by a General Electric J85 turbojet, Quail's performance was naturally tailored to that of its parent aircraft. It could be released at either high or low level, in the speed range Mach 0.6 to 0.9; and could fly up to 350 nm, with a limited number of pre-programmed changes of heading and speed. It remained in the SAC inventory from 1960 to 1978.

Such was not to be the story of a rather different missile, designed for carriage not only on the B-52 but on the Vulcans of the RAF (Plate 4.10). The Douglas GAM-87A Skybolt was a very advanced concept when its design study contract was awarded in May 1959. An air-launched ballistic missile with a range of some 1,000 miles from release could, it was argued, enjoy most of the advantages of its ground-launched 'cousins' in terms of speed, range and accuracy, whilst enjoying some of the unique tactical flexibility of the manned bomber and being comparatively less vulnerable, once airborne. Whereas missile silos could be monitored night and day by advanced reconnaissance equipments, an omnidirectional threat from a stand-off

PLATE 4.9   A McDonnell Douglas GAM-72 (later, ADM-20) 'Quail' decoy on release from its parent aircraft. It is remarkable that the diminutive missile could adequately mimic the radar return of the massive B-52. (*Boeing Aerospace Company*)

PLATE 4.10   Another story of expectation unfulfilled. The Vulcan/Skybolt combination would have carried the United Kingdom's strategic nuclear deterrent well into the 1970s. Feasibility studies indicated that the Vulcan B2 could carry up to 6 of these 1,000-mile-range- air-launched ballistic missiles, though only two dummy weapons were ever flown (1961). In the event, Skybolt's cancellation led directly to the transfer of the UK's strategic deterrent responsibility to the Royal Navy's Polaris submarine force in October 1967. (*British Aerospace plc, Military Aircraft Division*)

range of 1,000 miles would call for the permanent surveillance of literally hundreds of millions of cubic miles of sky.

Of course, a missile with the capabilities of Skybolt could not be small. In fact, over 38 ft long, its launch weight was a significant 11,300 lb. Nor was it ever likely to be a cheap item—development costs alone running at some $400 M at 1960s value. For that, a consortium led by Douglas and including Aerojet-General (for the engine), General Electric (for the re-entry vehicle) and the Nortronics Division of Northrop (for the navigation system)—would produce a fast (Mach 9 plus), extremely accurate means of delivering a nuclear weapon, virtually invulnerable to the defences of the day, and comprising some then very advanced components such as a two-stage solid fuel propulsion system and a stellar-monitored inertial guidance system. Even so (and despite some well publicised failures on test) it was not the problems of technology that led to the cancellation of the Skybolt project in December 1962. Escalating costs were certainly one factor and a steadily mounting political 'headwind', undoubtedly another. For the B-52 there were to be other options: for the RAF's Vulcans—none beyond the lifespan of its very much less capable Blue Steel missile (Plate 4.11). The result was that the strategic deterrent capability of the United Kingdom passed out of the hands of the RAF into those of the Royal Navy, with its first generation of Polaris submarine-launched ballistic missiles.

PLATE 4.11   Avro/Hawker Siddeley's Blue Steel stand-off missile was fitted to some squadrons of both Vulcan and Victor bombers from 1962. Whilst conferring up to a 200-mile capability for stand-off delivery, the liquid-fuelled (high-test peroxide and kerosene) missile proved both expensive and difficult to maintain. It was eventually phased out of front-line service with the RAF in December 1970. (*British Aerospace plc, Military Aircraft Division*)

With vastly more resources, and the luxury of several baskets into which to put its eggs, the United States pressed ahead with ballistic (and, later, advanced cruise) missiles capable of delivery from land, sea, sub-surface and air. The next major weapon system to benefit the B-52 was the Boeing AGM-69A Short-Range Attack Missile (SRAM). Comparatively small (14 ft long and some 2,200 lb in weight), SRAM nevertheless packs a very solid punch. Its low RCS and supersonic (Mach 2 plus) speed over flight times measured, typically, in a few minutes combine to make it practically impossible to intercept in the course of its 30-to-100-mile flight from release to target. And, with the OAS modification incorporated, a B-52G/H can carry eight such missiles mounted on a rotary launcher in the massive bomb-bay— a configuration which frees the underwing stations for the carriage of 12 ALCMS. SRAM's power source is a Thiokol solid-fuel two-pulse rocket motor which is, in fact, re-startable. Its guidance is inertial, using a highly accurate system designed by General Precision/Kearfott. First brought into operational service in 1972, SRAM remains a potent element of the B-52's offensive armoury.

CONVENTIONAL BOMBING

By the mid-1960s the B-52 had resurrected another operational role—that of conventional bombing (Plate 4.12)—which it was actually to take to war. In fact, the first combat experience of the already 10-year-old 'Buff' was in the skies over Vietnam in June 1965, and it performed in that role and theatre for the best part of eight

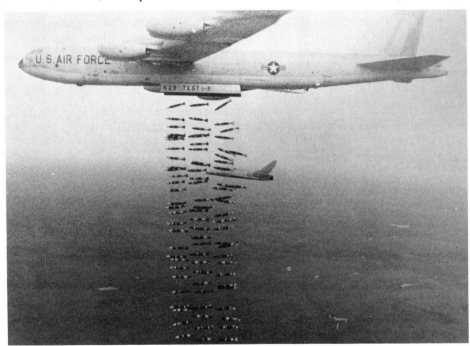

PLATE 4.12   An early 1950s photograph of a B-52D releasing its very impressive load of 500-lb bombs—though not, as suggested, actually on its attendant F-100 'chase' plane. (*Boeing Military Airplane Company*)

years. F model B-52s were first into action, flying out of the Pacific island of Guam and carrying up to fifty-one 750-lb bombs against Viet Cong installations north of Saigon. Twenty-seven of the bombs were carried internally; the remainder on underwing racks, again positioned inboard of each inner engine pairing. These missions (code-named Arc Light) rank as some of the longest offensive air operations ever mounted—typical 7,000 nm round trips (see Figure 4.5) being matched only by the epic Vulcan raids on the Port Stanley area of the Falkland Islands in May 1982.

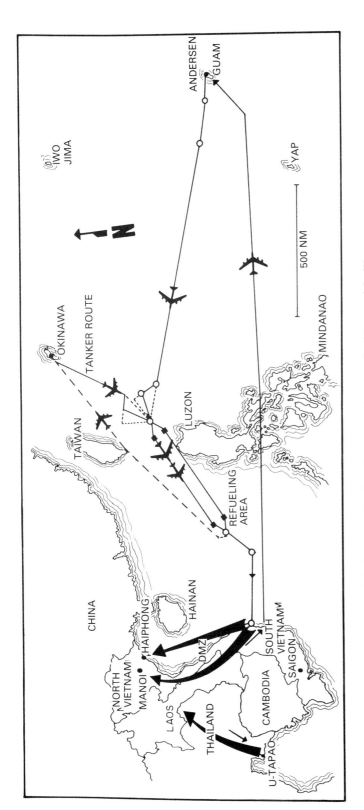

Fig. 4.5 Over-simplification of a very complex plan. On this map of the Western Pacific and South-East Asia are shown typical B-52 routes into and out of the war zone. The westbound route shows the general flight-path taken by the B-52s before arrival at the mainland of South Vietnam, whence they dispersed on a variety of runs to targets in the North. Most recoveries were made to the South and thence back to Andersen AFB, Guam. However, diversions were sometimes made from these basic routes to meet critical timing requirements, because of aircraft mal-functions, to carry-out additional refuellings or to escape the worst of the weather in refuelling 'brackets'. (*United States Air Force*)

However, when it came to ordnance, the B-52 had a handsome margin over the Vulcan's 21,000-lb bomb-load. D model aircraft were specifically modified for the South-East Asian theatre and the so-called 'Big Belly' B-52 was able to carry no fewer than 42 of the 750-lb or 84 of the 500-lb variety internally, plus a further 24 of either mark of bomb on its underwing pylons—a total of no less than a staggering 60,000 lb of ordnance on each long-range sortie: and 'staggering' may also have been an apt adjective for the old 'Buff' as it forced its way into the air from Guam—and, later, from other bases in Thailand and on Okinawa. At the height of the bombing campaign, well over 3,000 such sorties were being flown every month; and though the average over the 8-year period was much lower than this, the sustained weight of attack on South and North Vietnam, Laos and Cambodia can readily be imagined. It is beyond the scope of this book to speculate as to just what effect this terrifying bombardment had on the duration—let alone the outcome—of the Vietnam war. However, what can be clearly adduced is the part which strategic bombing was allowed to play, with many of the earlier political constraints removed, in bringing about the resumption of peace talks between the protagonists in late 1972. The decisive factor here was undoubtedly the sustained high-altitude bombing attacks by B-52Ds and Gs, supplemented by F-111 low-level night precision attacks on selected surface-to-air missile (SAM) sites and airfields in the 11-day operation codenamed Linebacker II. As an indication of the complexity of contemporary air bombardment in a high-threat sophisticated air defence environment, the variety of supporting aircraft types and roles is worth comment. McDonnell Douglas F-4 Phantoms of both the USAF and US Navy (USN) vere used for combat air patrol work in those areas over which North Vietnamese MiG fighters could be expected to operate. They were also employed in a number of other support roles, ranging from bomber escort to the laying of chaff to confuse the enemy's radar picture. This last was also one of the roles for which unmanned or remotely piloted vehicles (RPVs) were used. Teledyne Ryan 147-series RPVs were carried by DC-130 transport aircraft and frequently recovered by CH-3 helicopters. They were also used for reconnaissance and bomb-damage assessment during Linebacker II. To add their weight to the proceedings, Republic F-105 Thunderchiefs of the USAF and Vought A-7 Corsairs of the USN undertook suppression missions alike against SAM and anti-aircraft artillery (AAA) defences; whilst USAF Douglas EB-66 Destroyers, USN EA-3B Skywarriors and Grumman EA-6B Prowlers and US Marine Corps (USMC) Grumman EA-6A Intruders all helped supplement the B-52s' on-board ECM systems.

To assist even further in this work, B-52s flew in clutches of three, flying sufficiently close to each other in the vital task of seducing and saturating enemy defences as to ensure mutual ECM support—particularly in the most vulnerable minutes of approach to and departure from the target area. At those times, not only was each bomber committed to a period of steady, straight and level flight for the purposes of gyro-stabilisation of the bomb system; but its open bomb-doors significantly increased its RCS and, hence, its vulnerability to acquisition by enemy radars. In-flight refuelling of the B-52s on their longer-range missions was carried out by Boeing KC-135 Stratotankers of the USAF (Plate 4.13), operating out of bases on Okinawa; whilst additional tankers, based in the Philippines and Thailand, were on hand to pass fuel to the tactical aircraft involved in the battle. In all, rather more than 250 aircraft were involved in each of the raids—up to 90 on each of three waves. Of the 15 B-52s lost by enemy action, all fell victim to surface-to-air missiles; and history has suggested that a greater weight of attack might profitably have been placed against SAM sites in North Vietnam.

PLATE 4.13   Airborne fuel delivery for a SAC B-52. The USAF has adopted the 'flying boom' method of aerial refuelling, as against the 'probe and drogue' method used by aircraft of the RAF, RN, USN and several other air forces. (*Boeing Military Airplane Company*)

Operation Linebacker II signalled the first (and, to date, the last) use since the end of World War II of sustained strategic bombing in the classic sense. In the course of nearly eleven days between 18 and 29 December 1972, with only Christmas Day for respite, USAF B-52s flew 729 sorties against targets in North Vietnam with an overall attrition rate of just over 2%.[2] Their estimated 15,000 tons of bombs are claimed to have destroyed or damaged over 1,500 buildings, 500 rail targets, 10 airfields, more than a quarter of North Vietnam's reserves of petrol and 80% of its electrical generating capacity. Although that contribution may not have been decisive in war-fighting terms, it was almost certainly so in bringing the North Vietnamese back to the peace negotiations in Paris—and may there have played a role not unlike that of just two B-29s over Japan 27 years earlier. In terms of concentrated force applied in a fairly restricted area and in a short timeframe, Linebacker II was without equal during the conflict in South-East Asia. However, it has to be set in context of a total of 125,000 B-52 sorties over the 8 years of that conflict—during which, incidentally, those aircraft released no fewer than 2.63 million tons of bombs. By comparison, during the 5½ years of World War II in Europe, Bomber Command had to fly almost three times that number of bombing missions, to deliver just 36.3% of the B-52s' total tonnage—an indication of the massive increment in offensive power over less than three post-war decades.

BACK TO DETERRENCE

Another four years later, the decision was taken to equip the B-52, for its nuclear deterrent role, with a weapon which would help ensure its even greater survivability in any future conflict. The Boeing AGM-86B ALCM actually entered service with the B-52G squadrons of SAC in December 1982; and it had equipped the H model some two years later. The requirement for greater stand-off range had been realised long before (and not only in the USA); indeed, a long-range Subsonic Cruise Armed Decoy (SCAD) with a range of several hundred miles had been earlier considered and rejected. The ALCM now deployed is a 1,500 mile, 450-knot terrain-following missile, powered by a Williams International F107-WR-100 turbofan and weighing some 3,200 lb. The B-52G can carry up to six under each wing (Plate 4.14) and, in the near future, the H model will be able to lift an additional eight in the bomb-bay.

For airborne carriage the AGM-86B's wings, elevons and tail remain folded; but they extend for free flight within two seconds of release from the parent B-52. By that time the missile has a wing span of 12 ft and a length of 20 ft 9 in. Up to the point of release, the B-52's inertial guidance system feeds position information at regular intervals to the AGM-86B. Once it is flying solo (Plate 4.15), the missile's on-board TERCOM system takes over. This state-of-the-art equipment provides extremely accurate information on the missile's position by the comparison of real-time data supplied by the missile's on-board instruments (notably, a highly refined radar altimeter) with pre-stored information about the terrain over which the missile is flying. This information is extremely detailed and, by concentrating on ever smaller areas of terrain as the target is approached, ever greater detail can be defined and accuracy thereby enhanced. By the time the target is reached, absolute precision is virtually guaranteed. The process is not unlike that long used by aircrew, explorers and ramblers alike. In aircrew terms it equates to the progressive use of maps of increasingly larger scale as high-level cruise becomes low-altitude approach, acquisition of Initial Point (IP), IP-to-target run; and in the reverse sense for the escape and return to base.

In its own right, ALCM called for the sort of aircraft navigational accuracy that was incorporated in the OAS package already described; but the capability of a dual INS and the even greater enhancement which will be obtainable from the GPS Navstar serve also to improve significantly the delivery accuracies of conventional weapons. In addition to Mark 82 (500 lb), Mark 117 (750 lb) and Mark 83 (1,000 lb) bombs, these may now include the GBU-15 TV-guided glide bomb, the McDonnell Douglas AGM-84 Harpoon anti-shipping missile and an impressive quantity of air-delivered mines.

For its primary (nuclear) role, the effectiveness of the bomber against a series of threats is illustrated diagrammatically in Figure 4.6. From this it will be adduced that

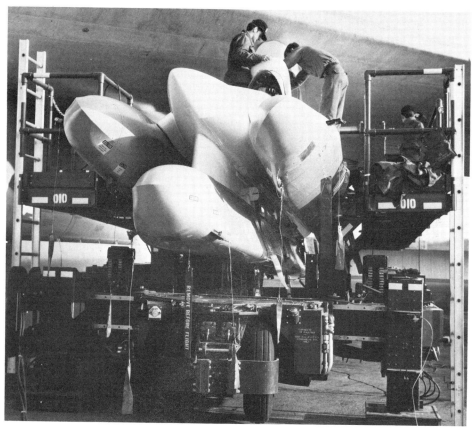

PLATE 4.14   A pylon-load of AGM-86B ALCMs being mounted under the wing of
a B-52G. (*Boeing Aerospace Company*)

PLATE 4.15   A Boeing AGM-86 released on a test-flying from the bomb-bay of a
B-52H. (*Boeing Aerospace Company*)

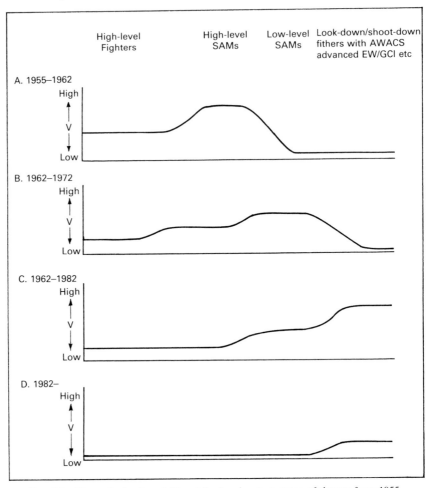

FIG. 4.6   Theoretical vulnerability of the bomber to a range of threats from 1955 to the present.(*Author*)

the B-52 retains a credible capability, despite the steadily enhanced effectiveness of modern defensive systems. This capability will be still further sustained by planned improvements to the aircraft's strategic radar system, a new phased-array ECM suite and enhanced navigational accuracy. For a conventional role in the 1990s (of which the G model would be principal exponent), the aircraft would need a range of improved sensors capable of detecting, classifying and tracking a variety of high-value targets at considerable range. Developments in synthetic (and inverse synthetic) aperture radar seem likely to offer promising avenues of exploration here. Secondly, an extremely accurate conventional stand-off weapon would be needed, with a Circular Error Probable (CEP) of 20 metres or less. This is a particularly demanding requirement for an air-launched weapon—and one that will be met only at considerable cost. It will thus become a matter of debate as to whether or not it should be fitted to such an old warhorse as the B-52: but that particular warhorse has shown a remarkable ability to survive in the face of challenges both technological and financial. As but one example of the latter challenge: it is estimated that the first four years' programme of the AGM-86B ALCM totalled some two-thirds of the eight years' production costs of the great bombers themselves. And that is but one of the many developments which the B-52 has spawned over the years. For the future, the already impressive and versatile armoury of the old 'Buff' can be extended yet further by carriage of the AGM-136A Anti-Radiation Homing Missile which offers another option for the vital wartime task of suppressing enemy defences. And who could, with certainty, claim that even that development would spell the end of the road for a very remarkable bomber (Plate 4.16)?

PLATE 4.16   The 'Buff' flies on. An impressive shot of a Boeing B-52H. (*Boeing Military Airplane Company*)

Meanwhile, the world of military aviation does not stand still; and already in the SAC inventory is a new and even more capable strategic bomber—the Rockwell International B-1B.

5

Approach by Stealth

Before looking in detail at the new generation of strategic bombers, let us examine some of the directions in which technology is moving to enhance their capability. This chapter will bring together a number of important avenues of research which combined to impart low observability or 'stealth' to future military aircraft.

Down the ages, fighting man has sought to exploit the element of surprise. Concealment and disguise were early forms of deception; and ambush, a commonly used tactic. Today, the impressive capabilities of surveillance and detection systems combine with sophisticated means of communication and information display to ensure that almost every movement of an enemy, actual or potential, is prey to observation— in the piping times of peace every bit as much as in those increasingly nervy days which would presage any future war; and, very much more so, during the course of war itself.

The speed of modern air-fighting machines is such as to allow aircraft (combat or support, fixed- or rotary-wing, manned or unmanned, tactical or strategic) to exploit to the full those innate characteristics of air power—flexibility and surprise; to apply force or to proffer assistance at long range, over a wide and diverse area and, above all, in timely fashion. By comparison with war in any other environment, speed is the very essence of air operations. But, of itself, speed is not enough. Once a prime element of surprise, speed *per se* no longer confers on the aircraft the degree of invulnerability it once did. Defences have become too sophisticated for that, and ways must be found to reduce or degrade the efficiency of defensive systems if the air power of today is to be applied as effectively as it should. Surprise is a characteristic now vested as much in the aircraft designer as in the tactician.

Over the years, military aviation has recognised the need for concealment and deception. Aircraft have long been camouflaged in an arresting variety of paint schemes, to reduce the capability of enemy detection by visual means. Decoy and spoof raids have been frequently used to conceal a true objective or target. In their efforts to escape detection, combat aircraft have been flown ever higher to combat the capabilities, successively, of guns, fighters and missiles. But, as Mr Gary Powers proved as long ago as 1960 with his U-2 spy-plane, high might have to be very high indeed. They have also been flown very low, to allow flight under the radar lobe and to take every advantage of terrain masking and of the enemy's known blind spots. But very low, particularly at night or in bad weather, may demand the assistance of terrain-following radar—which can itself be something of a give-away to alert enemy defences. Electro-optical and infra-red systems, however promising for the future, are only now beginning to give the same degree of confidence to aircrew flying, in indifferent weather, at the ultra-low levels required to defeat the most advanced detection and tracking radars. As we have already seen, the age of increasing sophistication in aids to navigation and target acquisition (radio, radar, infra-red etc) has spawned a whole industry of countermeasures and counter- countermeasures; which make the waging of modern war in the air a game of mind-boggling complexity, in which only the most skilled and highly trained can hope to survive— let alone succeed.

More recently, science and technology have been able to offer the airman yet further aids to the concealment of his intent and, indeed, of his very presence. With appropriate flair, the several different technologies currently being applied to this activity have been given the dramatic (if slightly sinister) sobriquet of 'stealth'. Earlier volumes in this series have covered various aspects of stealth technology: in particular, Air Marshal Armitage's book on remotely-piloted vehicles offered a most useful guide to the principles involved—particularly as they may be applied in the field of unmanned aircraft. In taking this on to the world of the strategic air offensive, it is inevitable that there will be some repetition of earlier work. But that is necessary if any sort of coherent story is to be told; and it may, again, serve to overcome the need for referral back to other sources.

First (to repeat a point already made) stealth technology is actually a mix of several different technologies. Between them, they seek to reduce the observability of an aircraft (or indeed drone, missile, tank or submarine). As applied to aircraft, stealth must increase the difficulty of detection— whether that be by eye, ear, radar receiver, thermal image intensifier or any other sensor. The range of technologies involved covers the suppression of engine exhaust smoke to the masking of on-board electro-magnetic emissions; taking in, on the way, aircraft design, engine noise suppression and camouflage schemes.

CAMOUFLAGE

The susceptibility of aircraft to detection by the human eye (supplemented, as may be, by image magnifiers and intensifiers) may still be reduced by careful camouflage, by the suppression of engine smoke and contrails, and by flight at very high or very low level. Let us first look at the avoidance of aircraft detection by paint and by the use of clean engines. The types of camouflage that have been used on fighting aircraft are almost as varied as the types of aircraft themselves. In large part, success depends on allowing the aircraft to merge with its background, though of course in practice this is very difficult to achieve. Not only does the background against which an aircraft may be seen vary immensely with route, height, time of day, position of the sun or phase of moon: but those aircraft do, on occasion, have to be seen—not least by friendly aircraft and by ground observers. The truly 'invisible' aircraft (if such could be created) might be rather safer over the heart of the enemy homeland than it would—at least to others—on the approach to its home base. Anti-collision and formation lights may do something to alleviate the problems—particularly in peacetime training, but such training can then less realistically simulate the conditions of war. However, the fact is that no combination of known finishes can make an aircraft even moderately invisible in all conditions of geography and light: and, anyway, hard high-gloss paints carry their own penalties in increased weight and frictional drag. For example, the weight of paint on a Vulcan medium-bomber, flying in the low-level role in the early 1980s, was some 174 lb. In the right conditions, it could make that very large and distinctive aircraft extremely difficult to spot from

PLATE 5.1   An impressive example of camouflage—though only over a specific terrain. A Vulcan bomber on a training sortie over Labrador. (*Author's Collection*)

a fighter at higher altitude (Plate 5.1). However, paint schemes became irrelevant to the very low-flying interceptor—or, indeed, the SAM or gun crew—because the Vulcan was just too big and could not be flown low enough to escape such detection. Nor was its disruptive-pattern camouflage of much value over the sea or desert terrain across which, parts of its planned operational profiles might well have caused it to fly. In other words, in the absence of a readily available 'chameleon paint', camouflage can only be a matter of compromise—at best, valuable during only certain phases of flight.

It is generally accepted that the most promising compromise, offering relative protection from view for longer periods, lies in a basic grey tone, with countershading to compensate for areas of highlighting or shadow (Plate 5.2). In this, the attempt is made to reduce the visually attractive differences between an aircraft's

PLATE 5.2   The relative effectiveness of light grey camouflage—particularly for the smaller 'fighter-type' aircraft. A pair of Royal Netherlands Air Force Northrop F-5s getting airborne. (*NATO*)

background and its own colour and luminance (or brightness)—which latter property becomes more important with increasing range, when the scattering of light by the atmosphere tends to merge colours. So-called 'active camouflage' has been trialled, with various lights and sensors constantly adjusting the luminance of individual aircraft components so that the whole is, as far as possible, at all times matching its background.

The texture of an aircraft's coating is also relevant to visual perception. Gloss paint can offer increased protection against the elements, but its reflectivity is also increased as against that of a dull matt finish. In an attempt to overcome the problem, radar ablative paints have been used—for example on the Lockheed SR-71 Blackbird (Plate 5.3). Rather than absorbing radiation, this type of paint tends to conduct it over the skin, avoiding some of the electro-magnetic hot spots that occur, in flight, on any aerodynamic surface. A still better degree of conductivity can be achieved by blending microscopic particles of metal (normally, iron) into the paint itself, to produce what is known as iron ball paint. Yet further advanced paints, of extremely complex manufacture, may be developed to enhance radar or infra-red absorbency. However their efficacy has yet to be proven and the results of such proof made available as a matter of public record.

ELIMINATION OF TRAILS

As for engines, the two obvious visual give-aways are from exhaust smoke and condensation trails (contrails). The latter are the trails of ice crystals, formed by the freezing of water vapour expelled with the products of engine combustion. Although all aircraft engines run at high temperatures, they also extract large quantities of water from the fuels on which they run. In conditions of extreme ambient cold (from about -24° at sea level to -45° at a height of 50,000 ft) the air in the wake of an engine will reach saturation point—the local heating effect of the engine exhaust being

PLATE 5.3   The distinctive SR-71 Blackbird, with a paint scheme to match its name.
(*United States Air Force*)

insufficient to overcome the increase in relative humidity caused by the addition of
water to the cold ambient air. The resultant cloud of ice crystals appears as a trail,
which broadens as it is diffused in the surrounding air. If that air is already at or
near saturation, the contrail will be slow to evaporate—and is in fact described as
'persistent'. Military pilots have long understood the dangers of contrails in assisting
the visual detection of their aircraft, and they are usually well briefed on the heights
to fly and on engine-handling techniques to adopt if contrails are to be avoided.
Given that the preponderance of military aviation in combat aircraft is now carried
out at low level, the problem of contrails is less acute than it once was. But, bear in
mind that they can actually form as low as ground level and, as will be suggested
later, it is not by any means certain that low-level flight will continue, for all time,
to offer an attacking aircraft quite the relative advantages it now enjoys.

Less easy to avoid (though less easy to detect and track when they do occur) are
wing-tip trails or vortices. These thin and transient trails are formed by a reduction
in pressure, usually at the wing extremities of a manoeuvring aircraft. Unlike contrails they need milder, but damp air for their formation and they occur invariably
at the lower altitudes. Similar effects may be observed over the upper surfaces of
wings and (though now of only academic interest to the majority of modern military
pilots) at the tips of propeller blades—in other words, anywhere a rapid reduction
of pressure leads to expansion and temperature reduction below the dew-point of

the surrounding air. As already suggested, the phenomenon is scarcely one to concern the crew of a large aircraft such as a strategic bomber, though it is of some immediate relevance to pilots engaged in hard visual combat.

The suppression of engine exhaust smoke is a different matter—and one that can be wholly desirable to military aircrews. The smoke trails from a whole generation of military jet engines have made the aircraft they power very much more easily detected by the eye (Plates 5.4 and 5.5), either directly or by the shadows they produce on the ground beneath the aircraft's flight path. The truly smokeless engine has not yet been designed—certainly if it is to be operated as flexibly and at such potentially high power ratings as are required by modern military aircraft. However, research and experiment have combined to reduce smoke emission from many engines, though often at some cost in reduced performance.

Smoke is a measure of combustion inefficiency in an engine, but the level of smoke is disproportionate to the level of inefficiency. In other words, engines which produce high levels of smoke are not necessarily those which are low on performance. That said, it is clearly desirable for aircraft engines to have as clean combustion as possible—to improve undetected penetration in war and, equally, to ease the environmental effects of low-flying training in peace. Several air forces now specify to the manufacturers of aero-engines products that are, as nearly as possible, invisible.

In defining invisibility in this context, consideration must be given to exactly how the jet efflux is to be viewed. For example, a jet plume that is invisible from the side may not be so when viewed along its length. To assist in applied design, opacity to light (or smoke number) can be plotted against the diameter of the engine's exhaust nozzle. As a broad rule of thumb: at a constant 'invisibility level', the smoke number for a small diameter nozzle will be relatively higher than that for a nozzle of larger diameter. The presence of carbon particles in an engine's exhaust emission will give rise to black smoke—the largest particles of which will be only of sub-micron size but, added together, can produce the familiar thick smoke trail so unwelcome to combat aircrew. The control of smoke emission demands at all times a correct fuel-air ratio within the engine. Naturally, this varies not only with throttle-setting and aircraft height, but even across the actual combustion process of the engine itself. For the purposes of smoke generation, the area in which the fuel-air ratio is most critical is that of the engine's primary combustion zone, where it is essential to maintain a weak mixture by ensuring a sufficient supply of air. In the business of smoke suppression (though not necessarily that of engine performance), mixture control is of more importance than the temperature of combustion. In general, the fitting of high-quality vaporising burners in an aero-engine does ensure good mixing. However, at the higher combustion temperatures experienced in a modern jet engine (and turbine entry temperatures of well over 2,000°C are not unknown) the selection of suitable materials can become difficult. Also at the higher temperatures, oxides of nitrogen (NOX) are generated in visible form, and the engine designer is often reduced to the business of trade-offs between the twin undesirables of NOX and smoke emission.

Smoke generation can also be influenced by the type of fuel or fuel additive used; by the fitting of a reheat system (virtually a *sine qua non* of current-generation combat aircraft); and by the type of engine control system that is used. Combustion

PLATES 5.4 and 5.5   A 'give-away' to any sharp-eyed interceptor pilot. A SAC B-47 Stratojet (above) emitting very obvious trails from its engine exhausts—in this case, amplified by the use of water injection. In the lower picture, the Hawker Siddeley/British Aerospace Buccaneer would be a very difficult target for any fighter pilot at the heights at which it is most 'at home'. However, even there, smoke would help alert the SAM or gun-crews of any target surface vessel. (*United States Air Force and NATO*)

design can, in general terms, take account of fuel type; and, these days, there is a high degree of standardisation over fuel grades for military use—certainly by the Western nations. Additives may, in fact, help some of the problems of smoke generation, though their use has to be carefully controlled in peacetime because of toxic products which are the unwelcome side-effects of many of the more effective of them. The use of reheat (or after-burner) does reduce smoke levels because the carbon particles are actually burnt out in the reheat process. However, reheat greatly increases an engine's fuel consumption and is therefore used sparingly—though, in practice, perhaps more often in a combat situation or on the run-in to a target, when detection by an enemy would be most dangerous.

Control systems are more likely to influence the production of white smoke on engine start-up—not, in itself, an important tactical consideration. It is associated with low combustion efficiency in the idle and sub-idle engine regimes and can, in fact, also occur at certain stages of the AAR process. However, in most circumstances, it is of little practical consequence and is, anyway, minimised by the incorporation of modern full-authority digital electronic engine-control systems.

In summary, the greater cycle efficiencies of modern aero-engines, with their high pressure ratios and combustion temperatures, certainly add to the problems of smoke control. High-compression delivery pressures and their associated temperatures demand high combustion temperatures which themselves demand more cooling air, leaving less available for smoke control in that primary combustion zone. The manufacturers of all modern aero-engines are working always at the edge of their complex technology and seeking always to improve a product which, in its natural environment, is working at the extremes of temperature, pressure, material tolerance, performance and efficiency. To help them in their demanding task leading manufacturers such as Rolls-Royce plc in the United Kingdom make use of the most up-to-date computer techniques to determine the most suitable designs for all the many components of their product. Such techniques are certainly used for the analytical prediction of engine emission control and, purely as an example, a computer read-out of the combustion temperature predictions for a typical military aero-engine is reproduced at Figure 5.1.

For our purposes, it indicates merely the immense detail into which the designer and manufacturer of modern aero-engines must dig if they are to provide their customer (in our case the military aviator) with the product that can most effectively do the job in a wide variety of circumstances.

NOISE SUPPRESSION

Aircraft engines are, of course, also a prime cause of another aid to aircraft detection—noise. Less immediately relevant to the air combat situation, noise can be useful in the early detection of an aircraft's approach and, as such, needs to be minimised. It is a bonus that noise suppression also helps overcome, at least in part, some of the environmental problems of peacetime low-level operational training; and useful again that, unlike many developments in military aviation, it does have a direct relevance to civil aircraft operations. Indeed, it has been primarily the

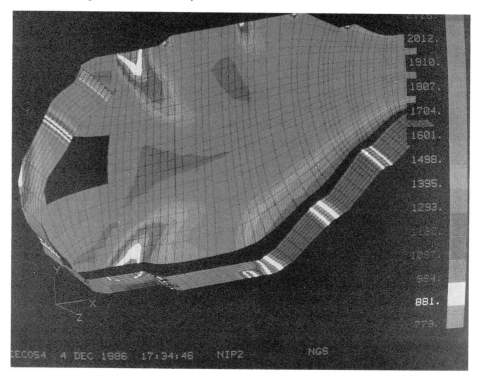

FIG. 5.1   Computerised predictions of combustion temperatures for a typical military aero-engine. (*Rolls-Royce plc*)

demands of the general public that have maintained the pressure on aero-engine
manufacturers to reduce the noise of their products. And noise regulations as applied
to civil airlines have become steadily more stringent. As an example, the British
Aerospace 146—generally accepted as the quietest of current pure jet airliners—is
being considered for yet further noise reduction as later and heavier variants demand
greater thrust from its Avco Lycoming ALF 502 engines. Incidentally, it is not only
aero-engines that make aircraft noisy—as anyone who has spent time with gliders
will readily acknowledge. A large passenger airline (or, for that matter, a strategic
bomber) would be very noisy in certain stages of flight—*eg* in the 'dirty' configuration
required for landing—even if it could be so operated without engines at all.

That said, it is the aero-engine that generates the most obvious problem of aircraft
noise. We have already looked at likely developments in military engine technology.
In the context of stealth, it is worth reminding ourselves that aircraft with propellers
not only burn less fuel (with consequent reduction in infra-red signature); they can
also be comparatively quiet—the trick being to silence the noise of the propellers
themselves. However, propeller-driven aircraft have inherent limitations on the
speed at which they can be flown. Such systems as advanced prop-fans, ducted and
unducted contra-fans used in conjuction with ultra high by-pass (UHB) ratio engines
will be able to power aircraft at speeds considerably in excess of those attainable
with earlier-generation turbo-props. However, one of the problems of engines such
as these has lain in the high levels of external noise they produce. As we shall see,

propellers are also rather bad news when it comes to the reduction of an aircraft's RCS—the blades of the large Soviet Bear aircraft, for example (Plate 5.6), being said to account for some 90% of its already significant radar detectability when taken head-on.

PLATE 5.6   A close-up of the very large contra-rotating propellor blades of a Tu-142 Bear-H, which are said to account for some 90% of that aircraft's 'head-on' detectability by radar. (*US Department of Defense*)

One of the keys to progress in the reduction both of engine noise and RCS will lie in the speeds at which future military aircraft will require to fly, particularly when they are in range of enemy early-warning, detection or defensive systems. If flight in those areas could be restricted to below (as a ball-park figure) about 500 mph, it would be theoretically possible to sustain it with propellers buried deep inside an aircraft body—with skin of a sandwich construction enclosing sound-baffles; with engine inlets so designed as to be virtually invisible to radar; and with jet effluxes which were, by present-day standards, comparatively slow, cool and silent.

INFRA-RED

The mention of 'cool' leads us to one of the two other characteristics of aero-engines which must be addressed if they are to play their part in achieving a genuinely stealthy aircraft. As has already been indicated, all engines produce heat; and aero-engines work consistently at temperatures far higher than those found in most other propulsion systems. Not only does the emission of infra-red (IR) radiation simplify the task of aircraft detection: but many anti-aircraft missiles are—and will undoubtedly continue to be—of the heat-seeking variety. And whereas earlier generations of such missiles needed to home in on large hot targets, technology has now developed to the point at which heat differentials can be very much more accurately measured—and heat-seeking missiles made capable thereby of discriminating and engaging relatively cool targets. A simplified diagram (Figure 5.2) indicates some of the hot-spots on a typical large aircraft—the engines being by far the most obvious in terms of IR emission. The even more generalised graph in Figure 5.3 indicates the potential for the detection of such emissions as compared with visual sightings

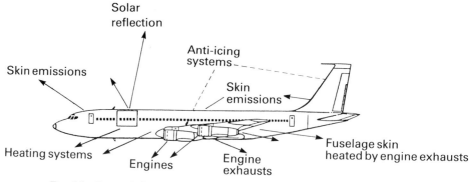

FIG. 5.2   Some obvious sources of heat emission from a typical large aircraft.
(*Author*)

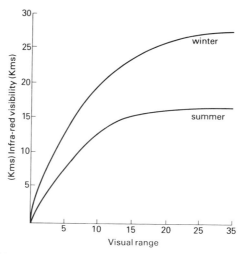

FIG. 5.3   Infra-red visibility v. visual range in North-West Europe

in North-West Europe. The capabilities of modern IR systems in comparison with those available by photography are well illustrated at Plates 5.7 and 5.8—albeit taking as subject a very non-military (and traditionally rather chilly) target. Unlike a church, a modern jet engine, in full reheat, may be putting upwards of 400,000 kW of heat into the surrounding air; and although this fairly quickly dissipates, it cannot be wholly absorbed and lost for a long time after the aircraft's passage. Designers can begin to attack the problem by the clever shielding of jet-pipes; but there is no perfect solution in that. Far more effective in reducing emitted engine heat is to enhance the effectiveness of the engine itself, *ie* by ensuring that as little fuel as possible is burnt for a given power output. Pressures on aero-engine designers to increase the Specific Fuel Consumption (SFC) of their products have, until recent years, stemmed from the need to reduce aircraft weight (or size) and running costs. Now those pressures are reinforced by the requirements to 'stay cool'. There may be some relief in the careful direction of cooling air to and around the hotter parts of engines: but practical considerations (and the efficiency of the engine as a means

PLATES 5.7 and 5.8   The same 'target' viewed by normal daylight photography and infra-red imagery. (*Royal Signals and Radar Establishment/Crown Copyright*)

of propulsion) limit what can be achieved in this area. Flight in reheat is, of course, to be avoided in all circumstances short of desperation when an aircraft is over hostile territory.

DESIGN

The final problem for stealth, as presented by the aero-engine, relates to its installation—and here we move on to the realm of the airframe designer and address the important role he has to play in the search for the 'invisible aircraft'. A basic measurement of an object's detectability is held to be its RCS—usually measured in square metres (m^2) and to which passing reference has been made. As has been pointed out in an earlier volume of this series, RCS is measured by calculating the amount of radar energy reflected by a target back to the observer (or radar receiver); and then calculating the size of sphere that would reflect the same amount of radar energy. The area of a disc of that same diameter is called the RCS. The two factors held to be of greatest significance in the determination of RCS are shape and the material used in the object's construction. It should be noted that RCS is not so markedly a function of the size of an object. To give one rather exaggerated example: let us assume, for argument's sake, that the RCS of a B-52 bomber to a given radar wave-band was 100 m^2. A fire engine, illuminated by the same radar, might well have a RCS at least double that value. The reason for this is that an aircraft (even a comparatively ungainly aircraft like the B-52) has been designed for maximum aerodynamic efficiency. As far as is possible within the limits set by its role, aerodynamically efficient shapes have been incorporated in its design; and streamlining has been featured to ensure its smooth (and, hence, efficient) passage through the air. The same principles have little application to the fire engine. For the role for which it was designed, strength and solidity are virtues together with space and load-carrying capacity; the large extendable ladder and its associated turntable have no place on our B-52. The result is that the fire engine is all square sides, sharp edges and right-angles which would reflect back any incoming radar signal; and holes, corners and open box-constructions which may even enhance that return. Fortunately, fire engines are not normally threatened by radar illumination—even, in their case, for the purposes of law enforcement.

But, however smooth and contoured an aircraft, does it not also have right-angles, box-like constructions and holes? Indeed it does—and in otherwise excellent military aircraft like the B-52, the F-4 Phantom and the MiG-25 Foxbat (Plate 5.9), those features are found in plenty. Up to the end of the 1970s, they were of less importance in aircraft design than were the often conflicting requirements of strength, weight, speed and load-carrying capacity. Now the accent is on smoothness, curves, embedded engines and obtuse angles. The RCS of an aircraft varies with the angle of interception as well as with the frequency of the threat radar. Against the types of radars likely to be fielded in the 1990s and beyond, RCSs of rather less than 1 m^2 will be the order of the day; and these are probably capable of achievement by such modern strategic bombers as the USAF's B-1B. Interestingly, they would not have been achieved with its predecessor, the B-1A; and a comparison of the two aircraft reveals the sharp spine and high angular intakes of the earlier aircraft as being two of the features which have been lost in the design of the stealthier B-1B.

PLATE 5.9   An impressive aircraft for its time; but the MiG-25 Foxbat (like many of its generation) is high on observability by radar. (*US Department of Defense*)

RCS is a function of four major factors. Size, shape and material have already been mentioned and will now be examined more fully, as will the fourth factor—aspect.

SIZE

Although it would appear that the size of an object should have a marked effect on its RCS, this is not necessarily so—as evidenced by the comparison of B-52 and fire engine. For a simple example, let us take a plate, of 1 m², viewed in a normal plane, *eg* as in a mirror. Illuminated by a radar operating at, say, 3 giga-hertz (GHz), its RCS would be about 12 m². However for another radar operating at 10 GHz, the RCS of that same plate might have increased more than tenfold—to 150 m², at least. Hence, the inadequency of any bold statement about an aircraft's RCS: it depends on the frequency of the radar being used against it. Another example of the effect of size on RCS can be seen in the decoy. As we have seen, for many years the trusty old B-52 carried small unmanned aircraft-like decoys called Quails, with RCS specifically designed to equate to that of the B-52 from which they were launched. This feature was built into the Quail by a series of measures to enhance its radar reflectivity. One such device is known as a Luneberg lens—in effect, a specially constructed reflection designed to optimise the electro-magnetic energy returned to the transmitting radar. Consider, also, three aircraft of roughly the same size—the B-52, B-1A and B-1B. Readily available information suggests their respective RCSs as being in the ratio of 100:10:1.

However, in the future it could be that size comes to assume greater relative importance in the detection of aircraft. One development, under consideration by several nations, is that of early-warning by high-frequency (HF) radars. Operating at a frequency of, say, 10 mega-hertz (MHz) a HF radar would have a wavelength of 30 m and, at the same frequency, the ideal half-wave dipole length for re-radiation would be 15 m—or roughly the span of a typical fighter-bomber of the late 1980s. This suggests that if HF radar were to be deployed (and there are many practical problems to be overcome in so doing), a whole range of future combat aircraft would have to be either very much larger or considerably smaller than they are now.

SHAPE

Let us now consider shape as a factor in the calculation of RCS. In general terms, any flat shape will reflect energy and sharp irregularities will enhance RCS. It is for that reason that radars are often calibrated by tri-hedral corner reflectors (Plate 5.10). The junction of two planes at 90° gives rise to a sort of double bounce of energy, which serves to enhance the radar return. Conversely, the reduction of a right-angle between two plates, by as little as a couple of degrees, can serve to reduce the RCS of those plates by a factor of 10.

PLATE 5.10   The enhancement of radar returns at the 'low tech' end of the market. A tri-hedral corner reflector, used for airfield radar calibration.

Translating that to an airframe/engine combination: the principal reflection points of a typical fuselage lie in those flat surfaces which are normal (*ie* at right angles) to the transmitter. It is thus important to avoid any 90° angles which might face the illuminating source; and as the angle between aircraft surface and radar can obviously vary with aircraft height, altitude and flight-path, the designer's task becomes impossibly difficult and perfection unattainable. Clearly (and obviously) RCS can never be reduced to zero. That said, our designer can do a great deal to reduce it. He can ensure that tailplanes slope in from the vertical and that wings blend into fuselage—features that are already evident on present-generation combat

PLATE 5.11   The McDonnell Douglas F/A-18 (in this instance a Canadian Armed Forces CF-18A from Baden Soellingen, in West Germany) showing design features which help reduce observability—and, incidentally, the advantages of a light-grey paint scheme. (*NATO*)

aircraft such as the MiG-29 Fulcrum and F/A 18 (Plate 5.11). Taken to the extreme, the ultimate shape for a reduced-RCS fuselage would look something like that reproduced in Figure 5.4. Of course, with 1960s technology, such a shape would have been impossible to control because of its inherent aerodynamic instability. Now that fly-by-wire has made instability the order of the day, by harnessing it in the cause of agility, such shapes may well come into their own in the design of stealthy combat aircraft.

Back to engines (again) and the inherently complex problem of inlet design. Traditional jet engine intakes have, naturally enough, been designed for efficiency in terms of adequate airmass flow into the engine at any likely combination of aircraft speed, Mach number, height, angle of attack or configuration—indeed, across the whole of the aircraft's flight envelope. They have also had to take into account the demands of easy access on the ground for inspection or repair, when time and aircraft exposure might well be at a premium. Although they vary greatly in size, shape and position on the aircraft, engine intakes can generally be said to offer a direct path for radar energy to pass into the very noisy area (in terms both

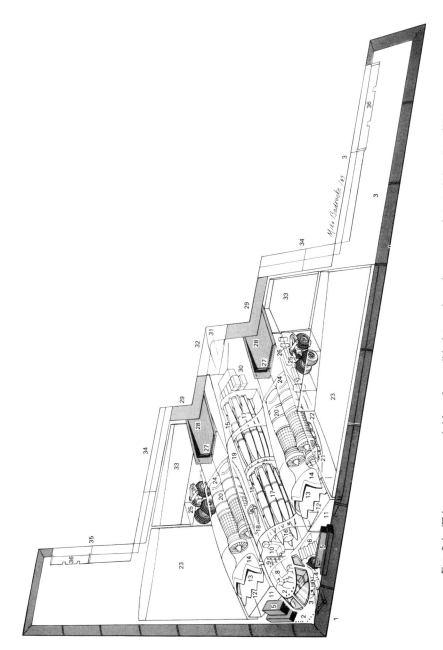

Fig. 5.4 This was one expert's idea of a possible future shape for a manned strategic bomber. (*Motor-books, USA.*) Compare with artist's impression of B2 on page 181.

of radar and of fact) of the low-pressure (LP) compressor—an area stiff with very unstealthy corner reflectors. If the engine is to remain outside the airframe, the designer must attempt to block that direct path of radar energy into the LP compressor—a difficult task if he is to guarantee the requisite airmass flow. A better solution would be to mount the engine (or engines) deep inside the aircraft's fuselage or wing structure, with an intake of zig-zag design, heavily coated with radar-absorbent material. Shock-cones, incorporated on some high-performance aircraft (primarily to decrease airflow to sub-sonic speed on entry into the engine), actually serve to reduce the RCS of the inlets they control by restricting the path of radar energy (cf that doyen of stealthy aircraft, the SR-71). However, as previously suggested, high supersonic flight may not be a pre-requisite of future manned combat aircraft—certainly for the strategic offensive role.

ASPECT

Moving on to another function of aircraft design, let us now look briefly at the question of aspect. As already suggested, in the context of RCS the shaping of an aircraft must be considered from every direction. This is particularly true of the more manoeuvrable, agile aircraft now in the inventories of many nations as air superiority fighters, fighter-bombers or ground-attack aircraft. In the future, there is no reason against (and every advantage in) making the longer-range manned bomber as manoeuvrable as it can be, for it will have to face many of the same threats as its smaller cousins; and it may, in the next generation, anyway develop into a smaller variant of itself.

Although technically difficult to achieve, it is important that the RCS of a modern aircraft is measured from all aspects—ideally, during the design phase when impending errors can be rectified. The methods by which this can be done are complex and deserving of more detailed attention, but they are beyond the scope of the present volume. Eager students without access to one of the specialist (and rather highly classified) research establishments may have recourse to a decided second-best—and study Maxwell's Linearity Equation, which has an application in the technique of Radar Scaled Modelling.

Let us take one large bomber as an example of the way in which various of its components affect the overall RCS of the aircraft. The Avro (later, British Aerospace) Vulcan was originally designed in 1947 to Air Ministry Specification B35/46. Known then only as the Avro 698, it was a futuristic design for its day. A large tailless delta aircraft of Aspect Ratio 3,[1] the Vulcan was one of six original designs to meet a tight and, for the time, very demanding specification for an aircraft to carry a 10,000 lb bomb-load over a still-air range of 3,350 miles by day or night from bases throughout the world. It had to be capable of carrying a wide range of conventional weapons and of being modified for reconnaissance duties. An initial all-up weight limit of 100,000 lb was later extended to 115,000 lb; but the Spec insisted on a 45,000-ft cruising altitude after 1 hour in flight, 50,000 ft after 2½ hours and as far beyond that as was achievable. The cruising speed was to be 500 knots (Mach 0.875) at continuous power over a target 1,500 mile from base. All that had to be achieved in an elapsed period of less than five years, with scientists, designers and engineers working beyond the boundaries of anyone's experience in areas positively alive with aerodynamic and structural uncertainties. And it had to be done without the benefit of experience of large jet engines or high-speed aerodynamics, without the advanced research facilities and wind tunnels, computers, sophisticated test equipment or exotic materials available to their successors.

The fact that not one, but three designs to Spec 35/46 eventually entered front-line service with the RAF (one of them still there in the AAR role) is the greatest

PLATE 5.12   A famous trio. All three of the Royal Air Force's 'V-bombers' entered service in the 1950s; all were eventually converted to air-to-air refuelling; and one (the Victor) is still in front-line service more than 30 years on. Pictured here are early marks of the Avro Vulcan, Vickers Valiant and Handley Page Victor. (*Royal Air Force Museum*)

possible tribute to Britain's post-war aircraft industry (Plate 5.12). The story is told elsewhere[2] and deserves to be read by all serious students of strategic bombing. For our purpose, suffice it to say that the Vulcan (Plate 5.13) was design ahead of its time—not least in the matter of design for stealth, a concept undreamt of at the time. Least beneficial from that point of view were, in fact, the massive tail and the exhaust ports from the large engines. However, those engines were deeply buried in a large and relatively smooth 'flying wing' from which there were remarkably few protuberances—the large (eventually, 21,000 lb) bomb-load being internally carried and the body of the aircraft having adequate space for all the special-to-role equipment which, on a smaller aircraft, would have had to be wing-mounted. The large (and potentially radar-resonant) cockpit in fact gave little reflection. The smooth shape of the canopy contributed to the Vulcan's RCS; and, designed as it was to fly

PLATE 5.13   The majestic Vulcan—a design ahead of its time. (*British Aerospace plc, Military Aircraft Division*)

at high altitude, gold-film heating was incorporated to prevent misting. Although transparent at very high light frequencies, this film behaved as if it were all-metal when illuminated by the lower frequencies of radar.

A modern variant of the gold-film treatment for cockpit transparencies might be to coat them with substances such as indium-tin oxide. The effects of this would be twofold; firstly, in retaining the purpose of the transparency by allowing a very high percentage of light (possibly in the high nineties of per cent) to pass unhindered into the cockpit; secondly (and more important from the point of view of the aircraft's illumination by threat radars), in greatly restricting the passage from the aircraft of the electronic emissions from equipments within the cockpit itself.

MATERIAL

As we have already noted, the ideal invisible aircraft would be transparent to the beams of all threat radars: we have also seen that this is an impossible specification. The aim of the designers and manufacturers of future combat aircraft will be to use, as far as possible, materials whose impedance is close to that of the surrounding air. A few such materials do exist—notably in the range of fibre composites; but those best suited to the reduction of an aircraft's electronic signature may not be sufficiently strong, sufficiently flexible or sufficiently easy to work as to make them suitable for the construction of combat aircraft—certainly, as regards some of the primary structures of those aircraft. For example: glass fibre has for some time been used in the manufacture of dielectric panels, such as those protecting many airborne radars. A glass-fibre aircraft would have a very low RCS and, indeed, small general aviation aircraft such as the Learfan have been largely so constructed—albeit for reasons of weight-saving rather than invisibility. It is reported that the 'paint' of such aircraft on air traffic control radars was too thin for comfort and that the civil aviation authorities insisted on their carrying two on-board transponders for reliable identification.

Other fibre materials—for example, composites of carbon or boron—are actually conductive and, used in sufficient concentration for strength, may reflect almost as well as metal. One solution has long been understood and, indeed, applied to ships, submarines and tanks as well as to aircraft. This is the coating of metal or other surfaces with any of a range of radar-absorbent materials (RAM). There are two principal families of such materials: so-called 'broad-band absorbers' and resonant materials.

Simply stated, broad-band RAM absorbs radar energy over a wide frequency

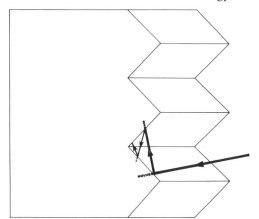

Fig. 5.5   The principle of broad-band RAM. (*Author*)

band by rapid attenuation over a short distance. As indicated (for illustrative purposes only) in Figure 5.5, materials coated with thick foam-like substances, cut in the shape of successive pyramids, can greatly attenuate incoming energy. Such coatings, resembling the construction of egg-boxes, are in fact used successfully on slower-moving and stationary objects—for example, in anechoic chambers used for the testing of radars. Claims have been made for polyurethane foams effective against frequencies as high as 100 GHz and, depending critically on the profile of the pyramidal indentations, down as low as the 100-MHz range. The low-density foam, usually carbon-impregnated, ensures dielectric loss; whilst the gradual transition of reflected energy, from that pertaining in free space to total absorption in the material, is affected by its pyramidal profile. The snag is that such facings are hardly conducive to optimum aerodynamic performance. They could only sensibly be used when faced by a radar-transparent skin.

A more general practical application of RAM for an aircraft's skin is narrow-band RAM or resonant frequency absorption (Figure 5.6). This works on the 'Salisbury principle'. In simple terms, the front face of the material reflects half the radiated energy whilst the next travels a quarter of a wavelength to the fully reflective back-plate; and back another quarter wavelength to combine with the 50% reflected from the front face. As a result, half of the emitted energy is returned 180° out of phase with the rest—and the result is destructive interference. Ideally, there would be no resonant radar reflection; and were it possible to obtain this ideal effect over the whole of an aircraft's surface, such an aircraft would be invisible to radar. However that would be true only for the radar frequency at which the distance between the front and rear faces of the aircraft's skin was exactly one quarter the wavelength of that frequency. The elimination of one specific threat, at any given time, would thus

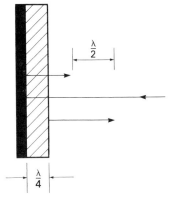

FIG. 5.6   The principle of narrow-band RAM or 'resonant frequency absorption').
(*Author*)

be achieved without any degradation of reflectivity from other radars and, as we know, single-frequency transmissions are not a feature of modern air defence systems. That said, narrow-band absorption can induce low levels of reflectivity over a modest frequency range.

Other types of RAM include some in which small metal spheres have been impregnated into the material itself, causing incoming radar signals to scatter and dissipate. The problem here is that widespread use of such material could give rise to unacceptable weight penalties on the aircraft; and the technique is therefore of more general application in the 'noisiest' areas of an aircraft's RCS, *ie* in engine intakes and around wing roots.

Of course, the effectiveness of any radar reflector is proportional to the rate of change of impedance between surfaces. As one obvious example: metal is a good reflector because, at its surface, the impedance of the air changes abruptly from an approximate 377 ohms in free space to conductivity at the metal itself. If this abrupt change in impedance could somehow be graduated, the resultant reflectivity would be reduced—perhaps quite markedly. In the search for ever lower values of RCS, points of transition on an aircraft's surface assume increasing significance. Discontinuities of all sorts have to be avoided. Thus, replenishment and inspection panels need to be as flush and as close-fitting as possible; and joints between differing materials must be virtually invisible to the eye and to the feel, if they are to escape detection by powerful and sophisticated modern radars. All such interfaces or discontinuities would also need to be electronically bonded to obviate sudden detectable changes in impedance—and, here, the use of gold film for sealing is an attractive (though expensive) option. Also interesting—and not merely in reducing an aircraft's observability—is the potential of so-called 'smart skins' for future combat aircraft. Experimental composites may be developed actually to conduct electricity to the point at which conventional antennae and threat detection sensors could be incorporated in the aircraft's own skin.

At Figure 5.7 is a simplified listing of the target areas on which future aircraft designers will have to concentrate if they are effectively to reduce the RCS of their designs. The values of RCS depicted in that table are purely illustrative, but designs

RCS (m^2)	FORWARD ASPECT	SIDE-ON	REAR ASPECT
1.0	–	*Main structural areas* – Fuselage – Wings – Tailplane	
1	– Main structural areas, plus – engine inlets	As above	Same, but including engine exhaust nozzles
0.1	– Control surfaces – Antennae – Aircraft nose	Same	Same (less noise)
0.01	– Protuberances	Same	Same
0.001	– Surface skins – Joint lines – Surface interfaces – Connectors – Ports – Material interfaces and transitions	Same	Same

FIG. 5.7   Aircraft design targets for the reduction of radar cross-section. (*Author*)

showing overall values greater than 0.1 m^2 are already well out of the race for stealth. And, as has already been indicated, that race will be an increasingly expensive one for its contestants. Not only are the techniques of combat aircraft design and manufature likely to be an order of magnitude more sophisticated than those which have stood the hitherto conventional test of strength, fatigue-resistance, lightness and repairability; but they will be worthless if they are to carry the sort of operational equipments which can themselves be easily detected by ground sensors. Thus, conventional radios, radars and transponders will have to be despatched to the museum. Future combat aircraft sensors will require very low probabilities of interception and will employ such complex and advanced techniques as spread-spectrum, passive or multi-static with, in the latter case, the relegation of all transmissions to a stand-off vehicle (or even a satellite) which must itself then be heavily protected. Certain it is that future technology will promise much—but always at a price.

LOW OBSERVABLE AVIONICS

The next generation of combat aircraft used for most of the roles available to air power will therefore be designed and manufactured to minimise their visual, aural, thermal and radar signatures. They must not put these achievements at risk by failure to reduce the potential give-aways of their own high-power on-board electronic systems. And this requirement will apply, as much as anywhere, in the area of the future manned strategic bomber and of any stand-off missiles that it might carry. Indeed, the longer flight times involved in strategic operations and their likely exposure to advanced, layered air defence systems positively demand that systems designed for navigation, target acquisition, defence suppression and penetration do not, in themselves, invite or assist enemy detection.

For future strategic operations it is probable that ever greater recourse will be made to penetration and escape by night or in poor weather. Developments in night-attack aids have been dramatic in recent years and show potential for even greater refinement. As will be well known to any student of air power, the ability to operate effectively by night can treble the time available for air operations in a typical central European winter. To take advantage of this potential, forward-looking infra-red (FLIR) systems are being developed in conjunction with state-of-the-art image intensifiers and advanced wide-angle head-up cockpit displays, to offer the combat pilot the ability to see by night almost as well as he can see by day—and with the added advantage that he can more easily acquire 'hot' targets. At the same time aircrew workload, which would otherwise not be sustainable in the high-threat environment of offensive operations, can now be greatly reduced by the automation of tasks and the presentation of information in easily assimilable fashion. There exist already many examples of comparatively low-complexity displays which can, on the one hand, offer the combat pilot a very high-quality remotely generated continuous map of his route, target area, obstrucions and enemy defences; and, at the same time, a FLIR picture of the outside world—with resolution at least as good as that hitherto achieved only by monochromic display. And there is potential for yet further refinement and development in the technology of the beam-indexed cathode ray tube. More of this later.

Another problem area being actively addressed (and with scope for much future development) is that of disseminating to the combat aircrew, in evaluated and usable form, the great mass of information that will be available to assist the successful completion of his task. Here we can see scope for exciting developments in the further miniaturisation of mass-memory equipments and dramatic reductions in time of access. Such equipments will also be free of some of the environmental constraints which currently inhibit their effective use in the harsher regimes of military aviation.

For now let us recall that, in the ceaseless advance of technology, there are relatively few instances in which something is gained for nothing. There are many examples where a less effective solution has to be accepted because the optimum is either unobtainable or unusable and others in which the advantages continue to outweigh the disadvantages. As rather over-simplified examples of each: the demands of long-range, heavy-payload, survivable offensive weapons systems preclude the benefits which can be enjoyed by small highly agile manned combat aircraft. Again: until such time as machines can be designed to think like men (and, despite impressive advances in the technology of Artificial Intelligence, it is unlikely that the full requirement will ever be met) the many applications of air power—more expensive, more complex and more demanding though they may be—will continue to need aircrew. To which all military aviators will echo a resounding 'hear hear'—possibly, even recalling the words attributed to one of their more distinguished colleagues on the comparative advantage of man over machine. Scott Crossfield, famous American post-war test-pilot, is reported to have asked:

> Where else would you get a non-lineal computer weighing only 160 lb, having a million precision elements, that can be mass-produced by unskilled labour?[3]

Modern avionics systems cannot be produced (or, at least, developed) quickly—and, certainly, never by unskilled labour. And that development often enough involves a compromise between conflicting requirements. For instance, IR imaging systems find favour by reason of their low observability. However, the effectiveness of any IR equipment is limited by certain unchanging laws of physics. It transpires that the amount of IR radiation emitted by any object is proportional to the fourth power of that object's absolute temperature. Obviously, the cooler a target or navigational feature, the less its IR emission and the greater the sensitivity required of the airborne sensor engaged in its acquisition. In consequence, the designer of the IR sensor must restrict himself to the wavelengths at which peak radiation will occur; and must also try to ensure that each of his sensor's component cells be given as much time as possible to 'see' the object to be acquired. The ideal IR sensor would involve a very large number of detector cells (in the high thousands, it has been suggested), so arrayed as to ensure virtually continuous cover of individual elements of the target. And that poses a significant challenge for equipments which are being carried, at speed, by combat aircraft—themselves subject to the many stresses of flight in a high-threat environment. By comparison, the designer of airborne radar has a rather easier time of it; but, as we have seen, radar emissions do not meet the need for low observability. With IR systems, the conflicting requirements of sensitivity, stability, uniformity and yield make it necessary for the designer to experiment with chemistry and metallurgy to produce the most effective substances for the construction of his sensor's components. Mercury-cadmium-telluride has, for some time, been favoured in FLIR applications, but indium antimonide, gallium and silicon are also candidates for consideration.

SUMMARY

It is clear that the search for low observability or stealth is taking the designers of combat aircraft, their components and their equipments down many a fascinating, but often confusing avenue. Whilst it is a fact that no aircraft can ever be truly invisible, we already know enough to declare that very significant measures can be taken to reduce its visibility to all detection means—visual, aural, electronic, electro-magnetic, thermal and radiated.

Furthermore, the comparatively straightforward retrofitting with RAM of existing aircraft, whose radar signature is unacceptably high, would be both an attractive and relatively cost-effective option. It has been reliably calculated that, spread over a fleet of 100 typical modern combat aircraft, such a programme would amount to about 0.1% of their procurement cost. Were the end result to be the survival of just one aircraft in war, the return on investment in hardware (to say nothing of the aircrew involved) would, as a conservative minimum, be tenfold.

The process of developing stealth technology is therefore a many-facetted one, currently being conducted in great and understandable secrecy. This book claims to do no more than offer its readers an idea of the problems involved. It will be a long time before their solution—partial or total—will be revealed in any detail, though it is known that aircraft such as the USAF's Rockwell B-1B (cf Chapter 6) have been designed with the requirements for low observability very much in mind. In terms purely of design, it will be fascinating to see whether future combat aircraft such as the American ATB and its successors into the next century are anything like that very stealthy-looking experimental aircraft, the Northrop YB-49 Flying Wing of the late 1940s (see Chapter 8). In aviation, future trends are often indicated long before they are capable of effective attainment.

6

Blackjack *v* B-1B

By comparison with combat aircraft of the Western world, information on Soviet aircraft, particularly in their years of development and early service, is extremely difficult to obtain. There are obvious reasons for this. Nevertheless, for many years now the Soviets have been producing some very interesting and clearly very capable aircraft—none more so than those which have emanated from the great design bureau of Andrei Tupolev. From the Tu-2 twin-engined bomber of World War II, through a series of brilliant designs, Tupolev virtually cornered the Soviet market in longer-range offensive aircraft with, successively, the Tu-14 Bosun and Tu-16 Badger (in all its many variants); the Tu-22 Blinder and, later, Tu-26 Backfire; and the now venerable, but still very much operational Tu-95 Bear—again, in several versions. In between times, he found it possible to challenge the Anglo-French Concorde in the supersonic transport business; but his Tu-144 (rather cruelly labelled 'Concordski') was less than successful and, after a series of mishaps, delays and disappointments, was finally withdrawn from service in early 1983—officially castigated by the Soviet First Deputy Minister of Civil Aviation of the day as 'too heavy and too inefficient'. Even Tupolev can't win them all!

What he has won is, nevertheless, impressive. And to show that everyone can learn by his mistakes, the latest product of the Tupolev stable owes not a little to the better features of the hapless Tu-144. As we have seen, the previous Tupolev bomber—the variable-geometry Tu-26 Backfire—was a subject of much discussion over its range capability. Was it or was it not a true strategic bomber?—an opinion which we have, anyway, learnt as being very much in the eye of the beholder.

BLACKJACK

No such question need be asked of Blackjack, as the latest Tupolev Tu-160 creation is codenamed. Reported as being under development in 1979, it was first sighted two years later, parked at the Ramenskoye test centre near Moscow—perhaps appropriately (or was it deliberately to confuse?) beside a pair of Tu-144s. Western analysts concluded that it had four engines and was similar in its configuration to (but rather larger than) the American B-1A. Certainly it looked capable of carrying a significant load of ordnance—presumably either free-fall or stand-off—as well as an impressive amount of ECM equipment and other defensive suppression aids. Nine years were to pass before, on 2 August 1988, Blackjack was ceremonially unveiled before Western eyes, when US Secretary of Defense Frank Carlucci and his visiting team were shown the aircraft (and allowed to climb on to its flight deck) at Kubinka air base, west of Moscow. More is now known of Blackjack, though its performance details are still closely guarded. Whether or not (as some experts had suggested) an excessively long period under wraps was an indication that its designers hit serious and continuing problems in its development, the fact is that Blackjack is now operational with the Soviet Air Force (SAF)—and in sufficiently impressive state as to be offered for inspection by a group of US visitors. What is not yet clear is whether Blackjack demonstrates as skilful and determined a harnessing of advanced technology as does the B-1B already in USAF front-line service. From reports of the Carlucci visit it would seem that cockpit environment, flight instruments and navigation aids are functional, but not startlingly new. There is, for example, no HUD and no artificial presentation of the external, though the aircraft does have the capability for terrain following. It is assessed as being unlikely that advanced fly-by-wire controls are incorporated—as they are on a growing number of modern Western aircraft, both military and civil.

Variable Geometry

Apart from its size, the most obvious feature of Blackjack is its use of variable geometry, a design feature with which the Soviets were already familiar through such proven combat aircraft as the MiG-23/27 Flogger, the Su-17 Fitter series and the Tu-26 Backfire. Variable geometry offers the pilot, in effect, a series of different aircraft to handle without ever changing his seat. For take-off and landing, at comparatively low speeds and minimum distances, there is an almost unswept (20° in the case of Blackjack), high aspect ratio machine: for the high-speed low-level dash towards and egress from the target area, there is maximum (65°) wing-sweep and a low aspect ratio—often a virtual delta platform. In between the two extremes is an almost infinite variety of in-flight wing-sweep settings—though, in practice, probably limited to mid-sweep for sustained high-speed cruise and enhanced (hopefully carefree) manoeuvrability. Again, the wings would be swept fully forward for extended loiter or long-range cruise when speed was not absolutely of the essence.

But if variable geometry offers several advantages to the pilot, it poses quite a few additional problems for the designer. Not only is there the question of strength with movement at the critical point of wing pivot. The carriage of underwing stores is complicated by the need to have them faired and always aerodynamically aligned with the airflow. The positioning of the engines is quite a problem too, particularly with larger aircraft. For example, rear-mounted engines may be fine on a variable-geometry fighter; but with an aircraft as large as Blackjack, such mounting would necessitate very long engine inlets, with consequent problems for the effective control of changing pressures from intake to exhaust. On the other hand, engines mounted beneath the inner (non-moving) part of the wing call for higher than normal tail sections, if horizontal stabilisers are not to be subject both to excessive thermal and sonic fatigue. Compromise is often the order of the day; and so it is with Blackjack—see the artist's impression at Plate 6.1, until recently the only reasonably authoritative depiction of the aircraft available to open sources in the West. But there can be no compromise on engine power to move such a large aircraft at supersonic low-level speeds and probably well in excess of Mach 2 at altitude. It seems likely that Blackjack carries variants of the Koliesov single-shaft turbofans

PLATE 6.1   For long, this artist's impression of Blackjack was all that the world at large had seen of the aircraft. Following the visit by US Secretary of Defense Carlucci to the Soviet Union (in August 1988) photographs were at last released. Incidentally, the air-to-surface missile depicted here on release from Blackjack is a '1600nm slus' AS-15 Kent. (*US Department of Defense*)

used in the developed Tu-144D. If so, total maximum dry thrust could be as great as 120,000 lb (static), with up to 200,000 lb available with after-burning. Variable ramps are fitted on each side of the dividers between the engine intakes.

Whilst clear evidence may as yet be lacking about Blackjack's engines, it is certain that the beast they power is big and heavy—possibly as much as 13% bigger than the B-1B and half as heavy again.[1] Part of the reason for that lies in geography and in the ranges which Soviet bombers might have to cover from secure bases within the Soviet Union to high-value targets on the US mainland. Another reason is that the Soviets probably still have some way to go before they can match the West in the micro-miniaturisation of components and systems—particularly of those sophisticated systems for advanced navigation, target acquisition, stores management, ECM and defence suppression which the strategic bomber of the 1990s must have if it is to be truly credible in its role.

Of course, the size of Blackjack allows plenty of space for carriage of the large quantities of fuel needed for an unrefuelled combat radius[2] of something approaching 4,000 nm—particularly when relatively long periods must, of necessity, be spent at low level. In the latter context, the shape of the big bomber's wing is of interest. Like Backfire before it, the wing pivots (*ie* the points on which the variable-geometry wing can swing forward and back) are rather further outboard on Blackjack than they are, for example, on the B-1B. This will offer both advantage and disadvantage in aircraft handling. On the plus side, it imposes significantly less structural stress on the pivots themselves, the comparatively shorter swinging portion of each wing acting to reduce bending movements in the area of the pivot. Again, the trim changes which accompany any movement, forward or rear, of a variable-geometry wing are obviously less marked the smaller the area of wing which actually moves. When a variable-sweep wing moves rearwards, so does the aerodynamic centre of the aircraft—although the centre of gravity (CG) may be virtually unaffected. One result of this is greatly to increase the task of the tailplane in aerodynamic balancing.[3] The nearer inboard the pivot point, the greater are the forces required to be balanced out. Trim drag is also greater—a significant factor in a large strategic aircraft. Both Blackjack and B-1B therefore feature outboard pivots housed in large wing 'gloves'; and on Blackjack a 3ft × 3ft vertical fence is raised on the middle part of each wing as it sweeps forward, possibly to improve aircraft handling (though a rather unusual means of doing so in the context of wing sweep).

The comparative practical disadvantages of locating wing pivots outboard of the fuselage include increased drag and less effective aspect ratio in the unswept position—both imposing limitations on cruise efficiency and manoeuvrability. The further outboard the pivot, the less the portion of moving wing—and, in consequence, the less the benefits obtained. In an effort to extract the maximum advantage of sweep from a wing which pivots about points some distance from the fuselage, the fixed (inboard) portion has to be extended further forward on the aircraft's fuselage; and this, in turn, will increase drag and reduce the quality of the low-level ride—a fact which imposes additional stresses on both aircrew and airframe.

All that said, the indications are that Blackjack presents a very carefully considered design, in which the inevitable need for compromise has probably been turned to good effect. From what little has been seen of it, it can be said to look good; and to the pilot, at least, that often indicates that it is good. Early impressions (and they can only be impressions) are that Blackjack does not incorporate the more advanced features of stealth technology. Although the basic similarity of design can scarcely be coincidental (Plate 6.2), there is markedly less wing/fuselage blending on Blackjack than on the B-1B. The large tailplane and very prominent dorsal fin look decidedly angular and, of course, the aircraft is very large indeed. On the other

PLATE 6.2   The Soviet Blackjack, on show during the visit of United States Secretary of Defense Carlucci to Kubinka Air Base west of Moscow in August 1988.

hand, the overall shape of Blackjack is clean and comparatively slender. A brief, but expert first look at the aircraft (by a senior USAF officer accompanying Mr Carlucci on his Soviet visit)[4] suggested that it had the contours and manufacturing smoothness of the XB-70—and that is indeed high praise. Clearly, there must be considerable reduction in overall RCS from the positioning of Blackjack's engines and the inlet-shielding afforded by the fixed inboard wing section. As for the inlets themselves, it seems likely that they also benefit from variable geometry, to permit flight over a wide range of heights and speeds.

Likely Ordnance

Blackjack's primary weapon will probably be the AS-15 long-range ALCM, about which little is as yet known. It is thought to have a range in excess of 1,600 nm and is almost certainly capable of launch from low level, as well as from height. It is one of a family of such weapons, closely related to the submarine-launched SS-NX-21 and the ground-launched SSC-X-4; and its configuration is similar to that of the rather smaller American GLCM of General Dynamics. However it is itself considerably smaller than the previous generation of Soviet air-to-surface weapons, such as the AS-4 Kitchen and AS-6 Kingfish, despite the fact that its range is increased by a factor of 10 or more on those earlier missiles. The guidance of the AS-15 is probably provided by a form of terrain comparison system, so that its accuracy could be in the order of 50 m CEP at maximum launch range. Its warhead is nuclear.

It has been suggested that Blackjack might carry up to 6 such weapons (or, as an alternative, 12 short-range attack missiles) on each of two internally-mounted rotary launchers. The total weight of ordnance, in a mix of missiles and free-fall bombs, is probably a maximum of some 18 tonnes. External weapons carriage is unlikely—at least in the near term. However, by the time that Blackjack is in full operational service with the SAF, it is likely also to carry the supersonic AS-X-19, now under development. This is a much larger missile, but with about the same range as AS-15. Such a weapon might be semi-recessed beneath the fuselage, for reasons of aerodynamics as well as of reduced RCS.

All in all, the Tu-160 Blackjack enters service with the SAF as a capable strategic penetrator of some versatility, but not sufficiently state of the art to throw Western air defence experts into panic. Whether it is later developed in ways which might cause greater problems for those experts, only time will tell. The aircraft certainly has size enough to incorporate an impressive array of offensive and defensive avionics—not to mention advanced weapons. However its basic design could probably not be sufficiently altered to allow it to operate in the truly low observable category.

THE ROCKWELL INTERNATIONAL B-1B

One aircraft that is clearly much better able to do so is the USAF's new B-1B bomber, designed by Rockwell International. Before ever it entered service, the B-1B had had a somewhat chequered history, extending over some 25 years in all. For it was as early as 1962 that the USAF first began to look at the sort of aircraft that would eventually be required to replace the B-52 as SAC's long-range manned bomber. The basic operational concept for this aircraft has remained virtually unchanged over the years, though the detailed specification has continually evolved. Even the descriptive acronym has varied—from the Subsonic Low Altitude Bomber (SLAB) of the early 1960s to the Advanced Manned Strategic Aircraft (AMSA) of the 1970s and the Long-Range Combat Aircraft (LRCA) of the present decade.

Canards

The first design to take the air was North American Aviation's massive XB-70A Valkyrie (Plate 6.3), of which only two prototypes were produced. Designed as a Mach 3 high altitude strategic bomber and first flown in September 1964, the Valkyrie was of large delta planform with 12 elevons on the wing trailing edge and hydrau-

PLATE 6.3   A rare shot of the Valkyrie—the experimental North American B-70 supersonic bomber which was a lineal ancestor of the B-1B. Clearly visible are the six under wing-mounted General Electric YJ93 engines. At the time, Valkyrie's 275-ton maximum all-up weight made it the heaviest aircraft ever built. (*United States Air Force*)

lically-operated drooping wing tips. It was also unusual for its day in sporting canard foreplanes, set high behind the crew compartment. An attraction of such foreplanes is that they do not suffer the lessening in effectiveness which is a feature of stabilising surfaces mounted to the rear of the mainplane, *ie* within the area of wing downwash. Indeed, because they lie in the upwash of the mainplane, their effectiveness is enhanced—to such a degree that care has to be exercised in controlling the movement of the aircraft's CG to maintain longitudinal stability. It is also possible for foreplanes adversely to affect the lift provided by the mainplanes—hence the normally high mounting of such devices. On modern high-performance combat aircraft, from the Swedish Viggen fighter through the Dassault Mirage V Milan variant and later Mirage 4000, Israeli Aircraft Industries' own Mirage development (the Kfir C-2) to present-day research aircraft such as British Aerospace's Experimental Aircraft Project (Plate 6.4) and the Dassault-Breguet Rafale prototype, canards have

PLATE 6.4   Canards (or foreplanes) to perform a different function on the British Aerospace Experimental Aircraft Project (EAP), seen here over the English Lake District on a test sortie from BAe's Warton Airfield. (*British Aerospace plc, Military Aircraft Division*)

become very much *de rigueur*. In these smaller aircraft they are closely coupled to the mainplane and enhance manoeuvrability, particularly in situations of high-lift or high Angle of Attack (AOA). Indeed, claims are made that lift enhancement can be as much as 50% in certain extreme conditions of flight. By comparison, the long-coupled canard configuration of the XB-70A has fallen out of favour. It should not be confused with the smaller vanes that appear on the nose of Rockwell's B-1B and which are fitted more as active control devices to improve ride at low level and high speed.

XB-70A to B-1B

The huge Valkyrie was powered by six General Electric YJ93 turbojets, giving a reheated thrust of well over 180,000 lb and offering a genuine Mach 3 capability at altitude. However, serious doubts were expressed about the survivability of such a large aircraft as a high-level penetrator; and, although test-flying continued until 1969 on the one surviving prototype (the other having been destroyed in a mid-air collision with a chase aircraft), the programme had, to all intents and purposes, been dead since soon after the initial roll-out.

If flight at 75,000 ft and at speeds in excess of 2,000 mph could not guarantee survival against increasingly effective Soviet surface-to-air missiles—what flight regime should be considered for the future manned bomber? The only alternative was to try to fly under the defences, with sufficient speed to out-run any fighter aircraft able to find its way through the electronic 'smokescreen' in which a large aircraft could effectively hide. Thus was born AMSA—and the original North American Rockwell B-1A (Plate 6.5), powered by four General Electric YF101-GE-100 twin-spool turbofan engines (offering some 120,000 lb of thrust with after-burning),

PLATE 6.5   North American Rockwell B-1A lifts off—one of four to be flown. Its own life was to be a short one, denied front-line service with the USAF. But it contributed greatly to the research, design and development of the B-1B. (*Rockwell International*)

and with avionics suites designed by Boeing (offensive) and AIL (defensive). Four B-1As were to be built, the first flying on 23 December 1974. The aircraft was large—though not as large as the Valkyrie. It was also of variable-geometry design, with a fully extended wingspan of 136.7 ft, a length of 152.2 ft and a height of 33.58 ft. The first three prototypes incorporated a crew escape capsule (which had been a not-altogether-successful feature of the smaller F-111 series of tactical fighter-bombers). The fourth B-1A reverted to the more traditional method of escape from high-speed aircraft—the ejection seat. After 8½ years of successful test flying, the Carter Administration decided that the project would not go ahead. Unit cost of the big bomber was assessed as being $100m and a growing body of influential opinion had anyway concluded that the task of strategic nuclear deterrence with manned bombers could more effectively (and certainly more cheaply) be carried out with the fitting of ALCMs to the old B-52. However, some limited test flying of the B-1A was allowed to continue under the Bomber Penetration Evaluation Study; and by the time that study had been completed (in April 1981), a total of nearly 2,000 flying hours had been accumulated on the four aircraft. It was with obvious relief to all engaged on the project when the US Government confirmed, in October 1981, its decision to develop an updated version of the aircraft—to be known as the B-1B.

The B-1B (Plate 6.6) is a multi-role heavy bomber with inter-continental range. It has a crew of four—pilot, co-pilot, Offensive Systems Operator (OSO) and Defensive Systems Operator (DSO). In essence, it retains many of the features of the earlier B-1A but has been extensively modified, particularly in its offensive and defensive avionics and by the incorporation of various features to reduce observability. About two-thirds the size of the B-52, it carries a significantly greater payload—of nuclear and conventional free-fall bombs and nuclear air-to-ground missiles. Its advanced systems for *inter alia* electronic jamming, infra-red counter-measures, radar location and warning will probably enable it to operate in the most sophisticated air defence environment predicted for the mid-1990s—after which time it could relinquish the role of penetrator to the ATBs and may revert to that of stand-off missile carrier or conventional bomber operating in less threatening environments.

Performance

The well-tried combination of variable-sweep wings and proven engines (now the Dash 102 variant of the B-1A's F101-GE power-plants) confer on the B-1B all the capability required for long-range and high-speed low-level penetration (Plate 6.7). Exact details are still classified; but an 'intercontinental unrefuelled' range is taken to mean no less than a 3,000nm radius of action which can, of course, be greatly extended by the bomber's compatibility with both KC-135 (Plate 6.8) and KC-10 AAR aircraft. Official statements of 'high subsonic' speed at low-level and 'low supersonic' at altitude may be conservatively assessed as about 550kts and Mach 1.2 respectively. The B-1B can operate from considerably shorter runways than can the B-52—again, functions of variable sweep and a high power-to-weight ratio. Maximum all-up weight is given as 477,000lb; and open sources indicate payloads of 24 AGM-69 SRAMs or gravity bombs carried internally; 20-AGM-86B ALCMs (8 internally); or 42,000lb of conventional bombs (500lb Mark 82 or 2,000lb Mark 84s) or combinations of all three. For extended range—say, on deployment to an overseas theatre—each of the aircraft's weapon bays can be configured to carry an extre 20,000lb of fuel. Additional roles could include long-range interdiction, sea surveillance, anti-surface ship warfare and aerial mine-laying.

PLATE 6.6   A USAF B-1B by Rockwell International in flight over the Western United States. (*Rockwell International*)

Systems-General

The aircraft has been described as a 'large computer system surrounded by fuel and engines' (Figure 6.1). In fact, four primary computers serve to control most of the major systems—navigation, target acquisition and weapon-aiming, stores management, engine control, fuel management, CG calculation, and so on. A Singer-Kearfott SKN-2440 INS is at the heart of the B-1B. Undoubtedly, it offers great accuracy over long range—200-ft drift after 3 hours' flight time having been quoted. An inertial navigation unit (INU) senses aircraft velocity, heading and altitude, whilst navigational data is drawn from vertical and horizontal accelerometers and two-axis gyroscopes. The extremely accurate accelerometers, which are maintained by the gyroscopes in a known frame of reference, provide the primary source of information to the system. Linear accelerations (both lateral and vertical) together

PLATE 6.7   The B-1B in one of its 'natural' environments. Of course, a terrain-following radar, advanced control systems, stability enhancement and rugged construction combine to ensure that altra low-level flying by the B-1B would not be restricted to areas of purely flat terrain. (*Rockwell International*)

PLATE 6.8   The already impressive radius of action of the B-1B can be greatly extended by the use of air-to-air refuelling. Here, a KC-135 tanker is almost dwarfed by its B-1A receiver in early trials of the system. (*United States Air Force*)

with angular change rates continuously monitor movement about all three axes and feed information direct to the B-1B's stability and control augmentation system. Dependable as the system has proved to be, there is no doubt that overall mission reliability would be greatly enhanced by the addition of a second INS. Indeed, this was to be the original specification for the B-1B, but tight financial control in the development phase led to its cancellation, along with a number of other non-critical items. As with most modern combat aircraft, the inevitable process of updating (particularly of avionics equipments) will apply in full measure to the B-1B during its in-service life; and wiring for that second Singer Kearfott INS has already been incorporated in production aircraft. A FLIR system is thought to be also on the USAF's

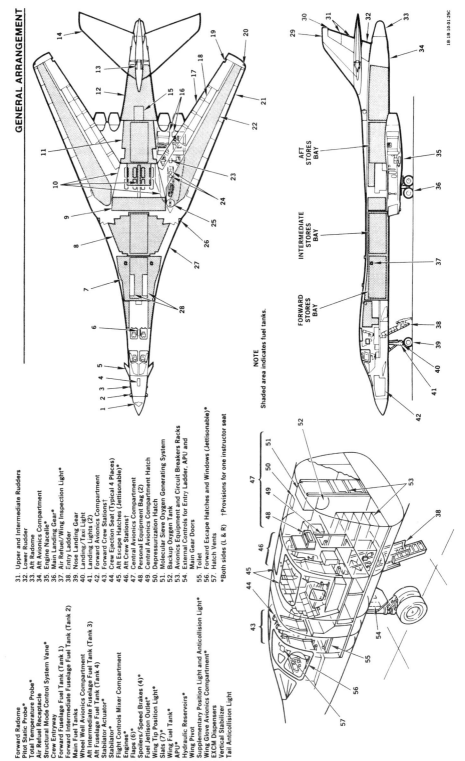

GENERAL ARRANGEMENT

1. Forward Radome
2. Pitot Static Probe*
3. Total Temperature Probe*
4. Air Refuel Receptacle
5. Structural Mode Control System Vane*
6. Crew Entryway
7. Forward Fuselage Fuel Tank (Tank 1)
8. Forward Intermediate Fuselage Fuel Tank (Tank 2)
9. Main Fuel Tanks
10. Wheel Well Avionics Compartment
11. Aft Intermediate Fuselage Fuel Tank (Tank 3)
12. Aft Fuselage Fuel Tank (Tank 4)
13. Stabilator Actuator*
14. Stabilator*
15. Flight Controls Mixer Compartment
16. Engines*
17. Flaps (6)*
18. Spoilers/Speed Brakes (4)*
19. Fuel Jettison Outlet*
20. Wing Tip Position Light*
21. Slats (7)*
22. Wing Fuel Tank*
23. APU* Fuel Tank*
24. Hydraulic Reservoirs*
25. Wing Pivot
26. Supplementary Position Light and Anticollision Light*
27. Wing Glove Avionics Compartment*
28. EXCM Dispensers
29. Vertical Stabilizer
30. Tail Anticollision Light

31. Upper and Intermediate Rudders
32. Lower Rudder
33. Aft Radome
34. Aft Avionics Compartment
35. Engine Nacelle*
36. Main Landing Gear*
37. Air Refuel/Wing Inspection Light*
38. Entry Ladder
39. Nose Landing Gear
40. Landing/Taxi Light
41. Landing Lights (2)
42. Forward Avionics Compartment
43. Forward Crew Stations†
44. Crew Ejection Seat (Typical 4 Places)*
45. Aft Escape Hatches (Jettisonable)*
46. Aft Crew Stations†
47. Central Avionics Compartment
48. Personal Equipment Bag (2)
49. Central Avionics Compartment Hatch
50. Depressurization Hatch
51. Molecular Sieve Oxygen Generating System
52. Backup Oxygen Tank
53. Avionics Equipment and Circuit Breakers Racks
54. External Controls for Entry Ladder, APU and Main Gear Doors
55. Toilet
56. Forward Escape Hatches and Windows (Jettisonable)*
57. Hatch Vents

*Both sides (L & R)   †Provisions for one instructor seat

NOTE
Shaded area indicates fuel tanks.

FORWARD STORES BAY   INTERMEDIATE STORES BAY   AFT STORES BAY

1B.1B.10-01.25C

FIG. 6.1 Rockwell International B-1B. General arrangement diagram. (*United States Air Force*)

shopping list for the B-1B; and, in due course it seems likely that the fitment of the Navstar GPS will also be considered.

Because of its low-level all-weather capability, the B-1B is equipped with advanced terrain-following radar (TFR) equipment. This is based on inputs from the Westinghouse AN/APQ-164 multi-mode radar, itself a primary component of the aircraft's offensive avionics package. Also featured are phased-array antennae; and the system is claimed to have a range capability of around 10 nm and sufficient definition to detect pylons and radio masts. 200-ft hands-off flight in all weather would be the sort of limits to which the system is designed to work; and there is the capability found in most modern TFR systems to select soft, medium or hard ride. To ensure that TFR emissions are minimised (and thus offer reduced warning of approach to enemy defensive systems), the radar beam is exceptionally narrow and emissions are intermittent. Radar scan patterns are at a minimum over relatively flat terrain, when TFR flying is clearly less hazardous. Information is passed from the TFR to computers and, thence, direct to the aircraft's flight control system for fully automatic response. The B-1B crew can also utilise the TFR system to fly a terrain avoidance regime, in which the pilot manually flies the aircraft to avoid obstacles presented on the multi-purpose cathode-ray tube (CRT) installed on his flight instrument panel.

The aircraft's stability control augmentation system plays a large part in reducing the effects of turbulence on low-level flight. To it has been added a stability enhancement function—a modified fly-by-wire system which allows the pilot to fly closer to the limits of aircraft stability and thus extract maximum performance in complete safety. This is particularly necessary at the higher weights at which the B-1B is now flying. In early B-1A development flying, the aircraft is said to have exhibited marked pitch-up tendencies as AOA reached its limit. A stall inhibitor system was incorporated, which prevented the pilot taking his aircraft near the critical limit of AOA. However at the higher all-up weights of the B-1B, greater latitude was required, and the AOA limit was found to be too restrictive for stable flight within the aircraft's expanded flight envelope. In effect, the stability enhancement function affords the pilot a degree of artificial stability to permit flight in what would, in terms of pure aerodynamics, be an unstable region of the B-1B's flight envelope. The concept of controlled instability—now a common feature of the agile fighter—has thus been adapted, in part, to the big bomber.

All this complex equipment is designed to allow the B-1B to fly safely and flexibly over as large a flight envelope as possible—assisting performance, at high and low level, over a range of varying speeds and weights. Necessary as that is, it does not equip the aircraft to carry out its assigned roles as a long-range bomber. For that, it needs another complete range of equipments—the performance specifications of which are, understandably, closely guarded. However, sufficient information has been released to allow at least an appreciation of the B-1B's capabilities, if not a detailed assessment of its effectiveness.

The aircraft's operational avionics systems can be divided into two: an Offensive (OAS) and a Defensive (DAS) Avionics Suite (Figure 6.2). In fact, as an example of the complex vocabulary (let alone capability) of modern military aviation, the

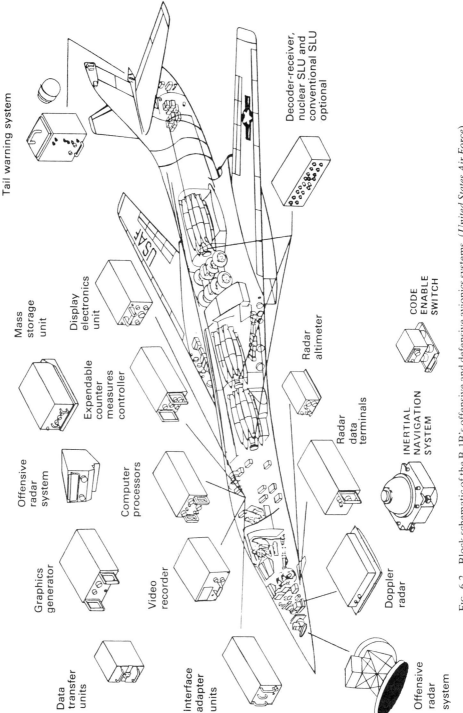

FIG. 6.2   Block schematic of the B-1B's offensive and defensive avionics systems. (*United States Air Force*)

correct designation for the DAS suite is 'Radio Frequency Surveillance Systems/
Electronics Countermeasures System—inevitably, RFS/ECMS. We will stick with
DAS—of which, a little more later.

Offensive Avionics

Meanwhile, for the OAS, Boeing is prime contractor; and a number of its components are the same as (or developments of) those already incorporated in the
larger updates of the B-52. In total, however, the OAS is certain to have even greater
capability than that available to the older aircraft. The SKN-2440 INS (already
mentioned) forms an important part of the overall system, as does the Teledyne
Ryan APN-230 Doppler velocity sensor. Avionics control units by IBM, multi-
function display units and video recorders by Sperry, and a Sanders electronic cathode ray tube for the display and analysis of threat information—all these are necessary features of the OAS. Clearly, a mass storage device is incorporated to help
control and disseminate the huge amount of information supplied by the sensors
and required for the operation of a variety of essential functions, from navigation
and weapons delivery to integrated test.

Although all these equipments are required for the B-1B to carry out its allotted
tasks, probably the most important single component of the OAS is the Westinghouse AN/APQ-164 multi-mode offensive radar system. This is a highly complex
and extremely capable state-of-the-art radar which combines functions which, only
a few years ago, would have required the fitment of several discrete units. Its primary
mode is high-resolution mapping, using advanced synthetic aperture techniques
including 'burst transmission' and automatic sequencing. These techniques produce
ground images, by day or night, irrespective of weather conditions. The basic principle of synthetic aperture radar (SAR) is that, as the platform (installed on the
aircraft) moves in relation to a fixed point on the ground (the target), continuing
differing radar echoes are received. If these echoes can be stored and compared, an
image of the target can be built up, which becomes more detailed and more coherent
the longer it is illuminated by the airborne radar. Simply, the effect is that of an
extremely long radar (ie as long as the flight path of the aircraft relative to the
target), with each of the successive elements of that radar providing an image of the
target. The principle could, of course, only be usefully exploited in real time when
computers were able to store and compare the mass of information provided and
present it in an assimilable form. The use of digital processing has even allowed
SAR to detect moving targets—a capability that was just not attainable with earlier
analogue processing techniques (Figure 6.3). Developments and enhancements of
SAR now allow the spotlighting of targets of specific interest, by steering the SAR
beam so that it maintains its illumination of the target despite aircraft movement;
and 'squinting' at targets which lie either obliquely ahead of or behind the aircraft.
The technique is thus particularly appropriate in the fields of reconnaissance or
surveillance. Fully developed, it is said to be capable of producing images approxi-
mating to those obtained by low-grade photography.

The radar-mapping mode of the AN/APQ-164 is supplemented by a conventional
real-beam ground-mapping function; and the equipment has the capability to detect
returns from weather or from ground beacons and to facilitate airborne rendezvous,

Principle of Synthetic Aperture Processing

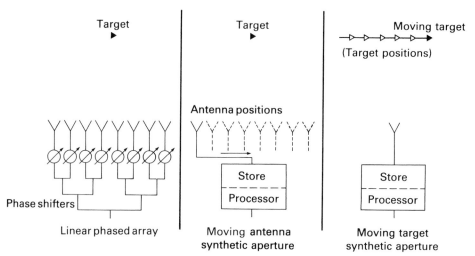

FIG. 6.3   The principle of synthetic aperture processing.

eg with AAR aircraft. For aircraft penetration, its functions include terrain-following and terrain avoidance (already described); and there are three distinct weapons delivery functions. These incorporate velocity update for the IN system, moving-target detection and tracking and extremely precise measurement of height above ground—this last being one of the key elements for the accurate delivery of weapons on target.

The offensive avionics suite of the B-1B is controlled by no fewer than six ABM AP-101F central computers, two micro-computers and a number of additional processors. The software for system management employs the very latest concepts of real-time processing control; and the programming language is also a much enhanced version of any previously used in an airborne application. It is clear that features such as these will offer later potential for growth and the ability to absorb the requirements of additional sensors and equipments. A feature of the avionics systems of the B-1B—both offensive and defensive—is their continuous monitoring and the capability to detect and react to faults. If any equipment were to fail, either through normal usage or as a result of battle damage, back-up sensors would automatically be brought on line and overall system performance maintained. There is thus a very high degree of redundancy built into the B-1B's role-related system—as, indeed, there is in its flight systems. Of course, multiple failures will eventually lead to system degradation; but even in that unlikely event, the software remains capable of selecting (and automatically bringing into play) the best available combination of equipments.

Again in an attempt to enhance flexibility, the B-1B carries two auxiliary power units (APUs) which supply high-pressure bleed air for environmental control on the ground. For the cooling of avionics equipments during flight, engine-bleed air is preferred. No ground-based ancillary equipment—be it hydraulic, pneumatic or electric—is needed to fire up the B-1B—a particularly important feature for operations away from main base. The APUs have the capacity to start the aircraft's engines—either singly or simultaneously, when a quick-reaction start or 'scramble' is called for. This last feature has long been admired by the crews of SAC who saw it as a particularly attractive characteristic of the old RAF Vulcan during the years in which that aircraft operated alongside the USAF's bomber force. As fitted to the B-1B, the APU s can also be used for rapid fuelling (or de-fuelling); and to maintain the environment and systems readiness of aircraft standing long periods of cockpit readiness.

Defensive Avionics

If the exact performance of the B-1B's OAS remains heavily classified, that of its defensive suite is purely conjectural. For obvious reasons, the USAF has been extremely coy about releasing any but the most meagre information about the systems which will protect the new bomber on its war missions. And it can be taken as no more than prudent judgement that what little has been published provides only an educated guess at the precise capabilities of those systems. What is known is that the AN/ALQ-161 ECM system, developed by the AIL Division of the Eaton Corporation, is the most capable and complex such system currently in service. It is also, without doubt, the most expensive: but it is, of course, designed to safeguard a very expensive aircraft and its highly trained crew to carry out potentially very hazardous operations. That said, it is a sobering thought that the B-1B's defensive suite is reliably reported to cover some 10% of the cost of the complete aircraft.

The defensive suite is designed to cover the complete spectrum of frequencies used in Soviet early-warning, ground-controlled interception (GCI), SAM and airborne intercept radars. Three steerable phased-array antennae provide all-round cover for the B-1B against HF signals, whilst the lower frequencies are covered by horn antennae. In the process of transition from B-1A to -B, developments were aimed at extending frequency coverage—both higher and lower, introducing a digital memory function, and improving the tail-warning system as an integral feature of the AN/ALQ-161. Again, the system is computer-controlled, the software having the capability of identifying and analysing every threat, and allocating jamming effort in a strictly prioritised manner. If necessary, the DSO has the ability to override the automatics and carry out manual jamming. In practice, his role is largely that of monitoring and supervising the kit. Jamming is effected by Northrop transmitters, working in conjunction with Raytheon antennae; and so capable is the system that threat signals can be detected, identified, analysed and jammed almost instantaneously. System integration has been so perfected that the defensive suite continuously monitors the output of its jammers at the same time as it is adjusting the reception of its antennae—thus enabling it to detect new threats whilst continuing to monitor and jam existing signals. Again, failures of individual components of the system are automatically compensated, and a high degree of redundancy is incorporated. Discharge of additional defensive aids (such as chaff and infra-red flares) can be effected automatically by the AN/ALQ-161 or, again, controlled manually by the DSO. Naturally, the impressive capability of the B-1B's defences is not achieved without cost. Monetary cost has already been indicated; but it is also worth noting that the weight of the system is in excess of 2½ tonnes, and that is thought to require up to 120 kilowatts of electrical power for full operation.

Electrical Systems

Mention of such impressive electrical power is a reminder of the complexity of the electrical system of an aircraft such as the B-1B. Developed for its cousin, the B-1A, it is undoubtedly one of the most advanced systems ever devised for the control of electrical power distribution in the air. Designed by a Division of the Harris Corporation, the EMUX (electrical multiplex) system has electrical control of all the B-1B's major sub-systems. In so doing, it obviates the need for an estimated 30,000 wire joins, which would have been required by earlier techniques to effect several thousand electrical connections throughout the aircraft. With EMUX, it is claimed that two 2-wire cables can be used for both control and signal transfer. The advantages for installation and maintainance are obvious, as is the weight-saving aspect of the now surplus electrical looms (estimated at some 80 miles in length). EMUX also confers considerable flexibility in the sense that later system modification, the addition or expansion of new systems and components can all be effected with minimum disruption of installed wiring. By its ability to collect and transmit electrical signals from any point on the aircraft to any other, EMUX can control a great variety of tasks—from the distribution of electrical power to and from the most advanced avionics systems to the more humble function of initiating the operation of the aircraft's landing gear. In itself, that constitutes an important, albeit less exotic example of how modern technology has been harnessed to the service of combat aircraft design.

Crew Environment

One impressive feature of the B-1B is said to be the attention that has been paid to the cockpit environment and to the ergonomics of life for the bomber's crew. Combat aircraft are not built for comfort, but some that have flown over the years, in air forces the world over, have made a fetish of discomfort. The Americans have usually done better than other nations in this regard, though it is probably unfair to suggest—as some have done—that while American designers have always been conscious of the need for aircrew, their British counterparts have built fine combat aircraft—and only then begun to wonder where their crews might be placed. Things are getting better but, by all accounts, the B-1B is an improvement on many of its predecessors.

Significant advances have been made in cockpit design and in the layout of controls, displays and instruments so as to afford aircrews the chance of using them to best effect (Plate 6.9). Human factors are self-evidently important if aircrews are to operate to best effect in a highly demanding, stress-inducing environment; and the design of their 'office accommodation' should be as well adapted to their needs as is possible. Technology has been able to help greatly in this process. Not only have new materials significantly improved seating, flying clothing and cockpit environmental control; but modern flight-control systems, the micro-miniaturisation of

PLATE 6.9   The flight deck of a Rockwell B-1B. Confusing as it may look to the non-professional, this layout is in fact extremely 'tidy' and functional—clearly a great advantage to the operators of this very complex and capable aircraft. (*Rockwell International*)

equipments, the speed and capacity of computer-driven systems, step-changes in information display, the rationalisation of warning systems and advanced techniques of lighting—all have played their part in reducing aircrew workload and avoiding unnecessary stress. The capability of advanced radars (like those now flying in the B-1B, Tornado, F-16 and other modern combat aircraft) is such as to offer aircrews detailed, easily assimilated pictures in a way not previously possible. Navigational way-points and targets can be acquired with pin-point accuracy and with little possibility of error or mis-identification, as indicated at Plates 6.10 and 6.11 where the ground-mapping radar picture (above) would be superimposed on that of the projected map display (below) to offer the aircrew a sort of '3-D' effect.

In the B-1B each OSO and DSO has no fewer than three CRT displays—like miniature TV screens, (Figure 6.4) but displaying images of far better quality. They can carry superimposed information, both written and pictorial, which precludes the need for constant cross-reference. They are so placed as to reduce to a minimum tiring eye and body movements. Integrated keyboards allow operators to interrogate their computers, asking 'what if?' questions and working through complex problems to achieve the best results. Multi-function equipments of enormous power and capa-

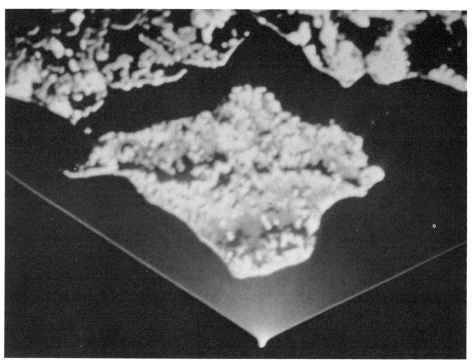

PLATES 6.10 and 6.11   Two views of the Isle of Wight, respectively from the ground-mapping radar (*above*) and the projected map display (*below*) of a Tornado GR1 of the Royal Air Force. (*Crown Copyright*)

bility can be brought into play by the touch of a few keys; and mega-memories can store millions of bits of information, which can be continually up-dated and almost instantaneously retrieved.

Test Systems

A very interesting state-of-the-art feature of the B-1B is its Central Integrated Test System (inevitably, CITS) which continuously monitors the in-flight performance of all the major aircraft systems, recording their status every half-hour of normal running, but diagnosing faults and automatically transferring functions as they occur. The CITS data from every B-1B sortie is, of course, preserved on magnetic tape for playback or print-out for the benefit of flight maintenance crews. As with similar advanced systems (such as the self-test facilities of many modern avionics equipments or the onboard check-out and monitoring system of Tornado) early problems were experienced with false or spurious alarms. Development, improved understanding and the beneficial effects of settling-in have all contributed to the ready acceptance of such systems as confidence-building equipments, which can greatly reduce the time previously spent on fault diagnosis and the unnecessary replacement of parts.

An extension of this philosophy is to be found in the USAF's Central Integrated Test Expert Parameter System (yes—CEPS). This is a more advanced, ground-based system for maintenance diagnosis which, for perhaps the first time in combat aviation, is bringing artificial intelligence to the aid of the technician. When fully developed it will provide, for each B-1B, a maintenance history and a complete record of modification state. It will thus operate as a data-bank, into which will be fed the processed and refined CITS data from each aircraft sortie. Detailed information on all ground servicing will also be recorded, so that it will become possible to make rapid evaluation and informed predictions. To date, such achievements have usually been hard-won—if, indeed, they were possible. CEPS should, once displayed, greatly ease the problems of the B-1B's maintenance engineers—men and women who, like aircrew themselves the world over, have often found themselves working in uncongenial environments, with inadequate information, against the tightest of time constraints.

From what is known of the CEPS project, it is being developed by a happy combination of theoretical designers from industry and hands-on maintenance men from the USAF. Here, as in so many other areas, it is vital that the one does not run out of step with the other. Too often in the past, designers and operators have been kept at a distance—usually by those who had little expertise in either role, but who feared that project control would be lost or that costs would escalate were the dead hand of bureaucracy not firmly imposed. They—and we—would do well to recall the experience of the great Professor R. V. Jones, whose brilliant research work for the British Air Ministry in World War II made him only slightly better known than did his constant brushes with authority: as so often, he did not endear himself to everyone because he was so often right. But what he did claim as one of the keys to success, in the many fascinating scientific researches he conducted, was the direct cross-fertilisation of ideas between scientist and operator. Sadly, that informed viewpoint is not always accorded the attention it deserves.

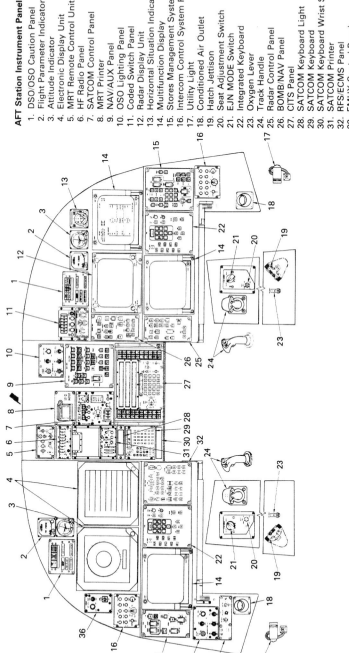

AFT Station Instrument Panels and Side Consoles

1. DSO/OSO Caution Panel
2. Flight Parameter Indicator
3. Attitude Indicator
4. Electronic Display Unit
5. MRT Remote Control Unit
6. HF Radio Panel
7. SATCOM Control Panel
8. MRT Printer
9. NAV/AUX Panel
10. OSO Lighting Panel
11. Coded Switch Panel
12. Radar Display Unit
13. Horizontal Situation Indicator
14. Multifunction Display
15. Stores Management System Panel
16. Intercom Control System Panel
17. Utility Light
18. Conditioned Air Outlet
19. Hatch Jettison
20. Seat Adjustment Switch
21. EJN MODE Switch
22. Integrated Keyboard
23. Oxygen Lever
24. Track Handle
25. Radar Control Panel
26. BOMB/NAV Panel
27. CITS Panel
28. SATCOM Keyboard Light
29. SATCOM Keyboard
30. SATCOM Keyboard Wrist Support
31. SATCOM Printer
32. RFS/ECMS Panel
33. EMUX Control Panel
34. DSO Lighting Panel
35. DSO Power Panel
36. Environmental Control Panel

FIG. 6.4   Diagram of the instrument panels and side consoles for the rear-crew members of the B-1B's airborne team.   (*United States Air Force*)

Conclusion

To conclude this inevitably incomplete survey of the Rockwell International B-1B—a brief word on its construction. So skilfully has work been carried out to reduce the observability of the beast that is reported to have only 10% of the RCS of its predecessor, the B1A—itself claimed as offering 10% the RCS of the B-52. The structure of the B-1B is mainly of various aluminium alloys and titanium, though some areas of fibre-composite material do exist. Wing/fuselage blending has been optimised, and the wing-sweep mechanism is pivoted outboard of the fuselage centre-point. Hydraulic motors actuate screw-jacks to effect wing sweep; and the outer wing can move from 15° to the now fairly standard 67° of sweep (Plates 6.12 and 6.13). Full-span leading-edge slats can be drooped for take-off and landing. Standard trailing-edge flaps are fitted to the outer wings, and conventional ailerons are replaced by an airbrake/spoiler combination—again on each outer wing. All control surfaces are operated by electro-hydraulic power, except for the outboard spoilers, which are fly-by-wire.

On either side of the nose of the aircraft are the small fibre-composite vanes, already mentioned (Plate 6.14). Controlled by appropriate accelerometers, these sense both vertical and lateral movement of the aircraft and electrically initiate damping in both pitch and yaw. They are thus of considerable value when the aircraft encounters air turbulence in low-level, high-speed flight—which is, of course, its natural environment. Similar considerations have dictated the positioning towards the aircraft's centre-line of the four General Electric F101-GE-102 turbofan engines, mounted in pairs under each fixed wing section.

In Memoriam

It makes a sad postcript to have to record that, for all his ingenuity and skill, the products of man are still susceptible to failure. On 28 September 1987 the USAF lost its first B-1B in a crash near La Junta, Colorado during a routine low-level training sortie. Three aircrew were killed—two of them riding as additional crew-members in the aircraft's non-ejectable 'jump seats', one because of a probable sequencing failure in his Weber ACES II ejection seat. The remaining three aircrew were able to eject safely. The accident investigators concluded that the multi-million dollar bomber had suffered no structural failure, no engine failure, no failure of its sophisticated flight control or avionics systems. It had simply run into a flock of birds, which had punctured the aircraft's skin and damaged the nacelles of one pair of engines. The effects were catastrophic—sudden loss of symmetric engine power followed by fire from fractured fuel or hydraulic lines. This was a 'million to one' accident that led to the incorporation of strengthening modifications on the rest of the fleet. For combat aircraft operating at high speed and low level, bird strikes are a fact of life; and such aircraft are already heavily strengthened in the areas most likely to be hit. That even these precautions failed to save the B-1B is proof—if proof were needed—that the search for the ultimate in combat aircraft design is indeed a never-ending process.

PLATES 6.12 and 6.13   A brace of B-1Bs, showing minimum (15°) and maximum (67.5°) sweep of its variable-geometry wings. (*United States Air Force/Rockwell International*)

PLATE 6.14   An impressive 'full frontal' of the B-1B with its small fibre-composite vanes on either side of the nose to enhance low-level 'ride'. (*Rockwell International*)

7

Enter the Missile

Another volume in this series will explore the actual and potential use of space in the conduct of air power operations. Here, it is necessary merely to sketch out the way in which missiles—both ballistic and cruise—have found their way into the armouries of several nations and have, specifically, taken their place alongside manned aircraft as components of strategic offensive air power. To examine why this should be so demands some elementary understanding of what these missiles are and how they can perform the tasks ascribed to them.

BALLISTIC MISSILE THEORY

First, let us look at the ballistic missile—'ballistic' because that is how it flies, affected for the greater part of its flight path only by the force of gravity, and thereby requiring great speed if it is to achieve any sort of range. Typically, a ballistic missile with a range of rather less than 1,000 nm would need to attain a burnout velocity of something approaching 2 nm a second: for the longer-range inter-continental ballistic missile (ICBM) that velocity will be over 4 nm/sec.

As indicated in Figure 7.1, if an object is projected at a given speed, parallel to the earth's surface, it will fall to ground when the centrifugal force of its forward motion fails to overcome the force of gravity which pulls it earthwards. In fact, there

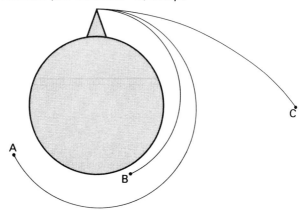

A: Centrifugal force = Gravitational 'pull'
B: Gravity overcomes centrifugal force (forward motion)
C: Gravitational 'pull' overcome – ie, 'escape'

FIG. 7.1   Missile theory: velocities and trajectory. (*J R Walker*)

132

is a theoretical point at which centrifugal force would exactly balance gravitational pull, allowing the object to continue to fly around the earth at a constant height. However, this is theoretical because it ignores the practical effects of aerodynamic drag which would cause the body gradually to slow down. Such drag is, of course, very much greater at the lower altitudes.

To take the process one step further: if the velocity of the object was further increased, there would come a point when gravitational pull was overcome so completely that the body would leave the earth's gravitational field. This is known as 'escape velocity'—some 6 nm per second which is, therefore, the practical maximum velocity of a ballistic missile. Anything greater than that and it would fail to return to earth to complete the task for which it was actually launched.

In order to achieve the high acceleration velocities needed to boost a ballistic missile into its required trajectory and to sustain it for the sort of range it is required to fly, an impressive quantity of fuel has to be available at launch—though much of it will be burnt in a very small period of time. Indeed of the total weight of the missile, only a very small percentage is taken up by the payload (or warhead). For a single-stage ICBM, some 93% of the total mass may be propellant—the remaining

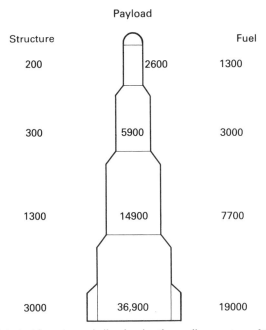

FIG. 7.2   A typical four-stage missile, showing the small percentage of the total system weight which can be allotted to payload. (*J R Walker*)

7% accommodating the missile structure, its engines and airframe, and the payload. Figure 7.2 shows a typical four-stage missile, in which the payload accounts for only 3% of total gross weight. From this it can be seen why missiles designed to lift large structures require such high initial thrusts—typically measured in millions of pounds.

Following the boost phase, a missile will follow an elliptical trajectory—the properties of the ellipse being outlined in Figure 7.3. For an ideal ballistic trajectory, the ellipse of the plane will include the missile launch-point, burn-out point, target and the centre of the earth. In practice, there is likely to be a slight variation between launch-point and burn-out point because it is during this (boosted) phase that any flight corrections must be made to maintain the missile on track to its target; and these may serve to deviate the missile slightly from its ideal ellipse. Missiles will also be affected by certain aerodynamic forces, particularly as they re-enter the earth's atmosphere; and the final part of the flight path to the target can also be affected by factors such as wind and warhead characteristics.

Figure 7.4 illustrates the flight path of a missile on an elliptical trajectory, given an earth which is both non-rotating and perfectly spherical. It can be seen that a number of different ellipses could be drawn to contain the missile launch-point,

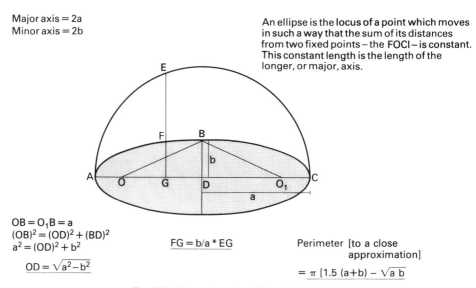

Major axis $= 2a$
Minor axis $= 2b$

An ellipse is the locus of a point which moves in such a way that the sum of its distances from two fixed points – the FOCI – is constant. This constant length is the length of the longer, or major, axis.

$OB = O_1B = a$
$(OB)^2 = (OD)^2 + (BD)^2$
$a^2 = (OD)^2 + b^2$

$OD = \sqrt{a^2 - b^2}$

$FG = b/a * EG$

Perimeter [to a close approximation]

$= \pi [1.5 (a+b) - \sqrt{a\,b}\,$

FIG. 7.3   Properties of an ellipse. (*J R Walker*)

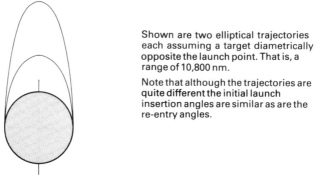

Shown are two elliptical trajectories each assuming a target diametrically opposite the launch point. That is, a range of 10,800 nm.

Note that although the trajectories are quite different the initial launch insertion angles are similar as are the re-entry angles.

FIG. 7.4   The flight-paths of missiles launched on separate trajectories but with similar initial launch and insertion angles. The earth here depicted is obligingly 'ideal'— both non-rotating and perfectly spherical. In practice, the missile designer has more difficulty. (*J R Walker*)

burn-out point and target; but only one of these would use minimum energy and would, thereby, be most efficient. Figure 7.5 shows the trade-off which can be made between burn-out angle and velocity over a selection of different missile ranges.

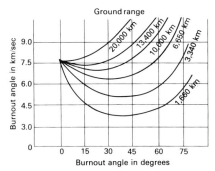

FIG. 7.5   The possibilities of trade-off between burn-out angle and speed over a selection of missile ranges. (*J R Walker*)

Source of Errors

The problem is that the earth insists on making things more complicated than that. It not only rotates, but it is not even spherical—its orange-shaped form being technically that of an oblate spheroid. If the missile were to ignore that fact and were rash enough to take it that the earth was 'near enough' spheroid, it would find (too late) that its target was not where it thought it was! Similarly with the earth's rotational effects: a missile fired on a trajectory which took no account of earth's rotation would find that the target had moved proportionately to the flight time and the angular movement of the earth at the latitude of the target. As the time of flight of an ICBM can be as much as 40 minutes, incorrect allowance for earth's rotation could result in a miss of impressive proportions. Both these factors are illustrated at Figure 7.6.

As its name suggests a ballistic missile behaves, like a bullet from a rifle, according to the laws of ballistics. Just as the aiming of a rifle critically determines the future trajectory of the bullet, so the initial boost-phase is a vital determinant of the accuracy of the ballistic missile. And just as the barrel of a rifle is short by comparison with the flight path of the bullet, so the boost phase of a ballistic missile is short in comparison with its flight path. Small errors up to the point of burn-out (when the missile's primary boost motors have used up all their fuel) can, again, result in very large misses in the target area. A number of factors affect guidance accuracy during the boost phase. First there is the need for the extremely accurate determination of the position of launch. The inertial guidance systems on which missile flight-paths depend are designed to sense movement, but they rely on being told the exact point at which the movement begins. For land-based missile systems, careful and accurate survey can determine launch position with great accuracy: the problem is very much more complex for mobile systems, including those launched from submarines. Again, it will be obvious that large errors in missile accuracy can accrue from any faulty alignment of their onboard inertial platforms; and, again, static-launch systems have advantages over the mobile variety—although some degree of wear, how-

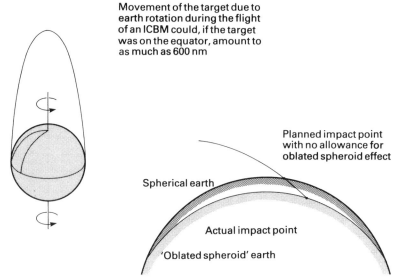

Movement of the target due to
earth rotation during the flight
of an ICBM could, if the target
was on the equator, amount to
as much as 600 nm

Planned impact point
with no allowance for
oblated spheroid effect

Spherical earth

Actual impact point

'Oblated spheroid' earth

FIG. 7.6   Figure 7.4 presumed an 'ideal' earth. Here are depicted the possible errors
accruing from the actual shape of the earth and the fact that it rotates. (*J R Walker*)

ever minute, can occur when missiles are maintained at a high state of readiness
over a long period of time. This is one of the reasons why missiles have to be brought
off-state from time to time—even though they may not have moved since their last
inspection.

After launch, missile attitude can be affected by factors such as gyro drift or
the imperfect sensing of acceleration by the onboard accelerometers: both can be
compared with the old-fashioned instrument error which has afflicted airmen since
first they were persuaded to put their faith in 'knobs and dials'. Most such errors
can now be compensated in the manufacture of modern instruments and components: those that remain will serve to ensure that guaranteed pin-point accuracy
will continue to elude mankind. However, precisely because such accuracy is being
sought, it is essential that other missile components behave 'as advertised'. Thus the
computer-generated signal to order engine cut-off (when the missile has attained its
required velocity) must be exact: the slightest anticipation or delay, or the slightest
drawing-out of the cut, can significantly affect the eventual range error of the warhead. The earth's magnetic field is another source of possible error. Although it can
be predicted accurately enough for most purposes, it is continuously changing; and
very small degrees of change can cause disproportionate errors in the long-range
missile shot. The same is true of the gravitational field, which can be subject to local
variation.

However, these are likely to be extremely small sources of error by comparison
with those encountered in the re-entry phase. Here, inaccurate predictions of atmospheric density or of wind velocity can be significant. The atmospheric effect begins
to influence the flight path of the re-entry vehicle at altitudes of about 45 miles,
where deceleration and the effects of heating become appreciable. Furthermore,
although short-range missiles, on very high trajectories, may re-enter the atmosphere at large angles of incidence (70° would not be uncommon) their longer-ranged

cousins, fired on optimum energy profiles, could be re-entering at much more modest angles—20° or so, for example. Thus, the longer-range missile might be subjected to atmospheric affects for a full minute or more of its flight path—which could result in the accumulation of quite large errors.

As always in these matters, not all potential errors will act in the same sense; indeed, some will serve to cancel out others. But this will not make the prediction of warhead accuracy any the easier—not least because some of the errors may be random. However, a few examples will give an idea of the extent of errors induced by inaccuracies in the guidance systems of missiles of even intermediate range. An accelerometer mis-alignment or inertial platform error of one-thousandth of a degree could give rise to a 300-m error at the target; an incorrect assessment of only 10m per second in the wind on re-entry could lead to 200m of error on impact—as could inaccurate assumptions of air density and geophysical conditions above and around the target area. Gyroscope drifts of 0.1° an hour could result in 250-m errors at target; and algorithmic errors in missile computer programming could affect warhead accuracy by about half that value.

The sum of all these errors denotes the accuracy of the weapon, and it will be clear that this cannot be exactly predicted. Such statistical evidence as can be accumulated from test firings (themselves very expensive to mount and measure and, thereby, necessarily limited in number) will give military force-planners a CEP—that is, the radius of a circle within which half of the missiles could be expected to fall. Typically, this could be anything up to 1,000m for a long-range missile; and in the late 1950s and early 1960s, when techniques to improve ballistic accuracy had still to be perfected, the only way to overcome inaccuracy was to increase the size and yield of the warhead. Thus were incorporated warheads well into the megaton range—the largest reliably recorded nuclear test (by the USSR) being that of a 60-megaton weapon—an astonishing equivalent of 60M tons of conventional high explosive. The collateral damage created by the detonation by such a weapon can be extrapolated (albeit imprecisely) from the known effects of the 20,000-ton equivalent detonations at Hiroshima or Nagasaki.

As with conventional weaponry, the accuracy and warhead effect of nuclear weapons are inextricably linked. Expressed simply: if the accuracy of delivery can be increased by a factor of two, the yield of a warhead can be reduced by a factor of ten. Nomograms can be constructed to assess the effects of various nuclear yields against a variety of target groups; and from these it can be seen that a small weapon, delivered accurately, can have the same effect as a much larger weapon delivered less accurately. In part it is this relationship which accounts for the development of cluster weapons in the conventional field and of multiple independently-targetable re-entry vehicles (MIRVs) for nuclear weapons. The total explosive effect of a given weight of warhead can be significantly greater if the charge is split into a number of smaller components distributed about the target area. But the point remains: increased accuracy brings very high returns.

Accuracy

Turning back to our ballistic missile delivery, how can errors be minimised and the accuracy of warhead delivery enhanced? There are, broadly, three avenues of exploration. The first—and most obvious—lies in the constant improvement of design and manufacturing techniques, to ensure that all those missile components which impact on accuracy are constructed to ever smaller tolerances and their reliability continually improved. Secondly, attempts must be made to eliminate errors which occur in the exo-atmospheric part of the missile's flight path. Thirdly, these efforts can be independent of, or co-ordinated with, measures to improve the terminal homing of the warhead itself.

In the ballistic (or unpowered) part of the missile's flight path, an assessment of the accuracy of trajectory can be made from a variety of sources—radar-tracking and the use of ground-based beacons being already well established. Advanced navigational systems can be applied equally to missiles as to manned aircraft; and the development of the GPS (described at Chapter 8) offers one such line of progress. Even more sophisticated methods may include the use of stellar tracking to update the inertial platform. In this case a star is tracked and, from the data received, a correction fed into the inertial system and through that into the guidance system. Figure 7.7 illustrates this technique in very simplified form.

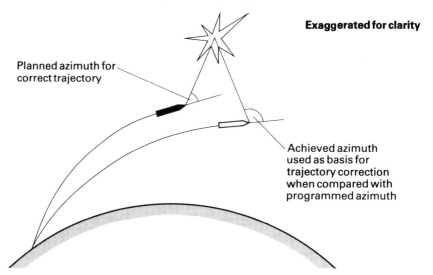

Exaggerated for clarity

Planned azimuth for correct trajectory

Achieved azimuth used as basis for trajectory correction when compared with programmed azimuth

FIG. 7.7   The principle of stellar guidance—heavily over-simplified. (*J R Walker*)

However, knowledge that a missile has deviated from planned flight path is one thing: correcting it is another. In the exo-atmospheric part of the flight path, some form of thrust motor or alignment impulse must be provided. It need not be great, but it must be applied with great accuracy if the cure is not to prove worse than the ailment. However, if the warhead is to be equipped with some sort of terminal homing device, then it is arguable as to whether or not the added complexity and weight of an exo-atmospheric flight-path correction system is cost-effective. One method of homing, applicable to fixed targets, is that of Terminal Scene-Matching. This pre-supposes the availability of an accurate radar picture of the target area, from which the position of the target itself can be precisely determined. Stored in digital form in the missile's computer, this predicted radar picture can be compared with the returns from a radar, operating in real time, within the re-entry vehicle. Corrections can be applied to the re-entry vehicle, proportionate to the amount of difference between the two pictures. Figure 7.8 illustrates this concept, which is another variant of Terrain Profile Matching (TERPROM) technology used in both manned aircraft and cruise missiles (and covered, again, in Chapter 8).

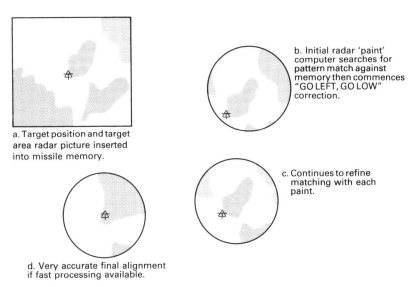

a. Target position and target area radar picture inserted into missile memory.

b. Initial radar 'paint' computer searches for pattern match against memory then commences "GO LEFT, GO LOW" correction.

c. Continues to refine matching with each paint.

d. Very accurate final alignment if fast processing available.

FIG. 7.8   The principle of terminal scene-matching. (*J R Walker*)

The possibilities open to scientists, technologists and designers in improving the guaranteed accuracy of a missile-delivered warhead on target are manifold and complex. They deserve deeper study by the student of air power and they will be more fully covered in other volumes in this series. Here let us merely list the possibilities that are available—and which must be explored and exploited, particularly given the likely development of anti-ballistic missile defences in the years to come. Trajectory-shaping (also referred to as fractional-orbit trajectory) injects the missile into a low flight path, so that it will break defensive radar cover later and allow defensive systems less time to react. Alternatively, a higher than normal trajectory can be used to capitalise on steep re-entry angle—which can also give problems to defensive systems. Terminal manoeuvring is another possibility; and it is even possible to arrange for a re-entry vehicle to fly a spiral, or random path during re-entry. A proposal in the early 1980s for a conventional airfield attack weapon as part of the United States' Counter-Air 90 programme had the re-entry vehicle decelerating to more conventional speeds and being navigated to the target endo-atmospherically, before dispensing its munitions. Although this particular project remained on the drawing board, clearly it was not felt to be beyond the bounds of the then-available technology.

Some Countermeasures

As with manned aircraft, chaff can be used to confuse enemy surveillance radars and to conceal missile approach. Indeed, because space-deployed chaff would not drop to earth, it could be used to provide a screen for the undetected approach of follow-on missiles—as, indeed, could the ionisation effects of a high-altitude nuclear detonation which effectively blacked out the enemy's communication and surveillance systems. Figure 7.9 illustrates these possibilities.

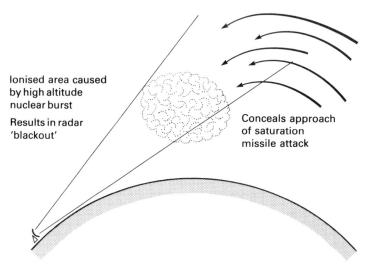

Ionised area caused by high altitude nuclear burst

Results in radar 'blackout'

Conceals approach of saturation missile attack

FIG. 7.9   The possibility of using 'nuclear blackout' to conceal the approach of missiles by ionisation effects. (*J R Walker*)

Warhead look-alikes (in the radar sense) are extensively used in modern ICBMs. In order to deliver the same radar signature, the decoy does not have to be of the same weight, density or size as the warhead it is trying to mimic. Given that weight is critical in missile design, even inflatable balloons can be used as warhead decoys, if covered with suitable metalised fabric. However, these would only be of value immediately after the re-entry vehicles had been deployed. Aerodynamic drag would begin to take its effect as the various objects reached the upper atmosphere, and the decoy cloud would soon separate from the warhead proper. Modern defensive systems, working at previously unattainable computer speeds, would then have sufficient time to react to obtain a valid interception solution on the real warheads. An alternative solution would be to use decoys which were smaller than the warhead itself, but with similar ballistic coefficient—simply, the weight of the vehicle divided by the presented cross-section and including a factor for drag coefficient. The radar signature of such decoys could be enhanced by the use of radar-reflective material or a radar-reflective lens—the converse of the technique used to reduce radar cross-section in low observable technology. Alternatively, the RCS of the warhead can be reduced by the sort of techniques already described in Chapter 5; but, given the critical nature of the shape of the re-entry vehicle, the scope for employing low-aspect angles is considerably less than that for manned aircraft. The effects of gravitational forces of up to 50g, of air-loads and of the high heat-loads experienced during re-entry, also make it more difficult for radar absorbent materials to be used in the way they can on aircraft subjected to very much lower stresses.

Of course, one way to ensure that other objects appeared to the defences exactly as if they were warheads would be to make them warheads. This is another advantage of the MIRV-ing process. As we have seen, a greater destructive effect will be obtained by using a number of smaller warheads in the same target area. They would also be much more likely to lead to the confusion of defensive systems—albeit at significantly increased cost, weight and complexity. As to the electronic warfare aspects of ballistic missilery and the defence against it, the range of techniques is closely comparable to that used in the more conventional offensive/defensive environment of the manned combat aircraft. Another volume in this series has already dealt with electronic warfare in some detail: suffice it is to say here that noise jamming, in all its manifestations, together with the more advanced techniques of range-gate and velocity-gate stealing are certainly not unknown to the ballistic missile and its re-entry vehicles.

As compared with the manned bomber for the role of projecting offensive power in the strategic sense, the ballistic missile has certain advantages. Firstly, it has a high probability of arrival. Once successfully launched, it is formidably difficult to stop; and this makes it an excellent weapon for deterrence, where a high Probability of Detonation (POD) is an essential element of the credibility on which deterrence is based. Life-cycle costs of missiles, though far from negligible, are certainly lower than those of a comparable capability based on manned aircraft: the budgets for manpower and maintenance are moderate, as compared with other systems. An important advantage of the ballistic missile is its speed of reaction. Modern solid-fuelled missiles can be kept at high states of alert for extended periods, and can be launched on warning of attack. This makes it extremely difficult, if not actually impossible, to contemplate successful pre-emptive first strike—the avoidance of which has been the over-arching concern of the superpowers for more than a quarter of a century.

The greatly increased accuracy now attainable from the ballistic missile not only increases its potency as a nuclear delivery vehicle, but also opens up some extremely interesting possibilities in the conventional field. Given accuracies of within about 30m (and some sources suggest that these can already be guaranteed), the technology now available in the design and construction of conventional warheads brings a whole range of targets, strategic and tactical, into the view of the conventional force planner. Indeed, where accuracy is less the objective than is the spread of panic and where the constraints of collateral damage are ignored, missiles are already being used—witness the employment by both Iranians and Iraqis of modified Soviet Scud surface-to-surface missiles in the counter-city aspects of their long war. The technological expertise of the more highly developed nations must surely demand that serious attention be paid to defence against the conventionally armed ballistic missile.

STRATEGIC DEFENCE

We have moved from the strategic to the tactical use of ballistic missiles. Let us revert, in order briefly to examine some developments in the defence against the ICBM; and let us first refresh our memories of the typical flight path of such a missile—this time with the accent on a possible defence against it. We have already seen that there are four distinct (though, of course, consecutive) phases of long-range ballistic missile flight: firstly, the launch phase—a relatively short (usually 3 or 4 minute) period of full thrust by the missile's main rocket motors. Given thrust levels of typically 20 tons and more, the launch phase sees the missile off its launch pad and beyond the point at which it has broken free of the Earth's atmosphere.

The boost phase of missile flight may occupy about the same length of time as the launch phase though, given that the missile has by that time achieved exo-atmospheric flight (*ie* flight outside the Earth's atmosphere) it naturally travels a very much greater distance than that covered by the earlier phase. During the boost phase the missile's launcher rockets separate from the missile itself—their essential work now completed—and fall away, to be burnt up on re-entry into Earth's atmosphere. It is also during this phase (sometimes referred to as a post-boost phase of flight) that the missile's warheads, safely lodged in their various re-entry vehicles (RVs) will be deployed—probably with a number of penetration aids, including decoys or balloons so designed as to give them, from the ground, every appearance of lethal RVs in their own right. This technique naturally complicates very greatly the task of the defender against missile attack, and it is the principal reason why much research effort is currently being expended on developing weapons which would take out an enemy's missiles before they had reached the point of RV or decoy release—*ie* during the albeit short launch phase.

Following the boost phase of flight, the warheads/RVs and decoys, together with any remaining elements of the now useless machinery, may travel through space for several thousands of miles and at speeds of something like 4 miles a second for periods up to 30 minutes. They are still several hundred miles above the Earth's surface at this time; and they are following ballistic trajectories so selected as to allow the RVs to re-enter Earth's atmosphere at the precise point and time for effective target strike. During this, the so-called 'mid-course phase', any necessary corrections may be made to RV trajectories in order to achieve on-target accuracy; and decoys and other aids to defence penetration may again be deployed. It is also a complicating factor in terms of defence against missile attack that the targets are, by now, comparatively cold and therefore considerably more difficult to detect by IR means.

The last (and shortest) phase of flight is the terminal phase. In the course of no more than one or two minutes the warheads re-enter the Earth's atmosphere at about 60 miles above its surface, to home in directly to their specific targets. In a full-scale ballistic missile attack probably thousands of RVs, decoys and other aids to penetration would rain down on selected targets, making this last chance for defence a very slim chance indeed. Hyper-velocity ground-launched missiles might well take out numbers of the incoming shower of deadly warheads; but their number and the difficulties of distinguishing between genuine warheads and still very convincing decoys, in an extremely short timescale, make it virtually impossible to guarantee more than limited success.

From all this, it is clear that for the greater part of the flight time from launch to detonation of an ICBM, its warhead (or, more likely, warheads) are exo-atmospheric. This does not mean, incidentally, that a ballistic missile must *sui generis* fly outside the earth's atmosphere. As already explained, it is ballistic because, like a bullet from a gun, it follows a trajectory dictated by the power initially imparted to it and, in the case of long-range missiles, later applied to achieve mid-course correction. Once that power has been used, the missile's flight path is governed solely by the laws of ballistics—whether it is flying in or out of Earth atmosphere. That said, because of the great distances involved, it is almost invariably the case that the ICBM and its 'cousin' the intermediate-range missile (IRBM) do fly exo-atmospherically—indeed, for the greater part of their respective flight times. In so doing, they obviously complicate the problems of anti-missile defence and compel the defender to seek to use the total missile flight time in which to engage—whether that be endo- (within) or exo- (outside) atmospheric. The problems of anti-missile defence are touched on later in this chapter (and, in more detail, in other volumes in this series); but, to put them into some sort of context and to anticipate consideration of some of the enormously advanced and complex technology which must be harnessed to defeat them, the simple table in Figure 7.10 may be helpful.

Missile flight Phase	Configuration	Typical flight Time (mins)	Possible counter
a. Launch	Missile a complete entity – ie, body, rocket and booster motors, control systems, warheads, decoys, penetration aids etc all together, to present a single target	3 – 5	- Particle-beam weapons - High-energy, space-based lasers
b. Boost and Post-Boost	Launch vehicle separates. First decoys may be deployed with re-entry vehicles (warheads)	4 – 5	- Space-based lasers - Ground-based lasers (possibly) - Kinetic energy weapons - Rocket-powered homing interceptors
c. Mid-course	Re-entry vehicles, decoys etc in space	Up to 30	- Ground-based lasers - Space-based kinetic energy weapons - Space-based electro-magnetic 'rail-gun' (?) - Anti-satellite missiles (may be air-launched)
d. Terminal	Warheads and decoys falling over a wide area, against many targets simultaneously	1 – 2	- Hyper-velocity ground-based missiles

FIG. 7.10   Technology *v* the ICBM. Some possible areas for future research.
(*Author*)

SDI

The vision of a viable defence against ballistic missiles has long intrigued its proponents; and limited progress had been made many years before the formulation of what was to become the United States' Strategic Defense Initiative (SDI). Both superpowers had experimented with ballistic missile defence systems before the first

Strategic Arms Limitation Treaty (SALT I) was brought into being with the signing of the US/Soviet Anti-Ballistic Missile Treaty in May 1972. One of the major provisions of that treaty was its restriction on the deployment of anti-ballistic missile (ABM) defences to one area around the national capital and one around an ICBM launcher area of each of the signatory powers. In the event, only the Soviet Union actually deployed an operational ABM system (around Moscow); and an amendment to the treaty later restricted any such deployment to one area in each nation.

Subsequent research on ABM systems and their components was also strictly limited by the ABM treaty, and development constrained well before the point of deployment. That said, research was both permitted and undertaken by the signatories to the treaty; and there was some debate as to whether or not it covered work based on technologies which were undeveloped at the time the treaty was signed. In an important speech delivered on 23 March 1983, US President Ronald Reagan called upon the American scientific community '... who gave us nuclear weapons, to turn their talents now to the cause of mankind and world peace, to give us the means of rendering these nuclear weapons impotent and obsolete'. Thus was born SDI (or 'Star Wars' in the arresting, but misleading catch-phrase soon coined by the world's media). In concept, it would bring together a number of technologies— several of them at the very forefront of current research—to permit identification, tracking, interception and destruction of ballistic missiles or their RVs.

The potentially large scale and the limited flight times of the threats against which SDI was to be developed are such as to ensure that it had to be a 'multi-layered' system. *Inter alia*, there would almost certainly have to be a capability for the interception of enemy missiles at their boost phase, *ie* at or soon after launch, when they were emitting massive amounts of heat and before they had complicated the problems of defence by releasing their RVs and decoys. Were it to prove feasible (and current indications are that this is so), boost phase defence would greatly reduce the number of targets to be engaged by subsequent defensive layers in the mid-course or terminal phases of missile trajectory—perhaps as many as ten independently targetable warheads and several decoys per missile launched. However, few—even among the more fervent protagonists of SDI—would suggest that boost-phase interception could do more than blunt the initial cutting edge of missiles launched in any massive pre-emptive enemy strike; other defensive layers would have to back that first line of defence and, given the greatly reduced timescales involved, those subsequent defensive systems would also have to be ever ready for action if SDI were to play its full and proper part in the deterrence of war at the strategic level.

One or perhaps two systems would be deployed to inflict further attrition of warheads and decoys during the mid-course phase of missile attack. Surveillance satellites might detect and subsequently control heat-seeking infra-red guided missiles or kinetic energy weapons, launched from other continuously orbiting satellites; whilst ground-launched interceptors could also be steered into position by very highly developed radars, or by passive electro-optical sensors, to launch their own anti-satellite (ASAT) weapons—a procedure which was proven as early as September 1985 in the successful interception of a Solwind P78-1 satellite by an ASAT carrying F15 fighter. But it is likely that, in any full-scale missile assault, a proportion of incoming and lethal warheads would escape even these defences; and there would, in consequence, be a need for a fourth defensive layer to destroy those threat vehicles which had survived beyond the point of re-entry to the Earth's atmosphere. Such terminal defences would comprise probably the most readily understood SDI techniques—land-based interceptor missiles, with extremely short reaction times and possessed of very high speed (Mach 6 or greater). As an example of the sort of speeds required, one comparatively early SDI-related experiment, carried out in the United States, involved the hitting of a moving target at some 12,000 ft with a kinetic-energy weapon. Accounts suggest that the weapon was terminally guided by onboard radar, at speeds of over 3,000 ft per second. Although the test was successful, it has to be borne in mind that typical RV speeds from an ICBM would be at least four or five times greater than that.

The whole SDI system—or, rather, complex of systems—would comprise exotic weapons ranging from ground-, aircraft- or satellite-launched interceptor missiles to space-based satellites incorporating electro-magnetic cannon, laser, or particle-beam directed-energy weapons (DEW). It would require a highly complex and extremely reliable array of emitters and receivers—again, land-, air- or space-based and employing both advanced radar and electro-optical acquisition capabilities. It would also have to be held together and, in the event, brought into action by command, control, communications and intelligence (C^3I) systems capable of handling almost staggering rates of information-flow—speeds of 30 megaflops (ie 30M complex calculations per second) having been recently suggested.

Indeed, although the 'kill' components of SDI have excited the imaginations of scientists, politicians and publics alike (and not always for the same reasons), it is probably in the area of surveillance, battle-management and communications where lie the most difficult challenges to modern technology. The age of the computer has made us increasingly blasé about numbers; but there is still something mind-boggling about the prospect of a system which must be capable of identifying, with absolute precision, and then tracking and engaging possibly 50,000 or more objects accelerating to speeds of 4 or 5 miles per second and to heights of at least 500 miles within an overall elapsed time of probably less than 20 minutes.

That said, the imperious advance of technology would seem to offer just such a promise. A varied array of different sensors already ensures that huge volumes of data can be made available for practical use at ever faster rates. New-generation communications and navigation systems are providing information with a speed and precision hitherto only dreamed of; and exotic new technologies—particularly in the application of directed energy—are likely all too soon to stand ready to take their places on the eternal see-saw of offensive/defensive capability.

As of now, it remains true that the most readily available form of ASAT system is a ground-launched interceptor missile with a nuclear warhead. Launched on a trajectory which would bring it close to its target, the effects of a carefully timed nuclear explosion would undoubtedly be to destroy or, at the very least, disable the incoming satellite. Although no longer of operational status, the United States did have such a system available in the mid-1960s. Nor would it be technically too difficult for the existing Soviet Galosh ABMs (deployed around Moscow) to be launched on trajectories which would allow them to intercept satellites in low earth orbit, rather than the ballistic missiles against which they are currently targeted. Indeed, any nation which possessed longer-range ballistic missiles (certainly of ICBM range and, if the payload were reduced, probably IRBM and submarine-

launched (SLBM) missiles too) could, in theory, launch such weapons on high trajectories with warheads set to detonate against satellites still in space, rather than after
re-entry.

In practice, of course, the problems are much greater than that. The timing of
such missile launches would be absolutely critical, as would the numbers required
to counter any likely scale and weight of attack. The detonation of even one—let
alone, many—nuclear warheads in space would have untold (and certainly unpre-
dictable) effects on the continued operation of all orbiting satellites and their communications—friendly as well as hostile. In any case, the theory of such an
interception suggests that it would be relatively easy to counter. A direct-ascent
ASAT would not only have to be launched a relatively long time before engagement
with its target satellite (and launched, incidentally, by a rather large missile); it
would also be following a pre-programmed trajectory and would thus be unable to
manoeuvre. In consequence, comparatively limited variation of flight-path, as a
result of its detection of the oncoming ASAT, would ensure the target's invulnerability; and all present-day satellites enjoy a degree of manoeuvre capability—if only
to assist their maintenance in planned orbit.

Rather greater flexibility in satellite interception could be gained by placing an
intercepting warhead itself in orbit, thus allowing it to engage anywhere along the
orbit of the target satellite without, for example, having to await its passage over
the ASAT's own launch-point. Existing Soviet ASAT systems are of this type and,
as far as is known, they rely on non-nuclear warheads. However, they have their
own limitations—not only in their comparative slowness of response (ie the time
between launch and engagement) but also in the fact that they can probably only
effectively threaten satellites in low earth orbit.

This last restriction would apply, also, to smaller interceptor missiles fired from
high-speed, high-altitude aircraft. Currently constrained from development by the
ABM Treaty, such a system would overcome a number of the disadvantages of those
already described. Once fired, it would take considerably less time (minutes, rather
than hours) to reach its target; its launcher aircraft could itself counter the manoeuvring capability of the target satellite before missile-release; and, as noted, its feasibility has already been demonstrated.

Some of the technologies available for consideration in the context of ASATs are
the same as those necessary for an effective defence against ballistic missiles—and
here we return to SDI. Ground-based lasers, for example, of very high energy (5
megawatts and more) have been freely discussed as one amongst several SDI candidate systems. The laws of physics are, of course, immutable—though who is to say
whether they have all been as yet fully investigated? Among those that have is the
fact that the energy delivered by a laser decreases with the square of the distance
between laser and target. Another, is that a laser is a line-of-sight weapon (although
obviously laser, not human sight); and could, therefore, only be of use in attacking
a satellite or incoming missile, warhead or decoy that is overhead.

For the student of technology and its application to air power, an interesting
research project in the SDI context is that of the Airborne Optical Adjunct (AOA)
(Plate 7.1). Part of what is (perhaps surprisingly) a US Army programme, a Boeing
767 commercial airliner has been extensively modified as a technology demonstrator
to determine the capability of airborne optical sensors for the early warning and

PLATE 7.1   The Airborne Optical Adjunct—part of the United States' research programme into the feasibility of strategic defence. This is a Boeing 767—the like of which will not be seen in airline service! (*Boeing Aerospace Company*)

tracking of ICBM warheads on re-entry. Within a large cupola, mounted on the 767's upper fuselage, is an IR sensor of very long wavelength. The value of IR lies, of course, in its ability to detect the comparative heat of objects against their environmental background. Given the extreme cold of space and the great sensitivity of the sensors mounted on the AOA aircraft, it is said that they would be capable of detecting the heat of a human body at a distance of more than 1,000 miles in space. Clearly, much less than this is required to discriminate between ICBM warheads and the debris that may be accompanying them on re-entry to the Earth's atmosphere. The data obtained from tracking all such objects will be processed by extremely sophisticated computers on board the AOA, and transmitted direct to ground-based radars. It will remain to be seen whether technology can offer sufficient accuracy and flexibility by this means for the timely and very early warning of incoming threats.

Whatever the eventual outcome of the United States SDI as a complete and viable programme, it is certain that research now being carried out in a number of areas of very advanced technology will have fair claim to attention in the development of future weapons and defence systems. It is also certain that great strides will be made in other areas of research—specifically into the 'non-kill' elements of the SDI programme. Among several which will undoubtedly have potential for development—whether or not an effective deployable SDI programme comes into being—are:

- Advanced surveillance and acquisition systems.
- Missile-launch detection and tracking equipments;
- C^{3}I and battle-management systems; and
- Advances in system survivability, weapon lethality and target-hardening.

Indeed, research was already underway (and not only in the United States) in several of these areas well before President Reagan's announcement of the SDI programme. In that sense, SDI has provided not more than a focus of attention or spur—albeit a very sharp spur—to renewed efforts on the part of scientists, technologists, engineers and planners alike. It will be some time before it is possible to evaluate the outcome of their combined efforts: but it is already clear that the SDI programme will, in historical terms, come to be recognised as every bit as great a boost to technological advance, on a broad front, as was the United States' Apollo moon-shot programme nearly 20 years earlier. It may also be worth recalling that when, in 1961, the then President Kennedy announced that an American would be put on the moon and safely returned within that decade, the project was widely assessed as being by an order of magnitude too difficult and too expensive. As to the first— it was done. As to the second: *The Economist*[1] reminds us that the final bill came to around $25 billion in 1968 dollars, which meant that in each year of the Apollo programme America spent less on space than it did on women's hairdressing.

CRUISE MISSILES

A few words are necessary on the other type of missile capable of strategic employment. Just as we have already met an early example of the ballistic missile used in war (the Nazi V-2 of World War II) so we have learnt a little of an early cruise missile of the same period—the V-1 'doodlebug'. Modern cruise missiles have advanced greatly over the technology of the V-1, but the principles demonstrated in that early example of the genre are equally applicable today.

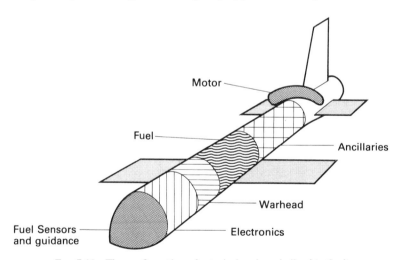

FIG. 7.11   The configuration of a typical cruise missile. (*Author*)

Figure 7.11. shows the configuration of a typical cruise missile with (Figure 7.12) some of the options available to a current in-service type. The cruise missile is, in effect, a small pilotless aircraft operating within the atmosphere at speeds associated with those of conventional aircraft, rather than missiles (see Volume 3 of this series for a fuller treatment of the RPV). Even with supersonic cruise missiles now close

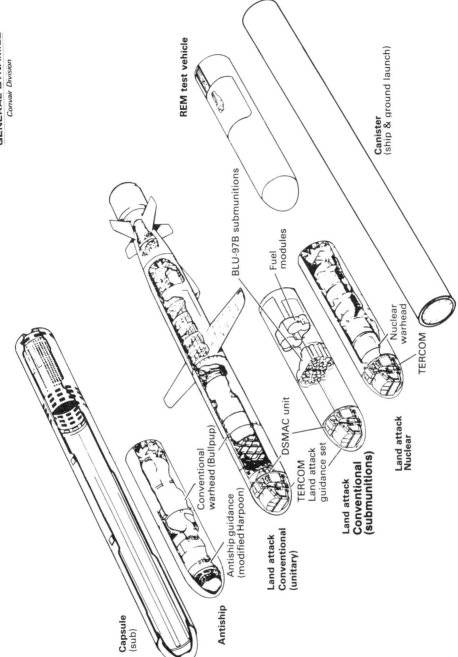

GENERAL DYNAMICS
Convair Division

REM test vehicle

Canister
(ship & ground launch)

BLU-97B submunitions

Fuel
modules

Nuclear
warhead

TERCOM

DSMAC unit

TERCOM
Land attack
guidance set

**Land attack
Nuclear**

**Land attack
Conventional
(submunitions)**

Conventional
warhead (Bullpup)

Antiship guidance
(modified Harpoon)

**Land attack
Conventional
(unitary)**

Antiship

Capsule
(sub)

FIG. 7.12   Some options already available to a present-day cruise missile—in this case, the General Dynamics BGM-109 sea-launched missile (SLCM). (*General Dynamics, Convair Division*)

to operational service, the speeds involved will still be an order of magnitude slower than those of their ballistic cousins.

The range and speed required of the cruise missile virtually dictate the choice of its engine. Indeed, at the shorter ranges it is possible to dispense with an engine altogether and to utilise the kinetic energy imparted to the weapon by the delivery vehicle. Even at low level, it is possible to reach distances of some 4 to 6nm from the point of aircraft release; and there exist a number of proposals for stand-off weapons using this technique to keep the delivery of aircraft out of the range of a target's immediate point-defence weapons systems. Released from high altitude and at higher speed, much greater ranges can be obtained. For ranges greater than 6nm from low level, a motor of some sort is required. The cheapest and simplest is a rocket, which can either be incorporated into the weapon design or merely strapped on to it. Designs exist for strap-on motors to give added energy to both the US Paveway series of laser-guided bombs and the GBU-15 glide bomb currently in service use. The value of the rocket motor is either to add energy in the form of a high-energy but short burn; or, at a lower thrust level for a longer period, to sustain the original energy imparted to the weapon, rather than to increase it. Whichever the application, the rocket motor tends to be cost-effective where the burn is short, rather than over the longer ranges; and rocket motors are generally confined to required ranges up to about 30nm.

Beyond that range, the advantage swings quickly towards the use of small turbo-jet engines—miniature versions of those used on manned aircraft. Again, there is a choice to be made. The engines may be either normal turbojets or more complex and expensive turbofans with large by-pass ratio. Certainly, the use of the latter type of engine is dictated by the range capability of the Boeing AGM-86 ALCM (Plate 7.2), as carried by the USAF's B-52 and B-1B bombers; or of the Soviets' AS-15, with a quoted range in the order of some 1,600nm. These powerful, but comparatively small engines are very efficient, and the range available from a limited fuel capacity can be increased by the use of special fuels. These may be either of higher specific gravity (SG) than normal (figures approaching 0.86 SG, as compared with the 0.77–0.8 SG of conventional aircraft engines); or, indeed, special fuels—such as those using a boron base, which have inherently higher calorific values.

The weight and structure of the cruise missile's engine and fuel tankage are major contributors to the overall dimensions and configuration of the missile itself. But the need is for the designer to reduce the size of the weapon to a minimum if the cruise missile is to operate from any one of a series of fairly restricted environments (*viz* the transporter erector launcher (TEL) of the ground-launched cruise missile; the torpedo tube of a submarine; or the aircraft pylon, where the need to minimise aerodynamic drag on the carrying aircraft must inevitably reduce the size of its store).

Cruise Missile Navigation

Unlike the ballistic missile (which travels for a large part of its trajectory unguided) the cruise missile flies its flight path in the aerodynamic regime and is effectively guided throughout. A number of navigation systems can be used, each with its advantages and disadvantages. The GPS (see Chapter 8) is certainly one candidate.

PLATE 7.2   A Boeing AGM-86 air-launched cruise missile (ALCM) flying over the
USA's Utah Test and Training Range in 1979. (*Boeing Aerospace Company*)

With probable accuracies of ±15 m in the target area, this system would not only be
acceptable for a number of target/warhead combinations, but could also be used
with a terrain data-base for ultra low-level penetration *en route* to the target. As
with the application of GPS to the manned aircraft, it would probably need the
backing of an inertial system which could maintain the missile's navigational accuracy during any period of interrupted or corrupted GPS signal. The whole system
would be difficult to jam—though not impossible, given time and money for its
development. Indeed, in the context of the future employment of a conventionally
armed cruise missile, outside the environment of the East/West super power balance, it is difficult to believe that an effective jamming capability will exist for a great
many years yet.

Another very useful navigational option, which would enable the missile to remain
independent of external aid, is that of TERPROM (again, described more fully at
Chapter 8). The advantage of this system is that it remains equally accurate throughout the route and up to the target itself. Against some targets, terminal homing
systems could actually be discarded. A disadvantage is that the missile flight path has
to be pre-planned; and limitations on the storage of the terrain database effectively
confine the missiles to fairly narrow corridors each side of a desired flight-path. In
the strategic context, this is possibly less of a problem than it would be in the purely
tactical scenario.

A technique which has further to go in development than that of TERPROM is
that of Terrain Character-Matching. In this case, the data base contains details of
the *type* of terrain—for example: built-up area, woodland, plain, railway line, road
and the like. As with TERPROM, use is made of a radar altimeter; but this time
the modification of radar return by the various characteristics of the terrain being
overflown can determine its type, for comparison with that in the onboard data base.
The technique is thought to offer acceptable *en route* navigation within normal
mapping accuracies and, used with a terminal scene-matching system, should be
sufficient to bring the target into the required field of view. Clearly it demands
rather less data storage for character-matching than for profile-matching and, thus, a

greater area can be maintained and carried in the missile's data base. A disadvantage is that weather conditions can materially affect the ground return. Snow is the obvious example, but flood must also be taken into account.

Enhanced Accuracies

As noted in the context of the ballistic missile, Terminal Scene-Matching is likely to offer great advances. At the slower approach speeds of the cruise missile, with more time for sensor acquisition and subsequent processing and with the vehicle itself designed for the aerodynamic environment—thus allowing more precise control during the final manoeuvres on to the target—accuracies of a very few metres can

PLATE 7.3   A convincing enough demonstration of the potential for cruise missile accuracy. In this sequence, a General Dynamics Tomahawk missile demonstrates its capability for pinpoint attack against critical land targets. (*General Dynamics, Convair Division*)

confidently be expected (Plate 7.3). This prospect of near pin-point accuracy opens up a range of new possibilities in the field of conventional warfare. First, it allows the comparatively small weight of warhead capable of being carried by the cruise missile to be used to much greater effect: as we have already seen, increased accuracy greatly reduces the size of warhead required to inflict a required degree of damage. Given accuracies with 10m, targets such as railway bridges over major features (rivers or gorges deep inside enemy territory) can become excellent and extremely cost-effective targets for the accurate conventionally armed cruise missile. Computer-controlled electrical signalling, now becoming the norm on many railway systems, also presents very profitable targets for pin-point attack. It is estimated that one highly developed European railway system coud be reduced to an estimated 20% of its capacity by the interdiction of only six vulnerable points. On another system, 30% of the track mileage could be virtually blocked by attacks on just three points. The more highly developed the system, the more vulnerable it becomes to precision attack at its vital nodal points.

Other obvious targets for such long-range attack are power stations and the large transformers of modern power-generation systems. Non-nuclear power stations (and, even more so, their nuclear variants) rely on the maintenance of extremely high pressures in the boilers which develop the steam required for large turbine-drive. If conventionally armed cruise missiles can be targeted with the accuracies now forecast, an attack on a power station would, in fact, become an attack on a specific boiler which, operating at upwards of 3.500psi, would need only to be pierced for the subsequent explosion to be devasting. Similarly, the main trans-formers which step down grid voltages to those usable by industry or in the home are, by reason of their great expense, few in number and with comparatively little built-in redundancy: another excellent target for a weapon of 5-m accuracy.

Vulnerability

Naturally, if it is to be effective, the cruise missile—like any other warhead carrier—has to be able to penetrate to its target. In the early 1980s, it was popular to discount this particular delivery means because of its supposed vulnerability to interception; but this is another of those cases in which practice proves to be very much more difficult than theory. Probably the most effective way to stop a cruise missile is to destroy its launch vehicle. However, for that reason, those launchers are either extremely mobile or extremely difficult to find—or both. The TEL of a GLCM can be placed on any one of a number of pre-surveyed sites and can be *en route* from one to another in a matter of minutes. A submarine which can fire cruise missiles (either vertically or from its torpedo tubes) is as difficult to find and attack as any other submarine: and there is as yet no breakthrough in the detection of deeply-submerged, still and quiet submarines poised to launch their missiles—whether ballistic or cruise. The earlier generation of stand-off missiles carried by aircraft, with ranges like that of the Soviet AS-4 (up to 250nm when fired from Bear and Blinder bombers) presented a problem—but not an insoluble one—to an efficient defensive fighter force. However, with stand-off ranges increased to 1,600nm in the case of the newer AS-15 or of 2,000nm-plus for the American ALCM, air defence systems will have great difficulty in positioning combat air patrols sufficiently far out to intercept the launch aircraft.

Defence against the cruise missile thus becomes effectively a defence against the missile itself. Again, the odds are not on the side of the defender. Foremost is the fact that the cruise missile is small—much smaller than a fighter aircraft. It travels fairly fast and at very low level, where ground returns can seriously affect air inter-cept radars. Its RCS can be extremely small—$0.1\,m^2$ being considered achievable by today's generaion of missiles and future developments expected to reduce that again by factors of 10 to 100. Taking, as an example, an airborne intercept radar with a good performance by modern standards, and assuming that it could detect a bom-ber-sized aircraft at 100nm: Figure 7.13 shows how the detection capability against

Target type	Typical RCS (m²)	Typical detection range (nm)
Bomber	25	100
Fighter	10	79.5
Cruise Missile	1	44.7
Cruise Missile	0.1	25.1
Cruise Missile	0.01	14.1
Cruise Missile	0.001	7.9

FIG. 7.13   Variations in typical detection ranges with decreasing radar cross-section
(RCS). (*Author*)

a typical cruise missile would degrade as RCS was reduced. Even an Airborne Early
Warning aircraft such as AWACS, with its much larger radar, would be able to
detect a cruise missile of 0.1 RCS at only about 50 nm. Figure 7.14 shows how
reduced detection range materially affects the resources needed to cover any given
arc of threat. The more stealthy the cruise missile, the denser must be the defensive
screen. But the range of the cruise missile allows for extended arcs of approach, so
exacerbating greatly the problem for the defender.

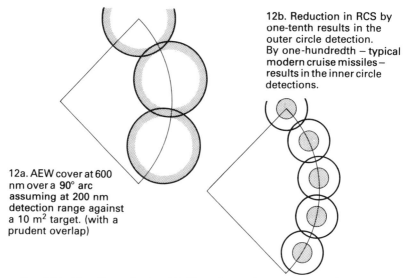

12b. Reduction in RCS by
one-tenth results in the
outer circle detection.
By one-hundredth – typical
modern cruise missiles –
results in the inner circle
detections.

12a. AEW cover at 600
nm over a 90° arc
assuming at 200 nm
detection range against
a 10 m² target. (with a
prudent overlap)

FIG. 7.14   The effects of reduced RCS on the requirement for radar (in this case,
airborne early-warning radar) cover. (*J R Walker*)

As Air Vice-Marshal John Walker has suggested in an earlier volume in this series,
current strategic bombers in the inventories of the superpowers can, as ALCM
carriers, claim truly hemispherical reach. The B-52, with a radius of action in excess
of 3,500 nm, mated with an ALCM of 2,000 nm range, has a combined reach of
5,500 nm—the distance from the equator to the pole. The same can be said of a
Soviet Bear-H/AS-15 combination. More practically, this reach could be turned to
tactical use to envelop targets—that is, to threaten them from wide arcs extending

through to a 360° capability. It is this potential which makes the cruise missile such an effective weapon system for deterrent use against a major continental power. Furthermore, its small size and the fact that significant numbers can be carried on board aircraft such as the B-52 and B-1B mean that the load of one aircraft would be extremely difficult to stop. That of three or four would soon ensure a total saturation of enemy defences over a small arc.

The development of the cruise missile will undoubtedly proceed along two main paths, each designed to make the task of its interception more difficult. The first will be to make the vehicles themselves more stealthy, not only to radar but to infra-red and visible wavelengths. The second approach will be to make them faster, which will have the effect of reducing the time available to the defensive system to effect an intercept. Already there is discussion in the open press of supersonic cruise missiles being developed by both the super powers. Nor is it a weapon purely for low-level attack. Missiles flying in the stratosphere at speeds perhaps as high as Mach 5 or 6 would pose major difficulties for any defensive system.

In any of its many possible forms, the cruise missile is indubitably a weapon of the future. Properly developed and deployed, it could provide a form of effective deterrence short of the nuclear option. Again, time alone will tell whether it will be so developed, given inevitably competing priorities for the allocation of scarce resources to defence.

8

What Next? Some Future Developments for the Strategic Offensive Role

In the course of this slender volume, much has been written about technology and much about the projection of air power at long range from the home base—strategically and offensively. For the great strength of air forces lies in their capability to take the war to the enemy, extracting every advantage of reach, flexibility and, increasingly, precision in the concentration of their power. From those capabilities stems the ability of the air to play its very full part in the deterrence and prevention of war. As we have seen, over the years technology has provided the means to enhance those inherent qualities perhaps more than in any other combat environment—save, perhaps, only that of submarine warfare. There the continuing struggle for mastery—of the hunter over the hunted, offence against defence—is of an order of complexity and challenge all its own. There, as in the air, technology has provided some powerful and sophisticated tools for the job: but good tools demand good workmen.

And if much has been written of technology, comparatively little has been said of the men who devise, develop, refine and eventually use that technology in the performance of their complex tasks. Indeed, such is not the purpose of this book. But the author would be failing singularly in his aim were he not to have encouraged and hopefully inspired his readers to learn more about the men behind the machines. The literature is plentiful enough; and a few suggestions for further reading are offered in the short bibliography that concludes this book. Whether the subject be the great scientists (Tizard, Jones, Oppenheimer, von Braun); the innovators like Whittle, Sikorsky, Barnes Wallis and Martin; designers of the calibre of Sopwith and R J Mitchell, Tupolev, Dassault and Johnson; the thinkers (Douhet, Trenchard, Mitchell and Slessor); or the airmen themselves (Ball, von Richthofen, Doolittle, Cheshire, Bennett and Yeager among them)—their stories hold endless fascination for the student of air power.

For it is people who make history—whether that history be of kings and empires or of those who serve them on (and, in our case, also above) the earth. This is to be no hymn of praise for mankind. There are those who would deny the claim to such treatment of the warrior and of those who support him in battle; and, anyway, few of that band would wish it. But it should not be forgotten that the god of technology is, in truth, man-made; and that its exponents are human too. In the course of the development of air power, the strengths and frailties of man have been many times revealed—perhaps never more directly than in the extremes of physical challenge to which the airman has traditionally been subjected. The air can be a harsh environment in which to fight—and survive; and though this is not a treatise on the physiological and psychological aspects of aviation medicine, a few comments on their application to long-range flying might not be inappropriate to a work on strategic air operations. The fact of the matter is that, all too often, at the very moment when its practitioners may be called upon to be at their brightest and best, they may well be approaching the limits of physical exhaustion. And though adrenalin can be a powerful antidote to tiredness—even fear—the long-range combat airman may be very grateful for a little further assistance from applied medical science.

THE OPTIMISATION OF SLEEP PATTERNS

It is a fact that sleep disturbance is frequently experienced by aircrew engaged in combat operations—and not, as the cynics would aver, always by reason of disturbed conscience. Clearly, for such aircrew to function effectively 'when it matters', some control over the patterns of sleep and wakefulness would be helpful—providing, of course, that such control was benevolent and did not carry the risk of unfortunate side-effects.

The normal healthy young adult (and the majority of combat aircrew will qualify under all four headings) has the ability, when tired, to pass very rapidly from wakefulness into a deep sleep—the so-called sleep of non-rapid eye movement. Sleep may be clinically measured in varying stages of depth but, for the sake of simplicity, let us concentrate on deep sleep, drowsiness (or light sleep) and periods of rapid eye movement (REM) when, although technically still asleep, the subject is actually hovering on the borderline between sleep and waking. Surprisingly, the phenomenon is not confined to the period immediately before waking; but is repeated, at varying stages and with irregular timing, throughout any period of normal sleep (Figure 8.1). I am, incidentally, indebted to Group Captain Tony Nicholson, Consultant at the Royal Air Force's Institute of Aviation Medicine for the information here assembled by the author in grossly simplified form. For a more detailed introduction to the subject, his recently revised AGARD publication[1] on 'Sleep and Wakefulness' is invaluable. As with virtually all living organisms, man's biological processes vary in respect to time in a way that is normally both periodic and regular—the so-called circadian rhythm. In man, as in many other species, the rhythm usually oscillates daily around the length of the solar day and is modulated by 'environmental synchronisers'—including light and dark, temperature, work schedules and sleep periods.

For the majority of tasks performed by a man whose body is following a normal circadian rhythm, performance rises during the day to a peak between mid-day and about 2100 hours each evening, falling to a minimum between 0300 and 0600 hours. For the night-bomber crews of World War II, this was obviously a factor of some significance. It is true that consistent sleep deprivation will modify man's perform-

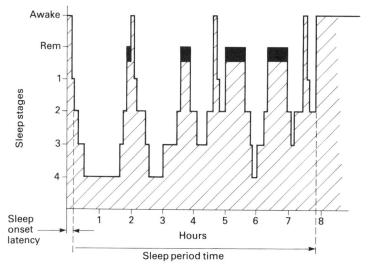

FIG. 8.1   Nocturnal hypnogram in a young adult. (*Advisory Group for Aerospace Research and Development, Paris*)

ance rhythms (usually adversely) though such modification may in part be ameliorated by practice, consciously applied effort and high levels of motivation—again, important features for the combat airman. Degradation in task performance can also interact with the circadian cycle itself, with decrements of between 10% and 35% being measurable for different stages of the cycle. At Figure 8.2 are schematic representations of a number of factors capable of modifying circadian behavioural rhythms.

Just as interruptions to the normal pattern of time cues (light/dark, day/night) can affect man's ability to perform to his optimum, so can any sudden shift in accustomed time routines—the well-known jet lag experienced by transmeridian travellers. There is also a cumulative effect in irregular work; and this has to be taken into account in the calculation of effective crew-duty hours for civil airline crews and the crews of long-range transport aircraft in peacetime. In war, of course, things may have to be different, but it would be a wise commander who attempted, as best he might, to give his crews adequate off-duty rest time during periods when such rest was likely to be most beneficial. The illustration in Figure 8.3 shows how such patterns might be organised in a peacetime situation, when the intent was to minimise any risk to airline passengers; in war, the commander would have to do the best he could to replicate those patterns if he was to obtain the best results from his people. A typical variation of performance against time on task is shown at Figure 8.4. As a guide towards 'doing his best', the commander should be aware that a period of sleep of about 4 hours in the evening of a long night's work will usually achieve significantly better sustained results than will the oft-preferred alternative of 'cat napping' (whose advocates, incidentally, included Winston Spencer Churchill during an excessively wearing and prolonged period of stress in the more than five years following his acceptance of the British Premiership in May 1940).

Some calculations of the rest periods required after a long-distance flight have rather more relevance to the pay-packets of civil airline crews than to war-fighting. I am

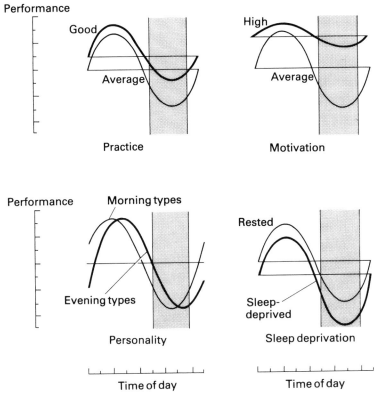

FIG. 8.2   Some of the factors which can modify circadian behavioural rhythms.
(*Advisory Group for Aerospace Research and Development, Paris*)

reminded by my colleague John Walker of guidance issued some time ago to intend-
ing travellers which, it was suggested, might avoid their rushing into potentially
expensive decisions too soon after subjecting their 'biological clocks' to long flights.
Briefly, it used the circadian cycle to produce a series of departure and arrival
coefficients, *viz*:

Local Times of Arrival/ Departure	*Coefficients for:*	
	Dep	*Arr*
0800-1159	0	4
1200-1759	1	2
1800-2159	3	0
2200-0059	4	3
0100-0759	3	3

The following calculation was then suggested:
(a)   Take the actual flight time in hours;
(b)   Divide by 2;
(c)   Add the number of time-zones crossed (providing they total more than 4);
(d)   Add coefficients for departure and arrival times (see above); to
(e)   Produce the recommended rest time, expressed in one-tenths of a day.

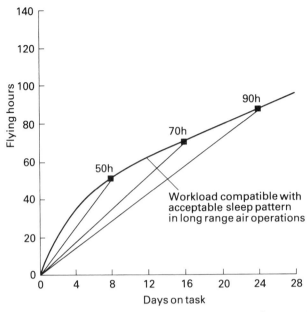

FIG. 8.3   Acceptable aircrew duty hours related to time on route in a normal peace-time situation. (*Advisory Group for Aerospace Research and Development, Paris*)

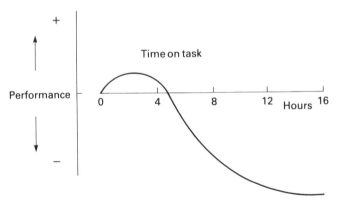

FIG. 8.4   Diagrammatic representation of change in performance with time on task. (*Advisory Group for Aerospace Research and Development*)

Thus for a 12-hour eastabout flight, say from the United Kingdom to Hong Kong, departing Heathrow at 2140 and arriving at the destination at 1750 the following day (both times local), the calculation would be:

$$\frac{12}{2} + 8 + 3 + 2 = \frac{19}{10} \text{ of a day}$$

or nearly 2 days' rest before investing heavily on the Hong Kong Stock Exchange. There are few firms which could afford to subscribe whole-heartedly to such a proposition, though their senior executives might support it unreservedly. Applied to war, it might attract even less support. Not only would the strategic bomber crew be ill-placed to take time off in the target area; but, even were that possible, the war could have begun and ended while they were resting. Clearly, there are adjustments to be made here!

Such adjustments might best be achieved by ensuring that aircrew engaged on sustained and intensive combat operations maximise their limited off-duty periods by sleeping as deeply as possible and as soon as practicable after debriefing from one mission; and by waking, without side-effects, to prepare for the next. In the context of sleep-inducement, alcohol (a favoured prescription of some in wartime) is not recommended. Not only does it act as a stimulant; but the amount required to induce sleep will leave the patient with some rather unhelpful side-effects. In recent years, much research work has been carried out on the identification of substances to regulate sleep patterns. The most encouraging results have come from the use of so-called hypnotic drugs—which are not the dangerous substances they may sound. Used properly, under carefully controlled medical prescription, hypnotics have been shown to be of value in the treatment of disturbed sleep patterns. Different preparations exhibit different characteristics of absorption, distribution and elimination—another reason why they must be clinically prescribed for combat aircrew and their effects monitored by qualified flight medical personnel. Of course they must be non-addictive and, ideally, they should be fast-acting and their effects rapidly or ultra-rapidly eliminated. It should be emphasised that medication now recommended for the regulation of some aircrew sleep patterns has been subject to the most rigorous testing and, properly used, does no more than ensure that limited sleep is sound sleep, from which awakening is both natural and free of residual effects; and as a result of which the performance of often complex and demanding tasks is unimpaired. A striking example of what can be achieved is illustrated in Figure 8.5. Here, the curve for 'acceptable workload' in the peacetime situation is compared with the results actually obtained by the controlled use of safe hypnotics during the South Atlantic conflict of 1982.

AIRCREW PROTECTION

Another area in which the needs of combat aircrew have long been the subject of experimentaion, simulation, trialling and often expensive re-equipment is that of protective clothing. The study is one deserving of a work in its own right. All that will be here indicated is that, depending on role, such aircrew may have to be protected against the physiological and/or psychological effects of gravity, extreme cold, overheating, fatigue, anoxia, noise, vibration, stress, dehydration, glare, flash, smoke, fire, blast, shrapnel, explosive de-compression, bird-strike, disorientation, ejection, exposure, trauma, immersion, impact and crash. They must be so equipped as to survive, by day and night, in conditions of nuclear, chemical or biological warfare; and, according to theatre of operations, to survive also in the arctic, jungle, desert, or at sea against the possibility of having to abandon their aircraft. All too often, the specialised equipment, clothing and accoutrements required for rather a lot of these situations must be worn or carried at the same time. Small wonder that modern combat flying is not quite the 'joy ride' which some would judge it from the

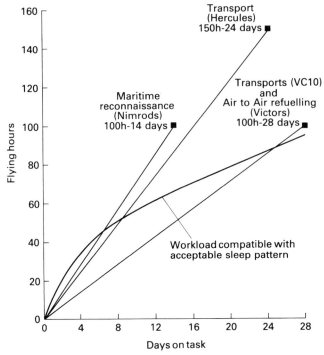

FIG. 8.5   Workload (flying hours) achieved by some aircrew during the RAF's
South Atlantic campaign in April – June 1982. (*Journal of the Royal Society of
Medicine, Volume 76, November 1983*)

safety of *terra firma*. Challenging, stimulating, rewarding and satisfying it may be:
comfortable, relaxed, carefree and easy it certainly is not—nor, in the view of most
exponents, ever has been.

— AND ESCAPE

A brief word on aircrew escape which, by its very nature, must often be undertaken in moments of high stress and great personal danger. In the early days of
military aviation, the parachute was almost unheard of. Even when it became a
practical proposition for crew escape, its use was rejected by those who considered
it might affect 'the fighting spirit'. If not rejected, then often scorned—rather as the
case for car seat-belts took so long to stick, against considerable opposition on such
misplaced grounds as manliness and civil liberty. In due course, parachuting became
accepted as a sport for those misguided enough to wish to abandon any perfectly
serviceable aircraft; and the wearing of a parachute came to be accepted as a matter
of normal prudence for those whose lives already held quite enough potential excite-
ment. Later, personal and aircraft dinghies were developed, saving the lives of
very many ditched aircrew; and comprehensive survival kits were incorporated to
enhance the life expectancy of those unfortunate enough to alight, voluntarily or
not, in one or other of the less attractive areas of the globe.

With the advent of high-speed flight (*ie*, anything in excess of about 350 kts in

PLATE 8.1   An early test of a Martin-Baker rocket-powered ejection seat, fired from a Meteor jet fighter in 1949. Later variants of this seat have saved the lives of over 6,000 aircrew of 73 air forces—and will undoubtedly continue so to do. (*Central Office of Information, London*)

normal controlled conditions) aircrew lost the relatively simple, if daunting option of 'stepping over the side'. So dawned the era of assisted escape—whether by ejection seat (explosive cartridge and later rocket-fired) (Plates 8.1 to 8.3) or in a few instances (notably the American F-111 and earlier B-1A) by an escape module or capsule which detached itself from the aircraft and enabled the crew to retain the relative comforts of a cockpit environment, both in escape and in the subsequent survival situation (Plate 8.4). Such devices are unlikely to be developed, having proved themselves an unnecessarily expensive, heavy and over-complicated means of prejudicing the success of aircrew escape—certainly at the altitudes at which most modern ejections take place.

On the other hand, as with most things to do with military aviation, development of the ejection seat has been steady and impressive. There were some concepts of assisted escape from very early military aircraft; but even a variant from the period immediately following World War II is, in every sense of the term, a museum piece today. Yet there are literally thousands of aircrew who owe their lives to the 'Martin-Baker let-down' and its counterparts in the USA, France, the USSR and other air forces. Priorities for future developments will probably centre on the achievement of greater stability of the seat after ejection and before the separation of its occupant; and on the better thermal protection of aircrew involved in high-altitude escape. For the former, full stability and a totally automatic ejection sequence will be controlled (like so much else) by micro-processors; for the latter, efforts will be concentrated on improvements to in-built insulation—within the practical limits set by cockpit environment, normal aircrew comfort and operational considerations.

In the United States wind-tunnel testing is reported to have been completed on an advanced technology seat designed for aircrew escape at speeds of up to Mach 3 and at heights up to 70,000 ft. Vectored thrust is said to be incorporated for safer ejection from low altitude, and a Kevlar fabric net may help overcome the difficult problem of flailing of the arms, legs and head—a feature of high-speed ejection. The Crew Escape Technologies (CREST) seat will feature an inertial measurement unit, pitot-static system and computerised control to direct the effective firing of the seat's own solid-fuel rocket motor[2]. The Kevlar fabric is said to act as a flow fence or protective cup, stagnating the airflow over the body of the ejecting crew member and obviating the differential pressures which can cause increasingly severe injuries from flailing at speeds as low as 100 knots.

As a footnote to the question of aircrew escape, photographs recently released in the Soviet Union indicate a unique method of downward ejection for crew members of the TU-22 Blinder (Plate 8.5.) The problem was never solved for the rear-crew members of the RAF's V-bomber force—an issue which aroused some understandable controversy at the time, not least because it conferred on some members of the always tightly-knit bomber crew an advantage which was denied others. Of course, the subsequent conversion of the Vulcan to the low-level role would have made downward ejection a very risky enterprise anyway; but by then it was too late to be considered and the necessary structural modifications would always have been both difficult and very expensive.

ADVANCED NAVIGATION SYSTEMS

As regards equipment, very real advances have been made in recent years in the solution of one of the most fundamental requirements of flight—and particularly of military flight—with the need to place weapons on or gather intelligence from targets

PLATE 8.2   Test Pilot George Aird ejecting from his Lightning aircraft at a fantastically low altitude at Hatfield, Herts. 13 September 1962. (*Syndication International*)

PLATE 8.3   A striking photograph of a present-day ejection seat in action. (*Martin-Baker Aircraft Company Limited*)

as precisely as possible. Three developments in aerial navigation are worthy of mention in the context of strategic air operations—though none is confined to such operations, nor to their execution exclusively by manned or unmanned aircraft.

PLATE 8.4   Another way to escape. This F-111 crew module is being test-fired down a sled at Holloman AFB New Mexico in 1965. On this test, a rocket of 35,000-lb thrust propelled the module to a speed of over 400 knots. (*McDonnell Douglas Corp, St Louis*)

Navstar Global Positioning System (GPS)

Apart from a very significant increase in accuracy compared to existing airborne navigational equipments, the Navstar GPS is a passive system with obvious benefit in terms of low observability (see Volume 1 of this series). Being satellite-based, it will be much more difficult to jam or degrade than are such radio-based systems as Decca, LORAN or TACAN; and its combination of world-wide coverage and extreme accuracy make it particularly suitable for long-range offensive operations. Although certain details of the Navigation System, Time and Range (Navstar) equipment remain classified, sufficient has been revealed in open literature to suggest an eventual accuracy of ±15m in position and 4in per second in speed—this latter, a most impressive figure in the context of weapon-aiming. One early test flight, using prototype equipment, is in fact claimed to have produced an error of less than 8m at the end of a five-sector flight of more than 4,200 nautical miles.

The space segment of Navstar GPS will consist of 18 satellites and 3 orbiting spares. A ground (or control) segment—in fact, a network of ground stations—monitors the satellites and feeds to their onboard micro-processors continually corrected data on position and time (Figure 8.6). For the user—whether on land, at sea or in the air—the system is completely independent of weather; and for the military user there is the added advantage of a well-developed anti-jamming capability. By integrating the GPS with a standard inertial navigator (IN) for altitude and heading reference, it has also proved possible to overcome early problems of blind spots, when line-of-sight contact with orbiting Navstar satellites was temporarily lost in rugged terrain, or by reason of powerful electronic jamming.

The IN system of future long-range (and, for that matter, short-range) aircraft would also be used to provide a close estimate of present position, velocity and time in order to reduce the search time of the GPS. The system will then interrogate any three of the orbiting satellites and establish a 3-position fix, by measuring the time taken to receive the satellite signal and multiplying that time by the speed of light. Each satellite carries four atomic clocks, which are said to accumulate a 1-second

PLATE 8.5   A unique escape system. The Soviet Tu-22 Blinder modified with down-ward-hinged under-fuselage hatches for the entry and possible ejection of all three crew members. It is a source of continuing debate as to whether or not the pilot is ejected upwards (in time-honoured and comparatively gentlemanly fashion). But the navigator/radar operator (in the forward of the three positions) and the elec-tronics operator/remote tail-gun controller (to the rear) are very likely candidates for downward ejection—the latter, suffering the doubly indignity (but added safety) of actually facing aft at the time of ejection.

error every 300,000 years: luckily, they can be corrected! However, the clocks in the aircraft's own GPS equipment are merely the crystal variety (though themselves highly accurate). Any time difference between the two is taken out by establishing the exact range of aircraft equipment to a fourth satellite.

Because of its accuracy, independent passive operation and relatively low cost, Navstar GPS is clearly destined to enjoy a very large market indeed. Being a satellite-based common user or shared system, it could even be used by combat aircraft, at high or low level and in all weathers, to maintain loose tactical formation without recourse to attention-getting radar emission. There have been estimates of a future requirement of something approaching 50,000 sets for the US military alone—and that is to say nothing of the vast civil and other military applications of the system. Already in commercial use for survey work and stellar observation, future appli-cations will almost certainly include traffic control by land and in the air and, as

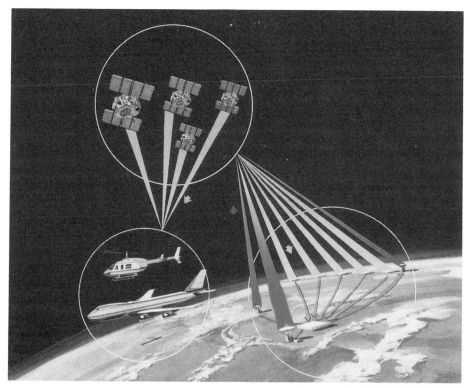

FIG. 8.6   A simplified 'artist's impression' of one of the many applications of the Collins GPS Navstar system. (*Collins Air Transport Division, Rockwell International*)

indicated at Plates 8.6 and 8.7, the day will surely come when it may be fitted as an optional extra in the family saloon. Had the Challenger shuttle disaster in January 1986 not severely delayed the satellite launch schedule planned by the United States, it is certain that the GPS programme would by now have reached an advanced stage. As it is, the fully developed capability of the system is only just around the corner.

Nor has that other superpower, the USSR, failed to exploit a similar capability. As indicated in Figure 8.7, the Soviet Glonass system is similar to Navstar, but is thought likely to consist of only 12 satellites when fully developed. This would suggest attainable accuracies of about 100 m in commercial use and perhaps half that in military applications. Similar capabilities are foreseen in the European Space Agency's Navsat system, though accuracies can be greatly increased—albeit at increased cost.

Ring-Laser Gyros

Other advances in navigation have been made possible by developments in two different areas: that of the ring-laser gyro (RLG) and TERPROM. To date, both are being considered as candidate systems for tactical aircraft; but the technologies involved are certainly of interest in other areas of military aviation—particularly, in the case of TERPROM, for low-level applications. In the United Kingdom, British

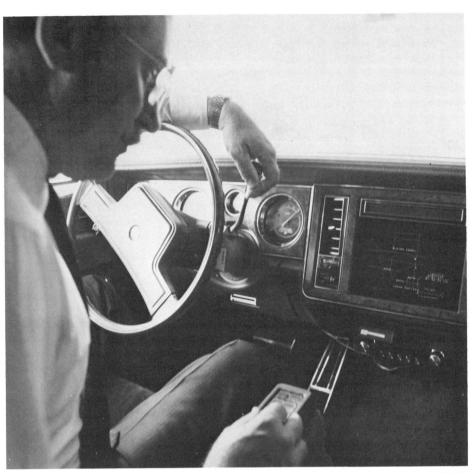

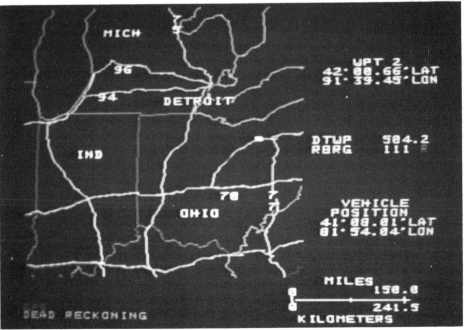

PLATES 8.6 and 8.7   An 'optional extra' with a difference. The saloon may look a little dated, but the global positioning system is pretty contemporary. This type of read-out may become a feature of future land-based systems. (*Collins Air Transport Division, Rockwell International*)

	NAVSTAR		GLONASS
21 (rising to 24 in mid-1990s)	**NUMBER OF SATELLITES**		9 (perhaps 12)
6	**NUMBER OF PLANES**		2 (rising to 3)
3 (rising to 4)	**SATELLITES PER PLANE**		6 (rising to 8)
20,233 K	**SATELLITE ALTITUDE**		19,100 K
55°	**INCLINATION**		63°
L₁ 1227 MHz L₂ 1575 MHz	**FREQUENCY**		1240-1260 MHz 1597-1617 MHz

FIG. 8.7   Some comparative aspects of the US Navstar and Soviet Glonass systems.

Aerospace has been active in both technologies for a number of years, but similar work has been in hand in the USA, France and elsewhere. The accuracies obtainable from IN equipments incorporating a RLG are not those of Navstar GPS; however, they represent a significant step forward from current capabilities. In fact, the device is not a true gyroscope, but assumes that description because, like all spinning mass gyros, its primary function is to sense angular rotation. The principle of the RLG can be somewhat simplistically stated as the measurement by laser light of movement or rotation of a block about its axis. A laser unit passes light in different directions inside a typically triangular closed block. Mirrors are used to direct the light and a photo diode detects differences in the received frequencies of the varying laser beams.

As illustrated by the schematic of a typical RLG (Figure 8.8), an annular chamber, triangular in design, is filled with a helium neon gas mixture which 'lases' when excited by electric discharge. Electro-magnetic waves are thus generated, to travel round the annular chamber in opposite directions. A photo-detector, placed in a fixed position, senses rotation of the unit about an axis perpendicular to the plane of the chamber. To this detector, the frequency of the electro-magnetic wave propagated in one direction appears to increase with rotation, while the frequency of the waves travelling in the opposite direction will appear to decrease. The difference between the two observed frequencies is directly proportional to the unit's rotational rate. In practice, when that rate is low, the opposing electro-magnetic waves tend to 'lock'; and, to obviate this, artificial movement is induced by a small motor. This picturesquely named 'dither motor' would, if uncompensated, give rise to inaccuracies in the read-out of unit movement, because the dither owes nothing to the true rotational rate of the RLG. Its effects must therefore be measured and the known value neutralised to produce a true reading in the gyro's output signals.

The RLG offers several advantages over the conventional mechanical gyro. It contains fewer components; it is unaffected by acceleration forces and can absorb higher rates of angular change; its outputs are digital; and it is inherently more

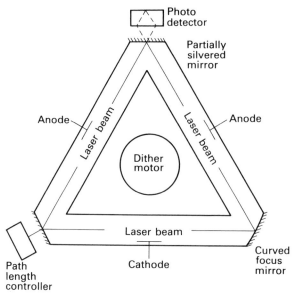

Fig. 8.8   Simplified schematic of a ring-laser gyro.

reliable. Improvements over conventional IN systems have also been proven—0.01% of movement being now detectable and accuracies of 0.1 kts being predicted for the near future *ie*, eight to ten times those of standard inertial systems. Finally, the RLG imparts another, potentially very significant advantage in that it greatly reduces the time of equipment alignment (or readiness for optimum operation) to some 4 minutes, as against typically up to 15 minutes for a conventional IN system. This is clearly of importance for aircraft requiring a quick reaction capability.

Terrain Profile-Matching (TERPROM)

TERPROM is another extremely accurate low-level navigation system with a potential for a variety of military applications. Its development by the Dynamics Division of British Aerospace has drawn heavily on such rapidly emerging technologies as very high-speed processing and large memory capacity. In outline, the system works by comparing or matching the profile of the terrain over which an aircraft is flying with that predicted by digital mapping. The prediction is carried aboard the aircraft; and a highly accurate radar altimeter is used to measure the actual terrain profile and constantly to calibrate and update the aircraft's own IN system. A further, very significant advantage of TERPROM lies in its ability to generate terrain-following commands and ground-clearance warnings by reference to the terrain profile some distance ahead of the aircraft. Clearly this is of value in flight over enemy territory, where the beam of a standard terrain-following radar can be used to locate the presence of an intruding aircraft. Further, by its inherent resistance to jamming and its capability for automatic operation at night and in all weather conditions, TERPROM offers a valuable adjunct to low observable operations. As the aircraft travels over a digitally mapped area of some 200,000 nm² (a figure likely to be greatly increased with the development of solid-state memory over the next few years) a computer takes regular samples of information both from the onboard IN system and radar altimeter. This information is compared with that predicted; and any resulting differences are instantly processed, by advanced Kalman filtering methods, to produce navigational corrections. As the process is repeated every 100m along the aircraft's flight path, its crew is provided with virtually continuous updating of position, velocity and height (Figure 8.9).

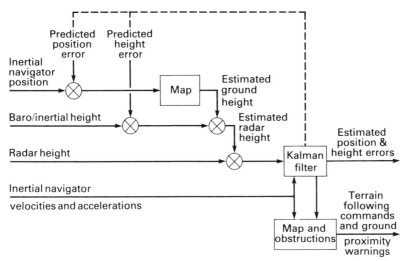

FIG. 8.9   Block schematic of the TERPROM process. (*British Aerospace plc*)

As well as offering high navigational accuracies, TERPROM significantly reduces the workload on combat aircrew operating at very low level and in adverse weather conditions. It is highly reliable, invulnerable to ECM and can be used throughout the aircraft's low-level profile—up to the point of weapon release. It can then be employed as an assured get-you-home facility, with automatic precision guidance on to the glide-path of approach to base—in zero visibility, and without recourse to any significant emissions, either from aircraft or ground. Truly a system of the future, with applications for manned and unmanned flight, fixed-wing or rotary.

AIRBORNE COMMAND POST—THE USAF's E-4B

The systems by which nations exercise the highest levels of command over the powerful strategic forces they have developed are complex, intricate and highly capable. Details of such systems are not only difficult to obtain (as, indeed, they should be); but it would demand a volume in its own right even to summarise such facts as are within the public domain. Nor are such systems, of course, exclusively related to strategic air power.

However, a glimpse into the world of higher-level control may be gained by a study of one system, operated by the Commander-in-Chief of the USAF's SAC—and, thus, with a claim to be included in any study of the use to which technology is put in the continuing development of long-range offensive air power. The United States' National Emergency Airborne Command Post (NEACP) is currently carried aboard one of four Boeing E-4B aircraft. The E-4B (Plate 8.8) is basically a Boeing

PLATE 8.8   The United States' National Emergency Airborne Command Post (NEACP), flown since 1975 in a heavily-modified Boeing 747-200B, initially as the E-4A. The latest variant, here pictured, is the E-4B. (*United States Air Force*)

747-200B, heavily modified as a highly survivable communications link between the nation's Command Authorities and strategic retaliatory forces. It is thus capable of operations in the environment of all-out nuclear war, when other means of communications may well have been lost.

The E-4A (later modified to E-4B standard) replaced in service the older (and much smaller) EC-135J Airborne Command Post—itself a military derivative of a Boeing airliner, the 707. It has more than five times the usable floor space of the older aircraft; carries three times its payload; and, with a flight-refuelled endurance of some 72 hours, is clearly a very much more capable and flexible system. As indicated at Figure 8.10, the heart of the E-4B is its Operations Team Area, situated amidships and allowing up to 31 staff members to operate, as necessary, a wide variety of circuits and systems—including automated data-processing (ADP), automatic switchboard, direct access telephone and radio circuits and 'hot lines'. They are also equipped with full inter-communication and audio-recording facilities. In operational terms, the aircraft's 'nervous system' lies in the Communications Control Area, divided into voice and data sections; and facilities also exist for conferences and briefings, technical control and crew rest. A 1,200-kVA electrical generator (the largest ever flown) is needed to power some 149,000lb of command, control and communications equipment—including computers, radios, acoustical insulation and furnishings. Full operation is possible with any two of the eight 150-kVA alternators off-line; and in order to cool both equipment and crew, the aircraft's pressurisation system is capable of delivering a massive 8,000ft^3 of air around the E-4B every minute. The ADP package alone consists of two processors, a 36-megabyte disk drive system, a tape-drive, two printers and eight remote keyboard-display terminals. The communications fit includes radio equipments to receive and transmit from very low (VLF) to super-high frequencies (SHF)—enabling the NEACP to communicate around the world via a network of satellites, air-to-air and air-to-ground systems and even the humble commercial telephone. In all, there are more than 50 external antennae on the E-4B—the most obvious being a steerable dish for

1. Operational team area.
2. Communications control area.
3. Technical control area.
4. Lower trailing wire antenna.
5. Aft lower equipment area.
6. Briefing room.

7. Forward lower equipment area.
8. Flight avionics equipment.
9. National command authority executive suite.
10. Forward entry.
11. Flight deck and upper rest area.
12. Conference/projection room.

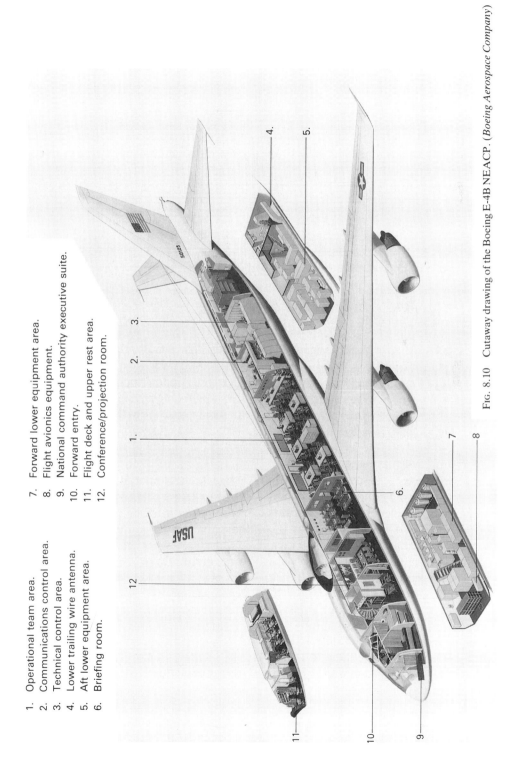

FIG. 8.10   Cutaway drawing of the Boeing E-4B NEACP. (*Boeing Aerospace Company*)

satellite communication, housed in a radome hump on top of the aircraft. At the other end of the radio-communications spectrum, VLF communication is effected by means of 5-mile-long trailing copper wire antennae which, fully extended, droop some 4,000ft below the aircraft in flight. The E-4B is protected against the effects of EMP and possible damage from thermal and transient radiation: it is, thus, survivable in a nuclear environment.

OTHER DEVELOPMENTS OF THE 'AIRLINER'

The E-4B is currently the most impressive example of a number of major projects by which the United States has sought to use large commercial aircraft for complex and esoteric airborne functions. Others have included a succession of derivatives of the old Boeing 707 including its larger variant, the E-3A (AWACS). 707 airframes have been adapted for a great diversity of roles, from the KC-135 Stratotanker, to the EC-135J Airborne Command Post and RC-135 family of electronic intelligence-gathering and reconnaissance aircraft. Yet another variant is the US Navy's E-6A TACAMO communications link (described elsewhere in this series); and another, highly specialised conversion is that which flies as the Airborne Laser Laboratory, involved with SDI-related experiments in the detection, tracking and guidance of missiles.

More recent derivatives include the C-18 series—707-323s now being converted for duty as EC-18B Advanced Range Instrumentation Aircraft; EC-18D cruise missile control platforms; and E-8As (formerly EC-18Cs)—vehicles for the airborne carriage of the Joint Surveillance Target Attack Radar System (J-STARS). These last aircraft will be fitted with a Norden multi-mode side-looking radar antenna, operating in synthetic aperture mode to detect and locate stationary targets and, with added Doppler, to locate and track moving targets. The information thus acquired will be fed back via the Joint Tactical Information Distribution System (or JTIDS) for accurate, real-time target direction.

Indeed, the trade in second-hand 707s has assumed an international aspect. Israeli Aircraft Industries is among a number of firms seeking to meet the growing military requirement for electronic warfare, airborne early-warning and tanker aircraft. The Boeing Military Airplane Company is developing its own variant of a tanker/transport 707 with guaranteed export potential; and the West German firm, Dornier, is converting three further 707-320s as trainer/cargo carriers in support of NATO's E-3A Airborne Early Warning Force. The ubiquitous 707 is also being considered as the airborne component of another NATO programme, the Multi-Service Electronic Warfare Support Group (MEWSG); and it is a sign of the times that suitable long-life aircraft are proving difficult to identify—so many being now in military use or being modified for it.

Other large civil aircraft have been pressed into military service with the US forces. The wide-bodied DC-10 has become the KC-10A Extender combined tanker and support carrier (Plate 8.9); and the Boeing 767 has become the carrier of the AOA to the SDI programme (see Chapter 5). Clearly old aircraft, if they have been well maintained, can take a long time to fade away—and may be subject to many changes in role, equipment and appearance before they do.

PLATE 8.9   McDonnell Douglas KC-10A Extender, combining air-to-air refuelling with a still impressive load-carrying capability, seen here engaged in the refuelling of a Lockheed SR-71. (*United States Air Force*)

RELATIVE PRICE EFFECT

A recurring theme throughout this volume, particularly in its later pages, has been the need to match requirements to resources in the inevitably costly field of modern military aviation. Before looking at the future of strategic offensive air operations, it might be salutary to touch briefly (and lightly) on the problem of their resourcing.

For a long time now, but increasingly in recent years (not least by reason of the high-technology 'explosion') research, development and production in the aeronautical sector of defence procurement have been subject to cost-escalation far higher than the average rise in defence budgets. It has been reliably estimated that, over the past two decades, real costs in this specific area of defence activity have risen by a factor of 6, while defence budgets have increased only by a factor of 2.

This Relative Price Effect (RPE) as it is known in the jargon of the day would, if allowed to continue, be a very serious matter indeed—particularly for Western nations in which government spending is properly subjected to extremely rigorous examination. RPE is, in fact, cited in support of some very gloomy projections of expenditure trends into the next century; and the gloomiest of all will claim that the affordable front-line combat strength of a medium-sized Western nation will be just one aircraft by the year 2020. Although such an air force would have a number of inherent advantages (reduced infrastructure and training costs among them) it would hardly be of value in the one area of military aviation that really matters—the projection of viable air-fighting capability.

On a more positive plane, RPE is one of the factors which continues to drive those involved in military aviation—be they scientists, engineers, industrialists, accountants or airmen—towards the pooling of resources, both human and material. This is certainly true within Europe and, perhaps increasingly, on a transatlantic basis— and, indeed, further afield. It has also become clear that new and emerging technologies can help restrain the cost-growth of military aircraft and their equipments— but only if the proper balance is struck between cost and capability. There is certainly more 'bang' to be had from the proverbial 'buck': but only so long as sensible, practical limitations are placed on an inherently explosive rate of technological expansion.

This is no argument for inaction. In historical terms, the growth of capability in military aviation has been nothing short of staggering; and this is due, in no small measure, to the initiative and enthusiasm of the many different disciplines engaged in it—and to their innate flexibility in applying technology to their needs. That very proper process will undoubtedly continue into the future because, without it, air forces would all too soon lose the dynamism and adaptability which have been among their most obvious characteristics. However, restraint must be exercised; and minds focused always on the practical, if the siren-call of emerging technology is not to lead us down one of two equally dangerous paths. The first is that from which it is so tempting to pluck all the many inviting technological prospects (some, possibly, as yet unripe) that the traveller becomes weighed down by his bag of 'goodies' and fails to reach his destination. Indeed, he may even have fallen out of a tree in attempting to reach that furthest, most tempting technological fruit. The second path is more insidious in its routeing. In following it, our hero is very much more selective in his choice of fruits but they are, without exception, the biggest and best of their kind—and each carries a cost. The end of the road is duly reached: but someone has there installed a check-out counter—and our man has forgotten his wallet. Truly, in this example, the best has become the enemy of the good—and has prevented its achievement.

From this, it is obvious that care and an informed caution are the necessary qualities to be applied by our traveller into the next century. To bring this little metaphor back to the real world: sensible expectations should be thoroughly examined and, once their potential advantages have been seen to outweigh the risks involved in their pursuit—they should be incorporated into a design that is then, to all intents and purposes, frozen until the equipment to which they are applied enters front-line service. Later bright ideas (of which there will be many) are the province of the mid-life update or the next generation of kit. The arguments about quantity versus quality of military equipment will rage interminably. But it is a *reductio ad absurdum* so to arrange matters that that single affordable combat aircraft is potentially the most capable in the world: 'on the day', it may just fail to start!

INTO THE FUTURE

Given current trends in national defence commitments and in the budgets required to meet them, it seems clear that, for the foreseeable future, new designs for genuinely strategic offensive aircraft will rest with just two nations—the USA and USSR. It is just possible that, well into the twenty-first century, the People's Republic of China might be added to that short list; but such thinking is purely speculative and there have, to date, been no indications of an autonomous national design capability for the production of such aircraft. Other nations (notably France, the United Kingdom and Israel) will wish to retain some capability to project offensive air power beyond the radius of action available to their current fighter-bomber forces. This they will do by the use of AAR and the development of increasingly effective stand-off air-to-ground missiles. The possibility of converting large transport aircraft as carriers of ALCMs cannot be discounted. However it is likely that, for some time to come, the constraints of technology and cost will ensure that such missiles would be nuclear-armed—and, therefore, in practical terms confined to the air forces of just five nations. The spread of strategic missiles will be similarly limited, though conventionally tipped surface-to-surface (and air-to-surface) missiles have already been used in a strategic sense—for example, in the Iran/Iraq war.

As has already been suggested, genuinely strategic missile development will be concentrated on improved survivability and penetrability. In other words, effort will continue to be expended on invulnerability to a pre-launch pre-emptive attack; on rapidity of response; on warhead protection throughout the flight regime, with the use of increasingly effective decoys against increasingly capable defensive systems; and on ever greater accuracy. As with all weapons systems, the greater the guaranteed accuracy at point of impact, the smaller the required explosive charge or yield; and, equally important, the less weapons that need be fielded. But that accuracy does have to be *guaranteed*—which has obvious connotations for systems reliability and survivability up to the point of impact.

For the manned strategic bomber, the future pattern has already been set and the options are, basically, two. The capability of modern air defences is such as to ensure that the penetrating bomber must combine extremely low observability to the whole range of defensive sensors with highly complex and effective self-defence systems and the ability to exploit to the full that still fundamental military requirement—surprise. With the decline of the bomber's capacity to defeat the enemy on his home ground, comes its relegation to an increasingly stand-off role—to the point at which it becomes merely a forward-based missile carrier and deliverer. Even at this stage a manned system does enjoy come clear advantages, as has been earlier indicated. For example:

- Given the availability of well-situated bases, it can be deployed over vast distances to meet changing or unforeseen threats.
- It can match those threats with a wide variety of weapons to cover a range of offensive options.
- It can be brought back to its home base if the threat recedes.
- If committed to an offensive mission, it can take every advantage of surprise and deception in its routeing; and can cope with the unexpected in ways that the unmanned system can not.
- It can offer a great degree of flexibility in the direction of its attack; and can apply human intelligence to any last-minute problems of target selection based on real-time intelligence.
- With obvious attractions for higher political and military direction it can, once launched, be re-targeted or recalled up to the point of its final committal; and, of course,
- It can be refuelled, re-armed and re-used.

For the few nations that can afford it, the manned bomber is, therefore, still a very relevant weapon of deterrence and of war-fighting. It also has a role in forcing the potential opposition to divert a significant proportion of his military expenditure from offensive to defensive systems. Of course, like any other complex weapons system, a modern strategic bomber can take anything up to ten years and more from initial concept to front line; and it will then be expected to remain for twenty years—possibly thirty—as a credible component of that front line. However significantly—even dramatically—its capability may be updated during its years in service, the designer of the basic airframe must be looking, as best he can, more than forty years or so ahead of his time; and there have been only two such timespans since the Wright brothers first (and very temporarily) overcame the effects of gravity in a heavier-than-air machine. It is considerations such as these which bring into sharp focus the almost unbelievable pace of progress in military aviation: it is such considerations which, equally, make so difficult the task of forecasting its future development.

FORWARD WITH THE B-2

For its next-generation strategic bomber, the United States has invested heavily in stealth technology—in all its applications. Until mid-1988, the work being carried out on an ATB was shrouded in a becoming veil of secrecy. Even after its roll-out at Palmdale, California on 22 November 1988, little is known about the performance of this revolutionary (and extremely expensive)[3] future addition to the USAF's front line. There is little doubt that it will be capable of operating at ultra-low level and will be possessed of a fair turn of speed—though probably in the subsonic range. It will also be able to cruise at high level and modest speed—conferring on it a long-range and a long loiter capability. It will certainly carry an impressive array of sensors for both defensive and offensive use; and, as forecast by General Thomas McMullen, Commander of the Aeronautical System's Division of USAF's Systems Command, the new bomber will have '... a formidable capability that could not be matched by any other system'.[4] In a later statement, dismissing criticism of the aircraft's capability against mobile targets, the USAF claims that it will in fact be 'our most flexible and adaptive system'.[5]

There had been much speculation about the eventual shape of the ATB (or B-2, as it is now known). Clearly it would incorporate every design device known in an effort to reduce its observability; and, as many had forecast, when it was first revealed by the US Department of Defense in April 1988, it was of flying-wing design. As indicated in the officially released artist's impression (Plate 8.10) the B-2 is basically a large delta, though with a distinctive zig-zag trailing edge which came as something of a surprise to the pundits: the full effectiveness of this planform has yet to be revealed. The overall effect is striking—and quite unlike that of any earlier flying machine. It seems to exude space-age technology, combined with menacing power. More prosaically (and more in line with the received wisdom of low observability), there are few corners and protuberances on the new bomber, and no vertical stabiliser or tail-plane. It remains to be seen whether the developed aircraft will incorporate some form of wing-tip stabilisation: certainly none was apparent from the artist's impression—nor can it yet be assessed from some of the early photographs of the B-2 (see frontispiece). What is certain is that the tendency to instability, inherent in any flying-wing design, will be compensated by powerful, computerised fly-by-wire flight control systems. There may well be some form of thrust-vectoring incorporated in the engine nozzles—although the official artist carefully avoided publishing any impressions of the aircraft's underside; and, at the roll-

PLATE 8.10   The ATB revealed—at least in an artist's impression released by the
US Department of Defense in April 1988. See frontispiece for photographs of the
B-2. (*US Department of Defense*)

out ceremony, almost nothing could be seen of the aircraft's trailing edge or engine
exhausts. Later photographs taken during the B-2's first flight (on 17 July 1989) are
rather more explicit (see frontispiece). The engine inlets are however clearly visible
as of curved and 'scalloped' design; with the engines (as expected) sunk deep into
the aircraft's wing. Some form of boundary-layer control is indicated by the shaped
'slots', which lie ahead of the main inlets. It is not yet clear whether these are the
only means of ensuring supply of intake air at high angles of attack; or whether
some form of additional auxiliary inlet is incorporated beneath the wing. In any
case, the primary inlets will throughout incorporate state-of-the-art design to
absorb, rather than reflect hostile radar emissions; and every care will have been
taken to ensure that the engines' back-ends will be as quiet and as cool as current
technology can make them. It appears that the actual exhausts are in fact mounted
above the inner wing, recessed within its zig-zag design.

Although official estimates of the aircraft's performance are obviously retained
on a very close hold, it has been calculated that its unrefuelled range could be in
excess of 7,000nm and that it will carry some 35 tons of bombs or missiles. So far as
can be judged from the few available photographs, the width of the aircraft's centre-
section is such as to accommodate a pair of rotary weapons launchers. Larger than
anticipated by some experts (at 69-ft long by 17-ft high and with a wingspan of some
172ft) the B-2 is expected to operate at heights from ultra-low level up to around

50,000ft. It will almost certainly remain subsonic for reasons of reduced observability and enhanced range. Its four General Electric F118-GE 100 engines are thought each to generate some 19,000-lb of thrust, which would certainly not be excessive for an aircraft weighing something approaching 150 tons at maximum take-off weight. Surprisingly, it is said to have been designed for a crew of only two—which says a great deal about the advanced nature of its electronics and computerised controls and instruments. The flight deck of the B-2 will be 'quite something'.

The US Department of Defense long ago announced that the ATB would make extensive use of new materials and step-change developments in electronics; and it is clear that weight reduction, IR reduction and containment, optical absorption and advanced metallurgical techniques will all have featured in the design of the new aircraft. New composite materials—developments of existing carbon-epoxy or fibreglass—have been put to extensive test and found to be both lighter and stronger than such conventional aircraft materials as steel or titanium. Coated with special paints, they act as absorbers or deflectors of radar signals; and research continues to ensure that they maintain their structural integrity at the extremes of humidity and low temperature to which any combat aircraft will inevitably be subject. Engines are being developed using denser fuel to increase range, yet producing a cleaner exhaust plume. ECM equipments to counter or 'spoof' the enemy's defensive sensors will be an order of magnitude more capable than those which equip even the powerful B-1B. They will need to deceive not only the next generation of powerful, long-wavelength and so-called 'carrier-free' ground radars, but also airborne surveillance and space-based sensors.

High-energy laser or particle-beam weapons could, at some time in the future, take their place as the twenty-first century variant of the defensive cannon. Another application of lasers may lie in their replacing electronic means of communication. Advanced bi-static radars could help keep the B-2 'quiet'—as will the almost certain incorporation of Navstar GPS for extremely accurate *en route* navigation and the updating of inertially controlled target-location systems. Much further down the line— indeed, approaching the domain of science fiction—some predict the development of equipments which will not only absorb incoming energy emissions, but actually recycle them to power onboard aircraft systems.

Given that the B-2 has now been revealed as of very advanced flying-wing design, it is appropriate that the prime contractor for this revolutionary new concept in strategic offensive aircraft is the US manufacturer, Northrop.[6] For it was the founder of that company, Jack Northrop, who designed the series of original 'Flying Wings' more than forty years ago. The huge piston-engined XB-35 was later developed as a YB variant—two of which were then converted into the jet-engined YB-49 and -49A (Plate 8.11).

The aircraft was devoid of any moving vertical surface—yaw control being provided by split, differentially operated control surfaces mounted at each wing tip. Given its extremely slender profile, whether viewed from front or side, it is clear why low fuselage drag was such a feature of the Northrop design. Again, the aircraft's mass being distributed across its impressive wing area, wing loading was low and the whole design highly efficient – it being claimed, at the time, to have the potential payload and combat radius of conventional aircraft half as heavy again.

That the aircraft failed to enter service was due to a combination of suspicion that

PLATE 8.11   An earlier 'Flying Wing' design, also by Northrop. This is the YB-49A, dating from the late-1940s. (*Northrop Corporation*)

anything so revolutionary could possibly succeed and indifference at the level of politico-military decision-making. There were also, it is true, certain practical problems that remained to be overcome—among them, the inability of the YB-49 to carry the largest of the (then very large) American atomic weapons, and some concerns about aircraft handling and stability, particularly at height. For the Northrop B-2 these practical difficulties will clearly have been overcome in the inexorable advance of technology: supercritical wing design, the development of composite materials, fly-by-wire (or fly-by-light) and the carefree handling of an inherently unstable design—all will play their parts. It will be instructive to see whether what will undoubtedly be a very expensive aircraft indeed can be fought through the many budgetary and other institutional battles that lie in its flightpath.

Postscript

It is instructive to compare the pace of bomber development in the two superpowers in historically recent times. For the 25 years following World War II, such development in the USA was comparatively rapid, large-scale and varied (*cf* the huge Convair B-36, the Boeing B-47 and -52, the supersonic Convair B-58, General Dynamics' swing-wing FB-111A and work on the very advanced Mach 3 North American B-70). Thereafter, there was a long lull in innovative bomber design, broken only in recent years with the development of the Rockwell B-1B and the Northrop B-2.

By comparison, the efforts of the Soviet Union have been both consistent and evolutionary, with results that have been little short of startling. It would be wrong to minimise the problems which faced Soviet designers and technicians in seeking to match the technology of the West from a very low base of experience in the years immediately following World War II. Lacking, in particular, any knowledge of jet engine development, the Soviets were reduced to the wholesale 'borrowing' of documents, drawings and equipments—to say nothing of (mostly German) designers and engineers. They were undoubtedly helped in some measure by a commercial agreement with the United Kingdom (in 1946) from which they were allowed to manufacture under licence the then advanced Rolls-Royce Nene and Derwent turbojets. From this and other Western sources, the design bureaux of Mikulin, Koliesov and Kutsnetsov went on to develop a whole range of extremely capable and advanced engines—Kutsnetsov also experimenting successfully with a particularly effective contra-rotating turbo-prop (the NK-12) used to power the mighty Tu-95/142 Bear at speeds approaching 550 knots. The variety of long-range Soviet bomber aircraft has, since 1945, been remarkable. Significant numbers have been produced of the massive Myasischev Mya-4 Bison, the versatile Ilyushin Il-28 Beagle and a series of Tupolev designs from the Tu-14 Bosun naval attack aircraft, Tu-16 Badger, the extensive Bear family and the supersonic Tu-22 Blinder, to the swing-wing Tu-26 Backfire and the still little-known Blackjack. Such consistent effort says much for the sense of purpose of the Soviets and for their firm belief in the continuing validity of the concept of manned strategic forces—a belief founded, not unnaturally, on a clear perception of the realities of both history and geography.

For the future it seems likely that, for both the superpowers, the strategic offensive mission—now made vastly more complex by the defensive capabilities that confront it—will continue to drive the development of airborne systems to the limits of available technology. It is highly unlikely that those limits have yet been reached across a broad spectrum of engineering disciplines; and progress will undoubtedly continue in aerodynamics, structures, propulsion techniques, artificial intelligence, information-flow, computerisation, flight displays and low observability—as, indeed, in the development of increasingly advanced smart, stand-off weapons. There is probably a great deal still to go for in these currently exploitable technologies before, in the very much longer term, we might foresee the long-range offensive mission mounted from hypersonic (Mach 20-plus) transatmospheric vehicles, covering the larger part of their mission profiles in space, but capable of re-entering Earth atmosphere and skipping back into space when necessary. The problems here are not merely those of technology, but of international agreement—and enormous cost. Whether there may be a military potential for such forward-looking concepts as the British Aero-

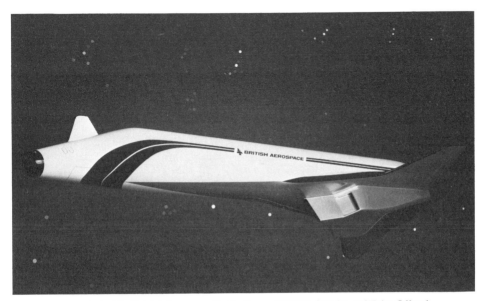

PLATE P.1   The British Aerospace/Rolls-Royce HOTOL (Horizontal Take-Off and Landing) Project—hopefully destined for the stars, though undoubtedly with many a hardship to negotiate en route. (*British Aerospace plc, Space & Communications Division*)

space/Rolls-Royce Horizontal Take-Off and Landing (HOTOL) project (Plate P.1) only time will tell. At the time of writing, that project is fighting for survival in its originally conceived role as a cost-effective satellite launching vehicle.

What is rather more readily forecastable is that time will not herald the dawn of any genuine, lasting global peace. The nature of man and the character of many of the power structures he creates will ensure the need for armed forces as far ahead as anyone can foresee. And, in turn, this will ensure that technology is exploited ever more fully in the interests of that perpetual see-saw of offensive/defensive capability. In time, nations may come to accept that the wars of the future cannot be won at any acceptable cost to their protagonists. Until then, ever more capable and potentially destructive systems will be created—hopefully to deter conflict by fear of that very potential for destruction: at worst, to be used as a means of its early cessation. For it will remain true for tomorrow's man, as it has been true down the ages, that whilst a firm defence may stave off defeat, ultimate success in war will demand bold offensive action.

Notes

Chapter 1

1. This has, more recently, been edited by David MacIsaac and reissued in condensed (but, still, 10-volume) form by Garland of New York (1976).
2. *Makers of Modern Strategy* (2nd Printing), edited by Edward Mead Earle, published by Humphrey Milford, Oxford University Press, 1944, (p.viii).
3. Combined Chiefs of Staff Directive for the Bomber Offensive from the United Kingdom, 21 January 1943
4. *Zeppelins and Super Zeppelins* by R. P. Hearne, published by John Lane, London, 1916, p.2.
5. John Terraine, *White Heat: The New Warfare 1914-18*, Guild Publishing, London, 1982, p.265.
6. Ibid, p.270.
7. *New York Times*, 14 October 1917.
8. Terraine, op cit., p.274.
9. *The Second World War*, Volume I, 3rd Edition, by Winston S. Churchill; Cassell & Co Ltd, London, 1950, p.133.
10. In the way of these things, it was revived nearly 30 years later in a project to sling three Gnat fighters beneath an Avro Vulcan bomber of the Royal Air Force (Figure 1.2). However, that project existed only on paper. The Convair B-36 Peacemaker (the largest bomber ever to feature in the United States' inventory) was actually used in trials for the carriage of a diminutive McDonnell XF-85 Goblin escort fighter. This combination never entered front-line service, though inconclusive launch and retrieval trials were continued, for a time, with an EB-29B/XF-85 pairing. For a slightly longer period in 1953 several GRB-36D aircraft were modified to carry Republic RF-84F Thunderflash reconnaissance fighters. This experiment was part of the so-called 'Fighter Conveyor' project, designed to carry fighter-type aircraft far forward of their normal radii of action; but it was overtaken by the development of air-to-air refuelling as a primary means of extending range/radius. It had, anyway, been anticipated no less than 37 years earlier when, in May 1916, a Bristol Scout had been air-launched from a Porte Baby flying boat. The GRB-36D was later used in trials of airborne stand-off missiles. Other applications of the pick-a-back principle were the pre-war British Short-Mayo flying boat composite (perhaps the most successful of such long-range projects) and Luftwaffe combinations of FW-190 fighters attached to unmanned bombers, filled with high explosive and acting as stand-off bombs towards the end of World War II. The results were less than successful.
11. AHB/11/117/1 (C) pp.17-18.
12. The distance the aircraft could fly on an operational sortie from base to target, allowing for possible diversions to evade enemy defences and sufficient fuel on return to fly to an alternative airfield, if weather or bomb damage prevented a landing at the home base.

Chapter 2

1. *The Strategic Air Offensive against Germany, 1939-45*, Sir Charles Webster and Noble Frankland, HMSO, 1961.
2. Webster and Frankland, op. cit.
3. A useful account is to be found in Volume IV, Annex II to Webster and Frankland, op. cit., to which this brief summary owes not a little.
4. Webster and Frankland, op. cit., Vol. IV, Annex IV.
5. W. J. Lawrence, *No. 5 Bomber Group RAF (1939-1945)*, Faber & Faber, London, 1951, p.192.

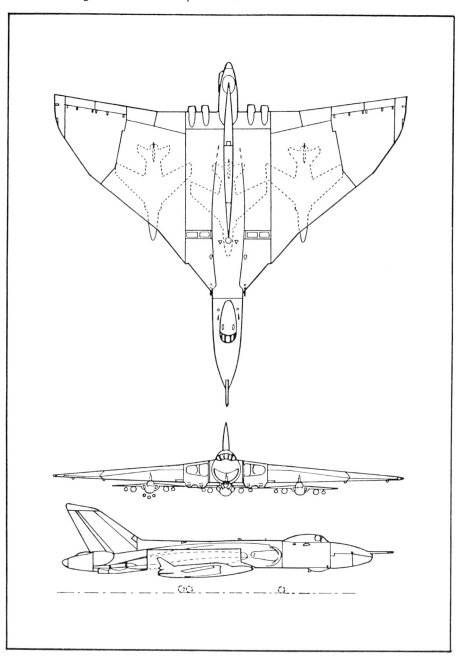

FIG. 1.2   The 'fighter support' variant of Avro's famous Vulcan bomber. As indicated, the concept involved the carriage of the three single-seat Folland Gnat fighters,
slung beneath the fuselage of the big bomber. Having been released to provide fighter
cover for the Vulcan, the Gnats would be expected either to land in friendly territory
or return for air-to-air refuelling by the 'mother' aircraft. The project was not followed
through. (*British Aerospace plc*)

Chapter 3

1. That option was never realistically available to the designers of the much larger Vulcan, though they did propose one variant which it seems M. Dassault did not consider for his Mirage IV. Unfortunately, the vertical take-off Vulcan never got beyond the drawing board!
2. A nice acronym for a very purposeful title: *Appareil de Recalage et de Cartographie pour Navigation Aveugle*.

Chapter 4

1. It should, incidentally, be added that the United States is far from being the only nation to deploy such weapons; and, as decoys or 'spoofs', not all of them are in fact harmless—as readers of Tom Clancy's *Red Storm Rising* (Collins, Glasgow, 1987) will readily recall.
2. A figure which, surprisingly, compares almost exactly with that of RAF Bomber Command during the period 1939-45.

Chapter 5

1. The Aspect Ratio of an aircraft's wing is defined as the square of its span divided by its area. Its value has a major influence on the vortex drag of a wing and on its lift capability at a given angle of attack.
2. Notably in Wing Commander Andrew Brookes's *V-Force: The History of Britain's Airborne Deterrent*, Jane's, London, 1982, to which I am indebted for this summary.
3. Quoted in *The Dictionary of Military and Naval Quotations*, edited by R. D. Heint Jr., US Naval Institute Press, Annapolis, 1966, p.304.

Chapter 6

1. For comparison with B-1B data (in brackets), Blackjack has a length of 177 ft (147 ft), a fully extended wingspan of 182 ft (137 ft) and a gross weight of 590,000 lb (477,000 lb)
2. Although there is, as yet, no firm indication of an air-to-air refuelling capability on Blackjack, it seems likely that one will eventually be developed.
3. Blackjack is reported as incorporating a fully movable vertical tail which (unusually for a supersonic aircraft) replaces more conventional rudders. Horizontal stabilisers are mounted at the intersection of the aircraft's main and dorsal fins.
4. Reported in *Aviation Week & Space Technology*, 15 August 1988.
5. The ATB has become the Northrop B-2 – of which, more in in Chapter 8.

Chapter 7

1. *Economist*, 3 October 1987.
2. J. R. Walker, *Air-to-Ground Operations*, Brassey's Air Power: Aircraft, Weapons Systems and Technology Series, Volume 2, Brassey's London, 1987.

Chapter 8

1. AGARDograph No. 270(E) (2nd edition): *Sleep and Wakefulness—a Handbook for Flight Medical Officers* by Group Captain A. N. Nicholson and Barbara M. Stone, published for the NATO Advisory Group for Aerospace Research and Development, Paris, 1987.
2. Reported in *Aviation Week and Space Technology*, 30 November 1987.
3. Latest official estimates suggest that each of the USAF's planned 132 B-2s may cost as much as $500M. However some commentators see that figure inevitably rising above $800M by the time the first aircraft joins the front line in 1992.
4. Reported in *Jane's Defence Weekly*, 30 April 1988.
5. Reported in op. cit., 3 December 1988.
6. With the Boeing Military Airplane Company and Ling-Temco-Vought (LTV) heading the list of companies involved in the development of the aircraft's systems, and General Electric taking the lead on the engines.

Bibliography

BETTS, RICHARD K., (Editor), *Cruise Missiles, Technology, Strategy, Politics*, Brookings Inst., Washington DC, 1981.

BROOKES, ANDREW, *The History of Britain's Airborne Deterrent V Force*, Jane's, London, 1982.

CROSS, ROBIN, *The Bombers*, Guild Publishing, London, 1987.

EARLE, EDWARD MEADE, *Makers of Modern Strategy*, Oxford University Press, 1944

HEARNE, R. P., *Zeppelins and Super Zeppelins*, John Lane, London, 1916.

JONES, R. V., *Most Secret War*, Hamish Hamilton, London, 1978.

KENNETT, LEE, *A History of Strategic Bombing*, Charles Scrivner & Sons, New York, 1982.

LAWRENCE, W. J., *No. 5 Bomber Group RAF (1939-1945)*, Faber & Faber, London, 1951.

MASON, R. A. & TAYLOR, JOHN W. R., *Aircraft, Strategy & Operations in the Soviet Air Force*, Jane's London, 1986.

PETTY, RONALD T., (Editor), *Jane's Weapons Systems*—various editions, Jane's Publishing Co., London.

POSSONY, STEFAN T., *Strategic Air Power: The Pattern of Dynamic Security*, Infantry Journal Press, Washington, 1949.

SWEETMAN, BILL, *Stealth Aircraft: Secrets of Future Air Power*, Airlife Publishing, Shrewsbury, 1986.

TAYLOR, JOHN R. W., (Editor), *Jane's All the World's Aircraft*—various editions, Jane's Publishing Co., London.

TERRAINE, JOHN, *The Right of the Line*, Hodder & Stoughton, London, 1985.

TERRAINE, JOHN, *White Heat: The New Warfare 1914–18*, Guild Publishing, London, 1982.

WALKER, J. R., *Air-to-Ground Operations*, Brasseys, London, 1987.

WEBSTER, SIR CHARLES & FRANKLAND, DR NOBLE, *The Strategic Air Offensive against Germany*, HMSO, 1961.

WHITFORD, RAY, *Design for Air Combat*, Jane's, London, 1987.

WRAGG, DAVID, *The Offensive Weapon: The Strategy of Bombing*, Robert Hale, London, 1986.

Self-Test Questions

Chapter 1   The Development of Strategic Bombing—the Role

1. List the several definitions of 'strategic' in relation to air power.
2. What difficulties faced those who attempted to forecast accurate figures for civilian casualties in World War II?
3. What factors militated against the development of precision bombing in the years up to 1940?
4. Compare the development of strategic offensive aircraft in the air forces of Germany and Britain in the years 1915-18.
5. What were the immediate and longer-term effects of the Condor Legion's attack on Guernica in April 1937?
6. Outline some of the tactical concepts considered by the protagonists of strategic offensive air power in the years between the two World Wars.
7. What comparable arguments hold sway today in the consideration of the most effective concepts of the application of strategic offensive air power?
8. Outline the development of genuine multi-role capability by reference to the de Havilland Mosquito.
9. What were the most important operational features designed into the Boeing B-17 Flying Fortress?
10. What were the six most significant technological developments for the role of long-range bombardment in the years up to 1939?

Chapter 2   The Development of Strategic Bombing—The Equipment

11. Outline the principal features of the bomb development up to the end of World War I.
12. Illustrate, by means of a simple diagram, the principal factors affecting bombing accuracy.
13. Outline (if necessary with a diagram) the principle of the tachometric bomb-sight.
14. Do the same for the vector (or impact) bomb-sight.
15. Apart from the effects of wind, gravity, aircraft speed and height, what other factors served to increase the problems of accurate bombing by aircrew during World War II?
16. List some of the aids to navigation developed during the course of that war.
17. Describe the workings of the German *X-Verfahren* system.
18. What were the advantages and disadvantages of the British H2S system compared with equipments such as Gee and Oboe?
19. Outline some of the defensive countermeasures devised by each side in the later years of World War II.
20. Briefly describe the development of the two main components of the Inter-Continental Ballistic Missile (ICBM) in the years to 1945.

Chapter 3   The Survival of the Strategic Bomber

21. List some for the roles of which existing aircraft types were modified for action in the South Atlantic conflict of 1982.
22. Give some contemporary examples of the employment of tactical aircraft on strategic missions.
23. What factors lay behind the decision to bomb the Port Stanleyj airfield in May-June 1982? And what were the effects of those raids?
24. Examine the capability of the Soviet Tu-26 Backfire for the role of strategic bombing.
25. Outline the arguments for and against the development of manned strategic aircraft, as against long-range missiles.
26. Describe the three most significant features of the USAF's FB-111, B-52, B-1B and B-2 bombers.
27. Outline, briefly, the development of the Dassault Mirage IV.

28. How do the Mirage IV's weapons delivery tactics now differ from those used in the early days of the aircraft's service life?
29. Briefly describe the *Air-Sol Moyenne Portée* (ASMP).
30. In what specific ways would the Mirage IV* have represented an advance on the capability of the then-existing Mirage IV?

Chapter 4   Something Old, Something New: the 'Buff' Flies On

31. Why has the Boeing B-52 been able to remain so long in front-line service with the USAF?
32. Indicate the ways in which the weapons delivery profiles of the B-52 have been influenced by the development of both offensive and enemy defensive capability.
33. Why is 'fatigue life' so important for the modern combat aircraft? And what steps can be take to extend it?
34. What are the principal advantages of Forward-looking Infra-red (FLIR) over radar for aircraft navigation and attack?
35. Describe the effects of Electromagnetic Pulse (EMP).
36. Outline the advantages of (a) Hound Dog and (b) Quail in B-52 operations.
37. List the various components of air power used in support of the Linebacker II raids on North Vietnam.
38. List the characteristics of the Boeing AGM-86B Air-Launched Cruise Missile (ALCM).
39. Outline the principles of the Terrain Contour-Matching (TERCOM) system.
40. How will technology help ensure the operational credibility of the B-52 for some years to come?

Chapter 5   Approach of Stealth

41. What are the primary advantages of air power?
42. List the principal means of aircraft detection.
43. What factors must be considered in designing an effective camouflage scheme for a combat aircraft?
44. Describe, briefly, the characteristics of 'radar ablative' paint.
45. In what specific ways do aero-engines give warning of aircraft approach?
46. Outline the factors involved in the elimination of engine smoke trails.
47. What features of aircraft design will tend to enhance 'low observability'?
48. Define Aspect Ratio.
49. Compare the physical properties of broad-band absorbers and resonant materials in the context of radar absorbency; and indicate how each might be used on a modern combat aircraft.
50. What features of aircraft design are most likely to repay study in the context of stealth technology?

Chapter 6   Blackjack v B-1B

51. Describe the advantage of variable-geometry in aircraft design.
52. What problems does it cause?
53. What is the likely ordnance of the Soviet Blackjack aircraft.
54. Indicate some of the reasons for the fitting of canards on combat aircraft.
55. What factors led to the decision of many air forces to move from very high-level to ultra low-level flight by their offensive aircraft?
56. In broad terms, what functions are computer-controlled on the USAF's B-1B aircraft?
57. Indicate some of the advantages of a terrain-following radar capability; and outline some of the problems involved in its use.
58. Describe 'controlled instability'.
59. Outline the principle of synthetic aperture radar.
60. What is EMUX? And what are its merits.

Chapter 7   Enter the Missile

61. What is 'escape velocity'?
62. By means of a simple illustration, indicate the principal components of a typical four-stage ballistic missile.
63. Outline the phases of ICBM flight.
64. Describe Circular Error Probable (CEP) and indicate its relationship to warhead size and yield.
65. Indicate some of the areas in which strategic defence research is being carried out.
66. Which 'non-kill' areas are likely to benefit most from SDI research?
67. Relate cruise missile range and speed to likely choices of engine.

68. Describe some typical systems of cruise missile navigation.
69. Indicate some likely targets for attack by highly accurate conventionally-armed cruise missiles.
70. Discuss the vulnerability of the cruise missile.

Chapter 8   What Next? Some Future Developments for the Strategic Offensive Role

71. Discuss the advantages and possible dangers of sleep patern optimisation for combat aircrew.
72. Describe the circadian rhythm.
73. List some of the hazards which may face any combat aircrew.
74. What are the disadvantages of an escape capsule?
75. Construct a simple diagram of a Global Positioning System (GPS).
76. Illustrate the principle of the ring-laser gyro (RLG).
77. What are the specific advantages of Terrain Profile-Matching (TERPROM).
78. What is Relative Price Effect (RPE)?
79. What are the continued attractions of the manned bomber?
80. Idicate some of the recent technological developments incorporated in the Northrop B-2 Advanced Tactical Bomber (ATB).

Index

Note: Aircraft types are listed under Aircraft, not under individual names

195